GROWTH, UNEMPLOYMENT, DISTRIBUTION AND GOVERNMENT

Also by Vani K. Borooah

POLITICAL ASPECTS OF THE ECONOMY (*with F. van der Ploeg*)

REGIONAL INCOME INEQUALITY AND POVERTY IN THE UK
(*with P. McGregor and P. McKee*)

THE STRUCTURE OF CONSUMPTION DECISIONS

Growth, Unemployment, Distribution and Government

Essays on Current Economic Issues

Vani K. Borooah
Professor of Applied Economics
University of Ulster

First published in Great Britain 1996 by
MACMILLAN PRESS LTD
Houndmills, Basingstoke, Hampshire RG21 6XS
and London
Companies and representatives
throughout the world

A catalogue record for this book is available
from the British Library.

ISBN 0–333–61729–0 hardcover
ISBN 0–333–61730–4 paperback

First published in the United States of America 1996 by
ST. MARTIN'S PRESS, INC.,
Scholarly and Reference Division,
175 Fifth Avenue,
New York, N.Y. 10010

ISBN 0–312–16158–1

Library of Congress Cataloging-in-Publication Data
Borooah, Vani. K.
Growth, unemployment, distribution and government : essays on
current economic issues / Vani K. Borooah.
p. cm.
Includes bibliographical references and index.
ISBN 0–312–16158–1
1. Economic development. 2. Unemployment. 3. Income
distribution. 4. Economic policy. I. Title.
HD82.B5774 1996
338.9—dc20
96–10819
CIP

10   9   8   7   6   5   4   3   2   1
05   04   03   02   01   00   99   98   97   96

Printed in Great Britain by
Ipswich Book Co Ltd, Ipswich, Suffolk

For Vidya, with love and gratitude

Contents

Preface

When you set out for Ithaka
ask that your way be long,
full of adventure, full of instruction

Ithaka
C.P. Cavafy

The roots of this book lie in a series of monthly articles I wrote for a business magazine, *Ulster Business*, in 1991 and 1992. The purpose of the articles was to set out, to a largely business audience, in a comprehensive but succinct manner, the key points surrounding different economic issues. Although the original articles have been considerably expanded and updated to form the chapters of this book, this purpose has not altered. The book is aimed at an audience that is sufficiently interested in economic issues to read (and, hopefully, buy) a book that sets out these issues clearly, comprehensively and, above all, seriously. This has implications for both the style and the content of the book. Clarity requires that the arguments be presented coherently, without obfuscation or resort to jargon. Comprehensiveness requires a wide perspective embracing theoretical, empirical and policy matters. Lastly, seriousness requires that the most up-to-date thinking on economic matters is presented in digestible form, but without violence to the integrity of the original arguments. Achieving this trinity of objectives has been the primary aim of this book.

The book is about four contemporary economic themes – growth, unemployment, distribution and government – and these comprise its four parts. Each theme is divided into topics and discussion of these topics forms the subject matter of the individual chapters. The chapters have been written as extended essays in, what I hope will be viewed as, a 'seamless' style of writing. In each chapter, I have tried to present a distillation of the main issues involved – theoretical, empirical and policy related – with the intention of presenting a coherent overview of the topic. This book is not a textbook and it does not attempt to detail the methods of analysis used in economics. Indeed, to read, understand and perhaps even enjoy this book does not require any prior knowledge of economics. It is, however, a serious book on matters economic and it aims to acquaint the reader with what, in my opinion, are important areas of economic interest. The choice of areas has been constrained by the boundaries of my knowledge.

ix

I am very grateful to the following persons and organisations for giving me permission to reproduce material from their works: Nicholas Barr, Nicholas Crafts, Timothy Smeeding, The Bank of England, The Central Statistical Office, The Employment Policy Institute, The OECD, The Joseph Rowntree Foundation and H.M. Treasury.

Many people have helped to ease the labour of writing this book though, naturally, I absolve them of the book's deficiencies for which I alone am responsible. Richard Buckley, as editor of *Ulster Business,* sowed the seeds by accepting my articles for publication; Victor Hewitt, on behalf of the Policy Planning Research Unit of the Northern Ireland Government, encouraged and sponsored the writing of the chapters on growth and on unemployment; Kevin Lee read and commented on some of the chapters and Beverly Coulter, Jacqui Ferguson and Sharon McCullough all helped, at different stages, with the preparation of the manuscript. To all of them go my warmest thanks. But my greatest debt is to Vidya Borooah who encouraged me to embark on this odyssey; who read, re-read, commented upon, painstakingly corrected and polished every chapter and helped improve enormously the clarity of the writing and thus the quality of the book. Without her encouragement I would not, for fear of angry Poseidon, have set sail; with her assistance, the voyage to my Ithaka proved to be smooth sailing.

Vani K. Borooah
University of Ulster

I Growth

1   Competitiveness

The last 40 years have, arguably, seen no economic event more remarkable than the rise – out of the ashes of the Second World War – of Japan, Germany and France and the parallel decline of the economies of the UK and the USA. In 1950, of the 16 countries whose gross domestic product (GDP) per capita are shown in Table 1.1, the UK was one of the richest. Compared to the UK, the per capita GDP of Japan, in 1950, was approximately one-quarter, Germany's was less than two-thirds and that of France was less than three-quarters. By 1987, Japan, Germany and France all had a GDP per capita (respectively 6, 9 and 3 per cent) higher than that of the UK. Indeed, by that date, with the exception of Italy,[1] Belgium and Austria, the UK was the poorest of the 16 countries shown. Although the USA maintained its position as the richest country in the world, the gap between it and its competitors had narrowed considerably: in 1950, Japan's GDP per capita was only 17 per cent of the USA's, but by 1987, it was almost 72 per cent of the USA's per capita GDP.

TABLE 1.1   *GDP per capita (UK = 100)*

	1950	1973	1987
USA	160.6	148.1	147.6
Switzerland	126.0	142.4	129.7
Canada	115.6	126.1	138.4
Australia	105.2	103.8	103.9
UK	*100.0*	*100.0*	*100.0*
Sweden	93.5	111.8	112.5
Denmark	93.3	105.8	108.4
The Netherlands	85.2	104.6	100.2
Norway	82.4	95.4	127.0
Belgium	74.7	93.6	95.5
France	70.5	100.7	103.2
Finland	62.6	91.8	103.5
Germany	60.1	102.5	108.6
Italy	55.7	92.1	98.3
Austria	50.9	86.8	95.8
Japan	26.8	89.3	106.3

SOURCE   A. Maddison, 1989, *The World Economy in the Twentieth Century* (Paris: OECD).

The engine for these reversals of fortune is generally agreed to be manufacturing – the decline of the UK and US economies may be related to a failure of their manufacturing sectors to hold their own against those of Japan and Germany. Table 1.2 shows the contrasting fortunes of these four countries (the UK, the USA, Germany and Japan) with respect to their shares in the world trade of manufactured goods. In 1950, the UK and the USA between them accounted for over half the share of world trade in manufactures, while Germany's share was 7.3 per cent and Japan's share was 3.4 per cent. By 1990, Japan and Germany collectively accounted for 36 per cent of the world's manufacturing exports and the combined share of the UK and USA had fallen to just under one-quarter. A comparison of the growth rates in manufacturing across Japan and the UK tells a similar story. The Japanese manufacturing output grew at an average rate of 15 per cent per annum over 1950-73; at 4.7 per cent per annum during 1973–89, and at 5.6 per cent per annum during 1979–89. The corresponding growth rates for UK manufacturing output for these three periods were, respectively, 3.1, 0.5 and 1.2 per cent.[2]

TABLE 1.2   *Shares of world trade in manufactures (per cent)*

	1950	1970	1979	1990
Germany	7.3	19.8	20.9	20.2
Japan	3.4	11.7	13.7	15.9
UK	25.5	10.8	9.1	8.6
USA	27.3	18.6	16.0	16.0

SOURCE   N.F.R. Crafts, *Can De-industrialisation Seriously Damage Your Wealth?*, Hobart Paper 120 (London: Institute of Economic Affairs, 1993).

Why should manufacturing be so important to a country's economic health? Although manufacturing over the past 50 years has rarely employed more than half of any country's work-force (and today employs less than one-third of the work-force in every industrialised country), for three reasons its importance to the national economy extends far beyond its contribution to employment or to output.[3] First, a major source of economic growth is improvements in production techniques that allow higher levels of output to be produced with a given level of resources. Such improvements are the consequence of expenditure on research and development (R&D) and the major spender in the economy on R&D is the manufacturing sector. Indeed, the Organization for Economic Co-operation and Development (OECD) estimated[4] that, in 1983, 60 per cent of R&D expenditure in the UK (and 70 per cent in the USA) was undertaken by its manufacturing sector.

Second, in addition to acting as an engine for economic growth, manufacturing also provides jobs that are well-paid. Hourly wage rates in manufacturing are, on average, usually higher than in the non-manufacturing sector. This may be so for a number of reasons: higher productivity in manufacturing enables higher wages, workers in manufacturing are older and better educated, the integrated nature of manufacturing places a premium on a stable, cooperative work-force and manufacturing is more unionised than other sectors. The combined result of these factors is that manufacturing jobs are good jobs.

Lastly, there are important links between the manufacturing sector and other sectors of the economy. Many services are provided on the backs of incomes generated by manufacturing. Services such as education, communications and financial services are generated in large part through the demands of the manufacturing sector. The view that manufacturing is important was encapsulated by the House of Lords in the UK when it said that 'manufacturing industry is vital to the prosperity of the United Kingdom ... Our manufacturing base is dangerously small; to achieve adequate growth from such a small base will be difficult.'[5]

How does one explain the rise of manufacturing in certain countries and its eclipse in others? Why should a group of countries, pre-eminent both economically and politically in the aftermath of the Second World War and in possession of large and thriving manufacturing industries lose, within the space of four decades, their economic superiority? Conversely, how did it come about that another group of countries, whose industries were destroyed by the war, were able over the same period to become so dominant in manufacturing? In providing an explanation for these events a word that is becoming increasingly fashionable is 'competitiveness'. Thus a 'loss of competitiveness' by the UK and US economies is usually cited as an important reason for their post-war economic decline while 'regaining the competitive edge' is upheld as the means by which this decline can be arrested and, perhaps, even reversed.[6]

Against this background, the purpose of this chapter is to provide some focus to discussions of competitiveness (for example, why have we lost it and how can we regain it?) by defining the term, identifying its major components and commenting on differences in the impact that these components have on the economy. The bottom line for competitiveness is the ability to out-sell one's competitors. Many factors, therefore, combine to determine competitiveness: price, quality, speed of delivery and after-sales service, are some of the more obvious ones. In defining competitiveness, this discussion takes the non-price factors as given and concentrates on 'price competitiveness'. Thus competitiveness, hereafter, refers to 'price competitiveness'. This is not because non-price factors are not important, but because easy access to technology means that many countries today produce a large range of industrial products to fairly uniform standards. Consequently, in the final analysis, for a number of industrial products it is price which determines whether one country's products are bought instead of another's.

The most important step, therefore, towards understanding what competitiveness is, is understanding how prices are determined. Economists offer two different views on price determination. The first is the *demand–supply* view whereby the role of prices is simply one of market clearing, that is one of equating the demand and supply plans of consumers and producers. While such a model would be applicable to some markets (most notably to markets for primary commodities and financial transactions where either auctioneers or jobbers determine prices), the vast majority of goods are traded in markets where firms set prices. Consequently, the concept of 'market-clearing' prices is not regarded as being applicable to industrial markets. Prices in such markets are generally 'sticky' in the sense that, notwithstanding variations in demand, they are not revised very often.[7] To explain pricing policy in such situations requires an alternative theory and this is provided by the theory of *mark-up pricing*.

In a famous article, R.E. Hall and C. Hitch[8] asked 38 firms about their price-setting methods and discovered that most firms typically set prices by first calculating the average costs of production and then adding a mark-up for profits. This finding, confirmed by subsequent surveys in both the UK and the USA, gave birth to the theory of mark-up pricing according to which prices represent a mark-up over unit costs. Proponents of this theory would further argue that fluctuations in demand and/or supply were not met by changing price, but by varying production and, as a consequence, running inventories up or down.

The costs of production constitute payments for a number of inputs (labour, capital, energy and raw materials) that enter the production process. However, for ease of exposition, the discussion here concentrates on labour costs, since labour is, usually, the most important input in production.[9] With this emphasis on labour costs, price (as expressed in a foreign currency,[10] which henceforth will be taken to be dollars) can then be expressed as the product of three components:[11] *unit labour costs*[12] × *profit margin* × *the dollar/pound exchange rate.* In turn, unit labour costs are given by the product of the wage rate[13] and the (reciprocal) of the level of productivity.[14] In terms of *rates of change,* the percentage rate of a change in prices may be written as the sum of three components: *per cent change in unit labour costs + per cent change in profit margins + per cent change in exchange rate,* where, in turn, the per cent change in unit labour costs would equal the per cent change in wages *less* the per cent productivity growth.

The significance of productivity growth is that a country could, without loss of competitiveness and with unchanged profit margins and exchange rate, secure an increase in real wages equal to its rate of productivity growth. Suppose, in the above relation for per cent changes, that both productivity and wage growth were, say, 5 per cent. Then, assuming profit margins did not change, prices would remain unchanged and real wages[15] would rise by 5 per cent. Indeed, the growth rate of productivity defines the increase in real wages that is possible, regardless of whether competitiveness was being gained or lost. For example, if productivity growth was 5 per cent and nominal wages grew by x per cent, then prices would change by $(x - 5)$ per cent and this would be positive or negative depending, respectively, on whether x was greater or less than 5. If prices did not change in other countries, then in the first case $(x > 5)$ competitiveness would be lost and in the second case $(x < 5)$ competitiveness would be gained. In any event, the growth in real wages, defined as the difference between the growth in wages (x) and in prices $(x - 5)$, would be 5 per cent. It is in this sense that Paul Krugman argues that competitiveness does not matter but only productivity growth does.[16]

Anticipating material contained in the next chapter, if one asked how productivity growth could be raised, then the answer would be a higher level of investment in all the things (modern plant and machinery, better technology, improved skills and so on) that make workers more productive. However, more investment requires, as a necessary condition, the availability of a surplus that can be invested and, in the stylised example presented here, this means higher profit margins. However, with a given productivity growth rate (say, 5 per cent) higher profit margins can only be obtained, without loss of competitiveness, if workers accept a nominal wage growth less than productivity growth. For example, if workers accepted a wage growth of 4 per cent, then in the context of stable prices, this would, with 5 per cent productivity growth, permit profit margins to expand by 1 per cent. Hence, the exigencies of generating an adequate surplus for undertaking investment that would raise productivity in the future means that workers have to sacrifice a part of their current productivity growth to higher profits.

This chapter takes up the question of improving competitiveness *in the context of a given rate of productivity growth.* That is to say, it focuses on the first and third items of the above relationship, postponing discussion of how to generate higher productivity growth to Chapters 2–3 and 4. In this context, if UK wage growth outstripped (given) UK productivity growth by more than it did in other countries, then UK unit labour costs would rise relative to those elsewhere. In turn, if unit labour costs in the UK rose faster (or fell more slowly) than in other countries, then the UK would lose competitiveness relative to these countries (in the sense that the prices of the UK products would rise faster than those of the products of other countries) unless this loss of competitiveness was offset by declining profit margins or by a depreciating exchange rate.

The third and last item in the above relationship is the exchange rate. A country's exchange rate represents the value of its currency (pounds) in terms of other currencies (dollars). It therefore reflects the demand for the domestic currency (pounds) relative to foreign currencies (dollars) and it translates prices expressed in pounds into prices expressed in dollars. An exchange rate depreciation[17] means that a given pound price is now quoted at a lower dollar price and hence depreciation, like a productivity increase, acts to improve competitiveness.

A country which, over a period of time, wishes to improve its competitive position, in the context of a given productivity growth rate, has, therefore, a choice of two policy instruments. It can try to achieve a lower rate of growth in unit labour costs than its competitors or it can devalue its currency. Although any of these methods would improve competitiveness, it should not be thought that, in themselves, they would restore an economy to sound health. Wage restraint or the freedom to devalue will not get a country out of anything other than a short-term hole. However, they might staunch the haemorrhaging in competitiveness brought about through large increases in unit labour costs and through overvalued currencies. There is only one way for a country to be competitive while, at the same time, making itself better off. This involves taking measures to increase the rate of productivity growth. The remainder of this chapter, however, focuses on more immediate issues, namely those of wage restraint and devaluation, leaving the issue of productivity growth to later chapters.

A depressing feature of economic performance in the UK has been its endemic tendency to generate wage increases in excess of productivity growth. Table 1.3 opposite shows the contribution that changes in productivity, wage rates, input prices and the cost of bought-in services made to profit margins and output prices during 1981–91. Over this period, growth in labour costs consistently outstripped productivity growth so that each year unit labour costs were higher than in the previous year. When combined with increases in the cost of bought-in services (which are mainly driven by labour costs), unit labour costs, in 1991, exerted an upward pressure on output prices of 5.7 per cent; the situation was rescued somewhat by a fall in input prices of 0.7 per cent which (with unchanged profit margins) resulted in an overall increase in output prices of 5.0 per cent.

TABLE 1.3   *Contributions to year on year percentage change in domestic output prices in manufacturing, excluding food, drink and tobacco 1981–91*

Year	Labour productivity 1	Labour costs 2	Unit labour costs 3 = 2 – 1	Input prices 4	Bought-in prices* 5	Margins (residual) 6 = 7 – (3 + 4 + 5)	Output prices 7
1981	2.0	6.4	4.4	2.9	2.8	–2.7	7.5
1982	3.1	4.4	1.3	2.3	1.1	2.2	6.9
1983	3.6	3.7	0.1	2.6	0.9	1.8	5.4
1984	2.7	3.5	0.8	3.0	1.1	0.3	5.2
1985	1.6	3.5	1.9	1.0	1.1	1.7	5.7
1986	1.7	3.1	1.5	–3.4	0.8	5.3	4.1
1987	3.0	3.4	0.3	1.7	0.8	1.6	4.4
1988	2.7	3.6	0.8	1.6	2.0	0.4	4.8
1989	1.9	3.7	1.8	1.8	2.2	–0.4	5.4
1990	0.3	4.1	3.8	–0.3	2.3	0.2	6.0
1991	0.2	3.7	3.5	–0.7	2.2	0.0	5.0

*Proxied by unit labour costs in the service sector.
SOURCE   *Bank of England Quarterly Bulletin* (August 1992), p. 298.

Table 1.4 shows that during 1979–88, unit labour costs in the business sector of every country listed (except Italy) grew more slowly than unit labour costs in the UK business sector; indeed, at 6.9 per cent, the average annual growth rate in the UK exceeded the OECD average by 2.2 percentage points. Since 1988 the gap between the UK growth rate and the OECD average has, if anything, grown wider and in 1988, 1989 and 1990 even Italy was able to boast of smaller annual increases in unit labour costs than the UK. Nor are these high rates of growth in unit labour costs in the UK a comparatively recent phenomenon. During 1960–73 the UK averaged unit labour cost increases of 4.8 per cent, while during 1973–9 this rose to 17.9 per cent. By way of contrast the corresponding increases for Germany were 4.3 and 4.9 per cent and for Japan they were 4.3 and 6.9 per cent.[18]

The conventional wisdom in the UK has been that the inability to control rising labour costs was, and is, due to the presence of strong trade unions at the bargaining table. However, even if this was true of earlier periods, it was certainly not true of the 1980s when, because of a number of factors (Mrs Thatcher's industrial reforms, the existence, since 1980, of unprecedentedly high rates of unemployment and a sharp decline in union membership), employers were, if anything, in a strong bargaining position relative to unions. Yet, as has been seen, labour costs continued to rise over the period. Two explanations have been offered for this.[19] First, most employers regard it as almost self-evident that pay increases must, at a minimum, compensate workers for cost of living increases and, if possible, workers should receive something over and above this minimum. Secondly, efficient firms, particularly in manufacturing, are often happy to pay this extra, secure in the knowledge that the surplus can and will be clawed back through productivity improvements. However, once a rate of earnings increase is established, it becomes the 'going rate' and less efficient firms are forced to concede similar increases in order to recruit and retain their employees.

TABLE 1.4   *Unit labour costs in the business Sector in OECD countries, 1979–91*

	Percentage change in previous period Average Annual Rate				
	1979–88	*1988*	*1989*	*1990*	*1991*
UK	6.9	7.4	9.7	10.0	7.2
US	4.9	4.2	3.1	5.0	3.6
Japan	0.9	−1.4	1.0	1.5	1.5
Germany	2.7	0.0	0.4	2.3	4.5
France	6.3	0.6	1.1	3.6	3.1
Italy	11.0	4.2	6.0	7.0	8.2
Canada	5.7	5.2	5.1	6.8	4.7
All above	4.5	2.5	2.9	4.3	3.8
Total all OECD countries	4.7	2.6	3.1	4.6	4.0

SOURCE   *OECD Economic Outlook* (June 1992), Table 60.

What if a country is unable to close its competitive gap by reducing the rate of growth in its unit labour costs below that of its rivals? If a country cannot reduce the prices of its products in export markets through domestic cost reductions, then to maintain competitiveness, it has no alternative but to depreciate its currency. Indeed, this is precisely the policy that the UK, willingly or unwillingly, has followed and this is exemplified by the fact that the effective exchange rate for sterling in May 1992, was 17 per cent lower than the average for 1980.[20] However, a country that, in the main, relied on defending competitiveness through exchange rate devaluation would only succeed in making itself worse off. This is because devaluation increases a country's exports by distorting the *terms of trade*[21] to its disadvantage. For example, a devaluation of sterling would mean that every pound's worth of exports would buy less in terms of imports.

The UK's entry into the European Community's (EC) exchange rate mechanism (ERM), in October 1990, robbed exchange rate variation of much of its force as an instrument for promoting competitiveness. Those countries which participated in the ERM undertook a commitment not to allow the exchange rate of their currency (against the other currencies in the ERM) to fluctuate by more than a given percentage above and below certain bilateral 'central' rates. In order to keep its participating currencies within these limits, the ERM provided for a number of mechanisms: intervention in the foreign exchange market, monetary policy and fiscal and incomes policy. Once a currency reached its bilateral limit against another currency, the central banks of both currencies were required to intervene in the foreign exchange market, buying and selling their respective currencies as necessary. If a currency remained under pressure for a period of time, interest rates could be raised to attract capital flows from other countries.[22] In the medium-term, resort could also be made to fiscal policy to influence aggregate demand or to incomes policy to restore competitiveness. If a currency diverged permanently from other currencies, a realignment within the ERM could take place but this had to be based on mutual agreement between the countries participating in the ERM.[23]

Proponents of the UK's membership of the ERM argued that exchange rate changes were never an effective policy instrument since the depreciation of sterling was simply a means of (partially) neutralising the loss of competitiveness brought about through excessive wage increases. The loss of this 'freedom' to vary the exchange rate was therefore, on this argument, seen as a good thing since it forced employers and unions in the UK to live with the consequences of their wage agreements. Indeed, it has been has argued[24] that the ERM provided useful political camouflage for countries struggling to control inflation but not wishing to state explicitly that this could only be achieved through higher levels of unemployment. Instead, membership of the ERM enabled high unemployment levels to be presented not as an objective of policy but rather as a consequence of the need to defend exchange rate parities within the ERM. For a while this magic worked. Although the period from the inception of the ERM in 1979 until March 1983 was a turbulent one, with a total of seven realignments, the period from March 1983 till January 1987 was a calmer period with a total of four realignments.[25] From January 1987 there were no realignments within the ERM until September 1992.[26]

The event that caused this magic to disappear was the unification of Germany in January 1990. German unification contained two important features. First, it enshrined a commitment made by Chancellor Kohl that the cost of unification would not be met from higher taxes. Second, the post-unification exchange rate between the West and East German currencies was established on a one for one basis.[27] The consequence of setting this highly uncompetitive value of the Ostmark was that large swathes of industry in the erstwhile East Germany went out of business leading to a dramatic rise in its unemployment rate. The social security payments and industrial support expenditures that West Germany had to undertake to deal with this problem, in conjunction with the 'no tax-increase' commitment, meant that the government deficit rose sharply with the result that inflationary pressures began to emerge. Alarmed by the rise in prices the Bundesbank, which is independent of the government and whose main objective is to fight inflation, imposed a monetary squeeze by raising interest rates to record levels.

Countries such as the UK, which were struggling to come out of recession, were badly affected. They were faced with the choice between maintaining their ERM parities by shadowing the German interest rises and thereby postponing recovery or seeking a realignment of parities. As it happened, the first option led, inevitably, to the second. The rise in UK interest rates required to defend sterling's ERM parity, in the face of the UK's high unemployment levels, was so large that it lacked all political credibility and, hence, could not be sustained. In September 1992, sterling and the lira left the ERM and the Spanish peseta was devalued. In November 1992, the peseta and the escudo had to devalue. In January 1993, the Irish punt was devalued by 10 per cent against other currencies in the ERM, the biggest devaluation by an ERM member since the establishment of the European Monetary System (EMS) in 1979.

The debate that has followed the collapse of the ERM has divided countries into two camps. There are those who, led by the French, favour a move towards monetary union and a single currency and there are others, of whom the UK is the most vociferous, who believe that leaving the ERM has given their economies, via exchange rate depreciation, a competitive edge which the system of fixed parities, embodied in the ERM, never permitted. Needless to say, the economic recovery of the UK that followed shortly after its departure, in September 1992, from the ERM has provided ammunition to the opponents of the mechanism who always viewed membership as a strait-jacket rather than as a life-jacket. In turn, this has led to a general revival of faith in the merits of 'competitively valued' currencies and, *ipso facto*, in a system of floating exchange rates.

However, as this chapter has argued, the exclusive reliance on exchange rate variations to promote competitiveness is bound to end in penury. If the objective of a country's economic policy is not merely to maintain or improve competitiveness but to also secure improvements in the standard of living of its citizens, then the key lies in generating higher rates of productivity growth.

This, in turn, requires investment which then requires real wage restraint: workers must be prepared to forgo part of their productivity achievements in order to generate the investment needed to establish a platform for future achievements. These matters, relating to long-term performance, are discussed in the next three chapters.

2 Accounting for Growth and the Productivity Slowdown

Productivity is about the quantity of output that is produced per unit of input and improvements in productivity relate to the production of more output with smaller input quantities. More often than not (as, for example, in the previous chapter) productivity is interpreted to mean 'labour productivity', that is to say it refers to output per unit of labour employed where this unit may be defined either as an employee or as an hour worked by an employee. In the previous chapter it was argued that growth in (labour) productivity is a major instrument (and, except in the short-term, the only instrument) for securing improvements in the real wage. This is one important reason why discussions of productivity are usually couched in terms of the efficiency with which labour is used. But there are other reasons as well for this emphasis on labour productivity: unit labour costs are a major component of the cost of producing value added with labour productivity constituting a major determinant of labour costs; moreover, wage negotiations between unions and employers usually contain, as an important subplot, negotiations about improvements in the productivity of the labour force.

However, while labour productivity is an important indicator of productive efficiency, it does not tell the full story in this regard. That is because output is produced by combining labour with many other inputs – capital, energy and materials – in a technically feasible manner. Any judgement on the efficiency of production, therefore, is better based on the productivity of a composite of inputs rather than on the productivity of a single input (labour). This type of productivity measure, which is expressed in terms of output per unit of composite input, is termed *total factor productivity*[1] (TFP) and is distinguished from productivity measures based on a single input (such as output per unit of labour or output per unit of capital). The difference between TFP and, for example, labour productivity may be illustrated through the following example. A highly capital-intensive plant operated with only a minimal amount of labour may show much higher levels of labour productivity than another, more labour-intensive, plant; however when all the costs of production

14

(that is, total amortised capital plus labour costs) are taken into account it may well turn out that the second plant is more efficient than the first.

In order to calculate the rate of growth of TFP, the rate of growth of output is used as a starting point. Two items contribute to an output increase: increases in the supply of factors of production (capital and labour)[2] and improvements in the efficiency with which factors of production are used, as a result of technological or organisational improvements. The extent by which output grows, over and above the amount attributable to increases in labour and capital, may, intuitively, be ascribed to productivity improvements. In essence the methodology of *growth accounting*[3] formalises this idea by decomposing the growth rate of output as the sum of the following: the growth rate of capital, the growth rate of labour[4] and a 'residual'.[5] Under the framework of growth accounting this residual is identified as *total factor productivity (TFP) growth*. In other words, TFP growth is that part of output growth which cannot be explained by the growth in capital and labour and which therefore must be ascribed to an increase in the efficiency or productiveness of capital and labour that results from improvements in technology or organisation.[6]

TABLE 2.1   *The sources of economic growth (per cent per annum)*

	(1) *Capital*	*(2)* *Labour*	*(3)* *TFP*	*(4)* *GDP*
1950–73				
France	1.84	0.18	3.02	5.04
Germany	2.27	0.15	3.50	5.92
Japan	2.93	1.63	4.71	9.27
UK	*1.75*	*0.01*	*1.27*	*3.03*
USA	1.37	1.17	1.11	3.65
1973–87				
France	1.48	−0.24	0.92	2.15
Germany	1.28	−0.49	1.01	1.80
Japan	2.29	0.66	0.78	3.73
UK	*1.12*	*−0.19*	*0.82*	*1.75*
USA	1.24	1.31	−0.04	2.51

Note: column (4) = columns (1) + (2) + (3).
SOURCE   N.F.R. Crafts, *Can De-industrialisation Seriously Damage Your Wealth?*, Hobart Paper 120 (London: Institute of Economic Affairs, 1993).

This methodology of growth accounting is used in Table 2.1 to identify, for the periods 1950–73 and 1973–87, the sources of economic growth (growth in the capital stock, growth in the labour force and TFP growth) for five countries: France, Germany, Japan, the UK and the USA. Every country in Table 2.1 experienced lower rates of GDP growth in 1973–87 relative to 1950–73[7] *and in every case the slowdown in output growth could largely be attributed to a slowdown in the growth rate of TFP.* More specifically, Table 2.1 shows that in the first period, 1950–73, almost 60 per cent of the annual growth in gross domestic product (GDP) in France and Germany was, on average, due to TFP growth; by contrast, in the same period, TFP growth in the UK and the USA contributed, on average, only 42 and 30 per cent, respectively, to their annual GDP growth rates. The poor economic performance of the UK, during 1973–87, can be traced to its relatively poor TFP growth performance. Between 1950–73 and 1973–87, as shown in Table 2.1, the average annual growth rate in GDP in the UK fell from 3.03 to 1.75 per cent – a decline of 1.28 percentage points; the fall of 0.45 percentage points (from 1.27 to 0.82 per cent per annum) in average TFP growth between the periods thus contributed 35 per cent to the decline in the growth rate of GDP.

TABLE 2.2   *Productivity growth in OECD countries*
(business sector, annual percentage)

	Labour productivity			Total factor productivity		
	1960–73	*1973–9*	*1979–88*	*1960–73*	*1973–9*	*1979–88*
Australia	3.2	2.0	1.1	2.9	1.2	1.0
Austria	5.8	3.3	1.8	3.4	1.4	0.7
Belgium	5.0	2.8	2.1	3.7	1.5	1.1
Canada	2.8	1.5	1.5	2.0	0.7	0.3
Denmark	4.3	2.6	1.5	2.8	1.2	0.8
Finland	5.0	3.4	3.2	3.4	1.7	2.3
France	5.4	3.0	2.4	3.9	1.7	1.5
Germany	4.6	3.4	1.9	2.7	2.0	0.7
Greece	8.8	3.4	0.2	5.8	1.5	−0.7
Italy	6.3	3.0	1.6	4.6	2.2	1.0
Japan	9.4	3.2	3.1	6.4	1.8	1.8
Netherlands	4.9	3.3	1.5	3.1	2.0	0.6
New Zealand	1.8	−1.5	1.4	1.0	−2.2	1.4
Norway	4.1	0.1	2.0	3.6	−0.4	1.4
Spain	6.1	3.8	3.4	4.2	1.7	2.1
Sweden	3.9	1.4	1.6	2.5	0.3	0.9
Switzerland	3.2	0.7	0.9	1.6	−0.9	0.2
UK	3.5	1.5	2.6	2.2	0.5	1.9
US	2.8	0.6	1.6	1.8	0.1	0.7

SOURCE   N.F.R. Crafts, 'Productivity Growth Reconsidered', *Economic Policy*, vol. 15 (1992), pp. 388–426.

Table 2.2 above shows growth rates of both labour productivity and TFP in the business sector of the Organization for Economic Co-operation and Development (OECD) countries for the periods 1960–73, 1973–9 and 1979–88. A number of features stand out. First, for every country and for every period shown in Table 2.2, growth rates for labour productivity exceeded TFP growth rates. Labour productivity increases both because of increases in TFP and also because of increases in the amount of capital available per worker. In the countries (and for the periods) shown in Table 2.2, the growth of capital exceeded that of labour and, hence, the amount of capital available per worker increased. A study of eight East Asian countries[8] also provides evidence that both capital accumulation and TFP change were significant sources of growth. Consequently, labour productivity grew faster than TFP. Second, there are wide disparities in productive performance across countries. For example, in 1960–73, Japan's labour productivity growth rate of 9.4 per cent was two and a half times greater than that of the UK and over five times greater than that of New Zealand. Third, for every country, growth rates of both labour productivity and TFP were highest in 1960–73; since then, irrespective of the productivity measure used, there has been a general fall in the rates of productivity growth. The last two features collectively constitute the post-war 'productivity puzzle'. Reasons for inter-country disparities in productivity levels and growth rates are discussed in the next chapter and this chapter examines the general slowdown in productivity growth that occurred after 1973.

In discussing the sources of economic growth (Table 2.1) the post-1973 sluggishness in output growth was largely attributed to the slowdown in TFP growth. Consequently, the general fall in rates of TFP growth that occurred after 1973 has been the subject of much discussion among economists[9] and four major causes for this TFP slowdown have been identified from a long list of possibilities.[10] The first was the slowing of the pace of new technological development that occurred after 1973. The second was the fact that the fruits of the electronic revolution, which was the major technological achievement of the post-1973 period, posed severe problems for the measurement of productivity and probably led to it being understated. The third was the collective of macroeconomic disruptions that affected the world economy after 1973 and the fourth was a deterioration, after 1973, in the quality of services provided by the capital stock. These causes are, in turn, discussed below.

Innovation is an important source of growth in TFP. Innovative new machinery, materials and processes all contribute to TFP growth by pushing an economy's production frontier (that is, the amounts it can produce with given quantities of capital and labour) outwards. Innovative new products and improvements to existing products also add to productivity both because they represent gains in quality and also because they often make production easier. In turn, innovation depends on the amount spent on research and development (R&D) although it should be noted there might be a considerable lag in R&D spending translating itself into an improvement in productivity.

Table 2.3 shows the growth that occurred in real (that is, inflation-adjusted) spending on R&D in five countries of the OECD over the period (and subperiods of) 1965–85. Although the pattern of spending growth varied across countries it is clear that growth rates in most countries fell in 1970–5.[11] The observed decline in R&D expenditure that occurred in many countries in the late 1960s and early 1970s, bearing in mind the R&D–productivity time lag, offers a plausible explanation for the post-1973 slowdown in TFP growth. Further evidence of the link between R&D spending and productivity was provided by Baily and Chakrabarti[12] who, in a study of the US chemicals and textile industries showed that the sharp fall in productivity growth rates in the former and unchanged growth rates in the latter were accompanied, respectively, by a slowdown of innovation in chemicals and an unchanged level of innovation in textiles.

TABLE 2.3   *Growth in total real R&D expenditure in OECD countries. Average, annual growth rates (%)*

	1965–70	1970–5	1975–80	1980–5	1965–85
France	4.09	2.81	3.70	5.80	4.09
Germany	9.49	3.77	4.90	3.30	5.34
Japan	14.94	6.03	6.77	9.25	9.19
UK	1.39	0.75	3.64	1.10	1.72
USA	2.03	–0.39	3.87	6.54	3.01

SOURCE   A.S. Englander and A. Mittelstadt, *op. cit.*

The slowdown in productivity growth generated by a slowdown in the rate of innovation has been compounded by the fact that much of the innovative activity of the 1970s and the 1980s has been in the fields of computer and electronic equipment. The effect of this has been that many of the fruits of such innovations have been mainly in terms of improved quality – faster and smaller computers and easier and more global communication through fibre-optic networks and satellites – rather than increased quantity. Furthermore, this quality improvement is not fully reflected in the measured output. To take a stylised example, a desktop computer with a 286 chip and a black and white monitor would be regarded as the same product as a notebook computer with a 486 chip and a high-resolution colour monitor. In other words, had the quality improvements of the 1970s and the 1980s been taken fully into account, the rates of output and productivity growth recorded for the post-1973 years would have been higher. The problem, therefore, in this argument, was more one of measurement than actuality. Although econometric estimates indicated that R&D expenditure was able to explain only a small part of the decline in the post-1973 productivity growth rates, Zvi Griliches[13] argued that this evidence, in view of the severe problems that the quality-enhancing innovations of this period posed for productivity measurement, should not be taken at face value. While one knows that R&D expenditure contributes positively to productivity growth, problems with measurement errors mean that, particularly with respect to the last two decades, one cannot, with any degree of accuracy, quantify its contribution.

At a broader level, the dramatic increases in the price of energy that occurred after 1973[14] set in motion two world-wide recessions, in 1975 and 1982 and a sustained increase in prices. In the wake of these events, many governments changed their policy objective from one of ensuring full employment to one of controlling inflation. The underuse of capacity, that resulted from the macroeconomic effects of the post-1973 energy price rises, was reflected in a suboptimal use of capital and labour which then contributed to the slowdown in productivity growth.[15]

Mancur Olson[16] attempted to explain, within the framework of political economy, why the post-1973 macroeconomic outcome was that of *stagflation*.[17] His starting point was to note the existence, in every society, of interest groups (unions, professional associations, producer cartels and so on) which lobbied government to gain certain favourable outcomes. The existence of these groups was likely to make society less efficient since such groups were more likely to be concerned with (and prepared to expend resources on) obtaining a larger share of a given national cake rather than with increasing the size of the cake. Thus, the larger the number of such groups and the greater their influence, the more society's resources would be diverted from meeting productive to meeting distributive ends. Since long-stable societies were more likely to have accumulated such groups (both in number and in influence) than societies with a history of instability, the former were likely to be less efficient and less dynamic than the latter.

As a corollary to the above argument, societies with a long history of stability were also likely to be slower in reacting to economic shocks. The oil price rise came at a juncture when interest groups in many countries, on the basis of their experience of the 1950s and 1960s, expected sustained increases in the real income of their members. Hence, the general increase in prices, which was the consequence of the rise in energy prices, resulted in wage demands that would secure the customary real earnings increase. In the changed conditions of the 1970s, with higher energy prices exerting downward pressure on demand, this was entirely the wrong response since it meant that the entire burden of adjusting to reduced demand fell on output and employment reductions. The result was stagflation. Countries like the UK, which had enjoyed long periods of political, social and institutional stability were particularly prone to such errors; on the other hand, countries such as Japan and Germany which, in the aftermath of the war, had to redesign and rebuild their institutional structures, were more flexible in their responses and partially countered the slump in world demand through wage moderation. Consequently, while the decline in the growth rates of GDP and productivity was, in the 1970s, an experience shared by all industrialised countries, it affected some of them more severely than others.

Attempts to provide a narrower (relative to the broad macroeconomic perspective outlined above) and more direct causal relation between energy prices and productivity growth are, however, fraught with difficulty. For example, Hudson and Jorgenson[18] argued that the importance of energy as a determinant of productivity growth stemmed not from its share in total costs (which was approximately 7 per cent for the major seven[19] OECD countries) but from its complementary relationship with capital. Since energy is needed to operate capital equipment, a rise in energy prices would make the use of machinery more expensive and, hence, cause the rate of investment, which is an important determinant of productivity growth, to fall. The problem was that the post-1973 level of investment remained too high to sustain this hypothesis. For example, for the OECD as a whole, the average, annual growth rate of capital, during 1960–73, was 5.6 per cent and this rate fell to 4.4 per cent during 1973–9.[20]

A more plausible hypothesis is that higher energy prices made unprofitable the old, fuel-inefficient plants built when energy prices were low and thus led to a scrapping of capacity. Since conventional measures of capital stock do not take account of such obsolescence the *measured* growth of capital was higher than actual growth was and consequently the *measured* TFP growth rate was lower than it actually was.[21] In addition, tougher environmental and safety regulations meant that part of the investment undertaken by firms was being diverted to 'unproductive' uses. The consequence of combining these energy and environmental effects was that, after 1973, a given stock of capital produced a smaller flow of services resulting in a smaller flow of output. A piece of evidence to support this hypothesis is that capital productivity has been falling in most industrialised countries – its average, annual growth rate, across the OECD countries, declined from –0.4 per cent during 1960–73 to –1.4 per cent during 1973–9.[22]

The general slowdown in productivity growth since 1973 is one part of the 'productivity puzzle' and, as this chapter has shown, our understanding in this respect is less than perfect and no specific explanation is watertight. The least contentious explanation that may be offered is a well-rounded one, which combines many of the specific elements noted earlier, whereby energy price rises triggered (possibly through the short-sighted responses of powerful and entrenched interest groups) a long recession and the consequent underuse of capacity, together with a decline in the quality of capital services, mixed with an undermeasurement of output and, leavened with prior falls in the rate of innovation, manifested itself in low rates of productivity growth. Lastly, it is possible that it may be a while before the innovation that has occurred, over the past two decades, in the field of electronic technology translates itself into higher rates of productivity growth. Electric power was introduced in the 1880s but it had little impact on productivity until the 1920s.[23] The power of fax machines, personal computers and mobile telephones to enhance productive efficiency may yet remain to be revealed.

In summary, therefore, improvements in labour productivity (that is, output per worker) are the consequence of more investment in either more capital or in new technology (R&D). Investment in capital could be in either physical capital, which is external to the worker or it could be in human capital, which is internal to the worker. However, the growth in the capital stock (whether physical or human) may raise the output per worker but may do little to raise the output per unit of resource (that is, labour plus capital). TFP growth requires innovation and new technology (that is, R&D expenditure) and these matters were discussed in this chapter in the context of a major area of debate in economics, the post-1974 slowdown in TFP growth. However, TFP growth is not what policy makers get excited about – that is reserved for growth in labour productivity. Measures to increase the growth rate of labour productivity, through increased capital accumulation, is the subject of the following two chapters. Chapter 3 asks about the constraints that the macroeconomic environment imposes on investment, but asks also whether the emphasis on macroeconomics is misplaced and whether the answers to productivity growth are to be found, instead, at the operation of the economy at a microlevel. Chapter 4 takes up the issue of education and training, which, in the context of economic policy, today occupies centre-stage and argues that accumulation is more likely to be effective when capital takes human rather than physical form.

3 Economic Policy and Productive Performance

The first chapter argued that it was only through rapid productivity growth that a country could aspire to become a high real wage economy, producing products that embodied large amounts of value added.[1] This chapter builds on this observation by considering ways and means for improving productive performance; however, before doing that it sets the context for the discussion on policy by examining the size of the productivity gap (expressed in terms of differences in productivity levels) that exists between some of the industrialised countries.[2]

The calculation of productivity levels poses some special problems. These arise because output in, say, the UK is calculated by deflating the value of production by an overall price index. This procedure expresses output in the UK as £x billion. An identical procedure for the USA would express output there as y billion. Unfortunately unless we know the appropriate dollar/pound rate of exchange it is not possible to compare the levels of output in the two countries. One possibility is to use market exchange rates to express output in a common currency. However, it is more appropriate to use exchange rates which equalise purchasing power between countries. Exchange rates calculated on this basis are known as purchasing power parity (PPP) exchange rates. Thus if it requires $200 to purchase a basket of goods and services that could be bought in the UK for £100 the PPP exchange rate is $2/£. Then the UK output of £x billion may be expressed as 2x$ billion and can then be compared to the y billion output of the USA. As any tourist knows market rates rarely coincide with PPP rates – many items appear very expensive in, for example, Scandinavian countries when the pound is converted into kroner at market rates. However, the calculation of PPP rates is itself problematical since it is difficult to, firstly, identify a common basket of goods and services[3] across countries and, secondly, to allow for quality differences across countries in the items in the basket.

In a recent study by international management consultants McKinsey,[4] based on value added in manufacturing per hour worked, Japan's overall productivity in manufacturing, in 1990, was 17 per cent lower than that of the USA and only slightly better than that of Germany. This aggregate finding, however, masked enormous variations in productivity between different sectors in manufacturing. For example, productivity in motor parts, car assembly and consumer electronics was much higher in Japan than in the USA[5] while in Germany it was much lower than in the USA.[6] On the other hand, in food manufacturing and in brewing, Japanese productivity levels were one-third that in the USA and half that in Germany.

The magnitude of the UK's 'productivity problem' may be judged from the fact that productivity in manufacturing in Germany (bearing in mind that Germany had the lowest productivity level in manufacturing in the comparisons cited above) has been estimated to be at least 50 per cent higher than in the UK.[7] To take a specific example, Ford of Europe estimated that, in 1990, it took 52.2 hours to produce a Fiesta in Dagenham, 33.3 hours to produce it in Valencia and only 29.9 hours to produce it in Cologne; a similar story could be told with respect to other Ford products.[8] Although, over the 1980s, the UK enjoyed a faster rate of growth in labour productivity in manufacturing than any other country except Japan (see Table 3.1) it has a long way to go before its productivity level is on par with that in the USA, Japan and Germany.

TABLE 3.1   *Growth in output per man-hour. Average annual percentage rates*

	1950–73	1973–9	1979–89
UK	3.4	1.1	4.8
US	2.8	1.3	3.4
Japan	9.5	5.1	5.4
Germany	5.8	4.2	1.8
France	5.7	4.6	3.2

SOURCE   *Treasury Bulletin*, vol. 3 (1992), no. 2, p. 27.

Against a backdrop of large differences in productivity levels between some of the major industrialised countries, this chapter turns to considering ways in which productive performance might be improved. There are essentially two views as to why certain countries have displayed a much better productive performance than others. The first view is that sluggish productivity growth (for example, in the USA and the UK) is the result of low rates of investment. This view – the implications of which are discussed below – may be termed a *macroeconomic* view of productivity. In contrast, another view emphasises instead the microeconomic factors determining productivity growth. According to this view the reasons for poor productivity growth are to be found largely in the manner in which individual firms operate rather than in the aggregate macroeconomic environment. This *microeconomic* view of productivity is discussed in the latter part of the chapter.

The *macroeconomic* view of productivity, which is well set out by George Hatsopoulos, Paul Krugman and Lawrence Summers[9] (hereafter HKS) emphasises the strong and positive link between capital formation and economic growth that has been noted by several economists.[10] HKS were careful to point out that their concept of capital was a broad one; it embraced both visible items such as plant and machinery and invisible items such as knowledge acquired through expenditure on R&D and the skills acquired through the willingness of firms to train workers or to take losses while developing new products or new markets. Under this view of capital, therefore, investment was defined as any use of business resources for the purpose of increasing the stock of capital. HKS argued that the main cause of poor productivity growth in countries like the USA and UK (relative to Japan and Germany) was that the former countries had low rates of capital formation (that is, investment) compared with the latter. Although there were many reasons for this low investment they could essentially be categorised as the high cost of capital leading to low demand for investment funds and the disincentives to saving offered by the fiscal system leading to a low supply of investment funds.

To understand the effects of capital costs on investment consider the following stylised example.[11] Firm A operating in the UK faces capital costs of 10 per cent while firm B operating in Japan faces capital costs of only 3 per cent. If a capital sum of £100 is to be repaid at the end of 2 years, then firm A will undertake the investment only if it will yield a return of £121 at the end of 2 years while firm B will undertake the same investment for a return of only £106 over the same period; on a 20 year loan of £100 the disparity is even greater – firm A will demand a return of at least £673 at the end of 20 years while firm B will be content with a return greater than £181 at the end of 20 years. Clearly, because of the difference in capital costs, Japanese firms will undertake many investments that their UK counterparts will not consider profitable. Moreover, it is in terms of *long-term investment* that UK firms will be most disadvantaged.

Estimating the magnitude of differences in capital costs between countries is not easy because firms raise money from borrowing and from equity so that the cost of capital cannot be measured simply by differences in interest rates. Normally the cost of equity will be higher than that of debt since investors demand higher returns on equity investments because such investments are more risky than debenture investments. Thus, two countries may have the same real interest rates[12] but different costs of capital. Using stock market multiples and taking into account taxes and depreciation, the cost of capital for a 20 year investment in plant and equipment in the USA in 1989 was estimated to be 60 per cent higher than in Germany and Japan.[13] Part of the reason for this is that the interconnections between finance and industry in Germany and Japan – whereby, for example, bankers sit on the board of directors of industrial companies and industrialists sit on the boards of banks[14] – allow for a much higher debt to equity ratio. Since debt is usually cheaper than equity, a lower cost of capital is the result.

On the supply side, the problem in the USA and the UK is that both countries have very low rates of national saving. National saving is discussed in detail in Chapter 16 but, briefly, it is the sum of household, corporate and government saving. In the absence of foreign borrowing, it can be thought of as the investment funds available to the country as a whole. The problem of low rates of national saving in the UK and USA is the result of low rates of household saving and corporate profits combined with large government deficits. Over the past 5 years, the UK household saving ratio, that is the fraction of household disposable income that is not consumed, though it had more than trebled from a low of around 3 per cent in 1987 to 11 per cent by the first quarter of 1992, has remained lower than that in its main European competitors. In 1991, the household saving ratio was 15.6 per cent in Italy, 13.7 per cent in Germany and 12.7 per cent in France. The volume of national saving is related to the surpluses and deficits generated by the different sectors of the economy. For example, government deficits, that is, the difference between current government expenditure and revenue, reduce the volume of national saving just as government surpluses cause it to increase. During 1960–90, of the OECD countries, Japan had the highest rate of national saving (31 per cent) and the UK and the USA, at 17 and 18 per cent, respectively, the lowest rates.

The argument that macroeconomic policy is an important influence on industrial development has also been put forward, in the context of the UK, by Walter Eltis.[15] His starting point is the observation that UK industry is relatively unprofitable compared to its major competitors. This fact has profound consequences for the performance of industry in the UK. Low profitability in UK industry leads it to rely on borrowing from financial institutions, rather than on internally generated profits, for financing its investments. To protect their investments, financial institutions monitor very closely the financial performance of their industrial clients. The lack of profitability in UK industry means that an adverse combination of external events could cause a firm difficulty in meeting its interest payments. This, in turn, could mean that its creditors did not renew its loans or else renewed them under punitive conditions possibly even involving changes to the firm's management. The result is that both creditors and borrowers have a common interest in avoiding long-term projects associated with new products or advances in technology (even though such projects, if successful, offer the prospects of large profits) in favour of low-profit, but safe, investments.

Thus industry in the UK is trapped in a vicious circle in which low profits lead firms to seek low-profit-making activities which, in turn, perpetuate their poor profit performance. By contrast, the higher profitability of French, German and Japanese industry means adequate margins for interest payments are possible, even in the face of economic setbacks. Consequently, industry in these countries, cushioned by adequate profits, is able to focus on quality and innovation, while industry in the UK, operating with more slender profit margins, is primarily concerned with keeping its creditors at bay. In order to break out of this cycle, UK industry has to become more profitable and this would, essentially, require action on two fronts. First, a significant part of any future productivity gains should translate into higher profits rather than, as at present, going almost entirely towards wage increases. This, in turn, would require unions and employers to accept that real wage growth would not keep pace with productivity. Second, governments should attempt, by avoiding policies that lead to excessive economic fluctuations, to create a stable macroeconomic climate. In the main this would mean pursuing budgetary policies which the markets regarded as credible, that is keeping public borrowing down to a level that would ensure that a stable ratio of public debt to GDP could be maintained at a low rate of inflation.

The problem of poor productivity growth can also be viewed from a *microeconomic* perspective. From this perspective, while the capital formation problem may be important in holding back productivity growth, the main problems lie not at the level of the aggregate economy but at the level of the individual firm and of the factory floor. In particular, problems such as poor design, slow product development, high rate of defects, unreliable delivery times – problems which, over the past 50 years have been responsible for manufacturing's decline in both the USA and the UK – cannot be explained away in terms of the general macroeconomic environment. Nor can macroeconomics explain why, within the same economic environment, some firms are successful while other firms fail.

Perhaps the best and most persuasive exponent of this microeconomic perspective on productivity is the MIT Commission on Industrial Productivity and its views are encapsulated in the work of Michael Dertouzos, Richard Lester and Robert Solow[16] (hereafter abbreviated to DLS). On the basis of eight detailed industry case studies – semiconductors, computers and copiers, commercial aircraft, consumer electronics, steel, chemicals, textiles, automobiles and machine tools – they identified six patterns of industrial behaviour, which, when taken together, best explained the poor performance of US manufacturing in the post-war period. These six patterns were: a reliance on outdated strategies, weaknesses in product design and development, failures of cooperation, short time horizons, neglect of human resources and government and industry working at cross-purposes. In the paragraphs that follow, the views of DLS with respect to some of these issues are summarised and discussed. Short time horizons have already been mentioned; discussion of human resources and of the role of government in promoting economic development is postponed since they are important enough to merit separate chapters and are dealt with later. This chapter therefore discusses only the first three of the above six points.

The industrial development of the UK and the USA was based on the large-scale manufacture of standardised products; the market for these products was provided, in the case of the UK, by its empire while the size of the domestic market in the USA was large enough to sustain this method of production. The increased industrial competition of the post-war period – engendered first by the rise, out of the ashes of the Second World War, of Japan, Germany and France and, second, by the more recent emergence of the industrial economies of Asia – combined with the greater affluence of today's customers has meant that the strategy of industrial growth through mass production methods is no longer viable. Instead successful industrial strategy today consists of producing low-volume, high-quality products for niche markets. This has enormous implications for industrial organisation: narrow specialism has given way to the multiskilled worker – this, in turn, has meant that industrial relations are cooperative rather than confrontational; price competition has given way to competition on the basis of quality – consequently, product innovation and defect-free methods are now of profound importance and close liaison with suppliers and customers are essential for survival.

Weaknesses in product design and development stem from differences, between countries, in attitudes towards industrial research. There is no doubt that both the UK and the USA are leaders in basic research – where they fail is in converting research ideas into marketable products. Indeed, in both countries, product realisation is a poor cousin of fundamental research. Conversely, the focus of research in other countries is not on the 'big idea' but on applied research and on product and process development. This difference in attitude towards research shows up in a number of areas which are crucial for industrial success. The first is design. The traditional approach is to design a product without enquiring as to how easy or difficult it would be to manufacture. A much better system – and one that the Japanese have always used – is for a multidisciplinary team to work on a product by simultaneously addressing the questions of design and production. Another area of weakness is product development. Kim Clark and associates[17] found that the Japanese needed only half as much time as the Americans to take a new car from concept to manufacture. This speed of product development was attributed to resolving conflicts at the outset and the simultaneous (as opposed to sequential) pursuit of the different development activities, with the entire matrix of activities being supervised by a 'heavyweight' project manager. Lastly, the different attitudes towards research show up in differences in attitudes towards product improvement. Emphasis on the 'big idea' means, very often, that the potential for subsequent, incremental improvements are undervalued. Nor is it recognised that the cumulative effect of incremental improvements may eventually exceed that of the original idea. The Japanese strategy is to introduce a product quickly to the market, find out its deficiencies, attend to the defects and, through close monitoring of customer feedback, make continuous adjustments and improvements to the product.

The third issue relating to poor productive performance is the absence of cooperation. The collapse of the command economies of Eastern Europe has focused attention on the differences that exist between the free market economies of the different Western countries. As Lester Thurow argues 'it is a new playing field: the "I" of America or the UK versus "Das Volk" and "Japan Inc."; the essential difference between the two is the relative stress placed on communitarian and individualistic values as the best route to economic success'.[18] In this conflict between, on the one hand, a philosophy which lauds individual enterprise and success (the Anglo-American model) and another which believes in 'hammering down all nails' (the German–Japanese model) there can be little doubt that, over the past three decades, it is the latter that has emerged the winner. This has important lessons for the losers. First, Japanese levels of efficiency can be attained by the West – the productivity of Japanese 'transplants' in the USA and the UK is almost as high as that of the parent companies in Japan. Second, to achieve these levels on an economy-wide basis will require, however, a fundamental change of attitude. In terms of industrial strategy, this change essentially means that cooperation must replace individualism.

This cooperation, according to DLS, would have to take many forms. First, there is cooperation between firms and their suppliers: without such cooperation methods such as just-in-time (JIT) – which eliminate the need for large inventories – cannot be implemented. Second, there is cooperation between labour and management: new systems of industrial relations are based on employee participation in shop-floor problem solving and in flexible teams that do away with traditional, narrow job descriptions. Third, there is co-operation between managers: in Japan and Germany the rotation of executives through all branches of operation (marketing, finance, production and research) is seen as a broadening of experience. Fourth, there is cooperation between producers and consumers: it is these links that encourage and make possible product innovations and improvements. Lastly, there is cooperation between government and industry: the state cannot act as a substitute for private industry but, by the same token, it cannot wash its hands of responsibility for industrial performance. What is needed is for the government to pursue policies which are in the best long-term interests of industry and which command its support.

To summarise therefore, from a macroeconomic perspective, a lack of investment, particularly in long-term projects, is the root cause of the poor productivity performance of manufacturing in the UK and in the USA. This lack of investment stems from a poor supply of funds to industry. This is partly due to small household surpluses and large government deficits, but partly also due to the inability of industrial companies to generate internal resources through adequate levels of profit. Many of the causes for the paucity of investment funds are amenable to correction through macroeconomic policy. Essentially this requires the provision of a stable macroeconomic environment, control of government deficits and a reform of the tax system both to encourage saving and to direct it towards industry.[19] Lastly, from the demand side, there must be a willingness to use available funds for long-term investment in industry and this requires appropriate monetary and fiscal policies to ensure low capital costs. At the same time, the work of the MIT Commission on Industrial Productivity makes clear that, at a *microeconomic* level, there are certain features of industrial management and organisation which may be identified as constituting 'best practice'. These are pursuing simultaneous improvements in cost, quality and delivery, staying close to customers and suppliers, using technology to strategic advantage, adopting flatter and less-compartmentalised organisations and seeking out innovative human resource policies. It is the constant pursuit of such best practice methods, in conjunction with macroeconomic policies that create a favourable climate for investment and growth, that constitutes the 'right' approach to sowing the seeds of productivity growth.

4 Human Capital, Education and Training

Human capital refers to the stock of acquired skills, knowledge and abilities of human beings. Underlying this concept is the idea that such skills and knowledge enhance productivity and, moreover, they do so by enough to justify the expenditure undertaken to acquire them. Thus, spending to increase the stock of human capital should be viewed as 'investment', not as 'consumption'. The return to investment in human capital is the increased amount of output that results from an expansion (and deepening) of skills and knowledge.

Although Adam Smith,[1] writing in 1776, had emphasised the importance of workers' skills as a fundamental source of economic prosperity, it was nearly two centuries later that the work of Gary Becker[2] provided a proper conceptual framework for the analysis of human capital. This extension of economic theory to encompass human capital was buttressed by the empirical work of Edward Denison[3] and Theodore Schultz[4] who established that there was indeed a connection between improved skills and knowledge and higher productivity. Until then, economists had persisted with a tripartite division between the factors of production (land, labour and capital) in which the contribution of labour to the production process stemmed from its *quantity* and not from its *quality*.

The fundamental insight that Becker provided was that the increased (future) earnings associated with investment in human capital should be set against the costs of undertaking such investment. These costs would be not just, for example, the costs of education and training (the direct costs) but also the earnings opportunities forgone while the period of education and training was being undertaken (the indirect costs). Thus, the theory emphasised the need for including all the costs, direct and indirect, associated with investment in human capital. Secondly, Becker stressed the distribution of income and wealth over the lifetime of an individual: underlying a person's decision to go to university is the calculation that the alternative of starting work immediately after school would, when evaluated over the person's lifetime, yield a less satisfactory income stream. Thus, in Becker's analysis, the rate of return on investment in human capital was obtained by evaluating the present value of the future stream of earnings that were likely to result from this investment. Rational individuals would invest in human capital up to the point where the return on such investment equalled the rate that could be obtained on alternative investment opportunities.

Broadly speaking, anything that serves to improve population quality should be regarded as contributing to human capital formation; thus improvements in nutrition, in health and in housing should all be regarded as increasing the stock of human capital. While this broad interpretation of human capital would command general acceptance, in operational terms most policy makers would regard education and training as lying at the heart of human capital. Until recently, explanations of the UK's poor economic performance tended to ignore the paucity of its skills base and emphasised instead factors (to name but a few) such as the high level of public spending and government intervention in the economy, entrepreneurial failure, stemming from a failure of incentives caused, in turn, by a distorted tax–benefit system and strong and (irresponsible) unions. Increasingly, however, economists who have been concerned about the poor productive performance of the UK, *vis-à-vis* Japan and Germany, have tended to apportion a major part of the blame to inadequacies in its educational and training system.

A number of independent researchers provide evidence for the 'skills gap' that exists between the UK and other industrialised countries and an excellent overview of this is provided by Sig Prais.[5] In international comparisons of mathematics test results for secondary school pupils, British pupils were outperformed by their counterparts in many Western European countries and in Japan, Korea and Taiwan. Indeed, it was estimated that average British pupils were a year behind average pupils in a European group, comprising The Netherlands, France and Belgium and 2 years behind average Japanese pupils. In terms of post-compulsory education and training, it has been shown[6] that, in 1990, only 37 per cent of 16–18 year olds in Britain were in full-time education; of the remaining 63 per cent only 15 per cent were in youth training. This rate is among the lowest in the group of the Organization for Economic Co-operation and Development (OECD) countries: in 1986, when the UK rate was 33 per cent, the average participation rate in full-time post-compulsory education, for a group of 13 OECD countries was 66 per cent. In turn, differences in the participation rates in post-compulsory education between the UK and other countries were reflected in differences in the skill levels of their respective work-forces: for example, during 1988–91, 64 per cent of the work-force in the UK had no vocational qualifications and only 25 per cent had intermediate vocational qualifications while, in Germany, the corresponding figures were 25 and 63 per cent, respectively.[7]

The most persuasive evidence for the hypothesis that a paucity of skills translates itself into low productivity is provided by a major, and continuing, programme of research undertaken at the National Institute of Economic and

Social Research (NIESR) in London. The general conclusion of this body of research was that, comparing like with like, the main difference between industrial plants in Britain and in Continental Europe was not in the quality of machinery used – which was often very similar – but in the standards of maintenance of machinery: because preventive maintenance, carried out by vocationally qualified staff, was routine on the Continent, breakdowns were rare; on the other hand, frequent breakdowns were an accepted part of British industrial life. For example, using matched samples of British and West German plants in the furniture industry, the NIESR[8] concluded that 'it was with the help of a thoroughly qualified work force [in Germany] that advanced machinery and advanced production methods were introduced, put into operation and fully exploited'. An important productivity-related benefit of better skills was provided by a corps of highly trained foremen who ensured that machinery could be adapted to specific needs, that machinery could be repaired without call on mechanics and that the flow of work met delivery dates.[9] At a broader level, it was found that the skill levels of UK workers in manufacturing were substantially lower than those of their German counterparts and that this gap in skills was largely responsible for the UK's comparatively poor export performance.[10] Indeed for three important export markets (the USA, Belgium and The Netherlands) the evidence was that the larger the proportion of workers in manufacturing with no qualifications in the UK, relative to Germany, the poorer the UK's relative export performance in that sector. In essence, a highly skilled work-force enabled firms to make rapid adjustments to the organisation of their production so as to produce quality products geared to the needs of a variety of specialised markets.

Given this background of low skill levels in the UK and given also the evidence that such skill shortages are often echoed in low levels of productivity, increased investment in human capital formation is crucial to improving the country's economic performance. The low level of skills in the UK stems from problems of both supply and demand. On the supply side, in direct contrast to the experience of most other industrialised countries, the UK is characterised by a large proportion of young people leaving full-time education between the ages of 16 and 18 years, either to enter employment or to enrol on the government's Youth Training Scheme[11] (YTS). To understand why leaving full-time education, after compulsory schooling, should be a popular option with British youth, one has to understand the nature of the alternatives. These alternatives are either to spend 2 years in post-compulsory further education[12] and then to seek employment or to progress from further education into higher education[13] and thereby postpone entering the jobs market for a further period of 3 years.

The first alternative is unattractive because the rate of return associated with employment after 2 years of further education is modest. It has been estimated[14] that young people who take vocational courses after post-compulsory schooling do not, over a lifetime, do any better than those who leave school at 16 years with the appropriate qualifications; the lifetime earnings for those who enter the jobs market after A-levels[15] is on average, for men, only 6 per cent higher than for qualified school leavers. This low rate of return to further education is due, in part, to employers in the UK being used to recruiting from the 16–17 years age group, either directly or through the YTS.[16] As a consequence, job opportunities for those seeking entry into the jobs market directly after a period of further education are limited. However, the low rate of return is also due to the fact that wages of qualified school-leavers are quite high[17] and that joining a YTS programme is financially more rewarding than staying on in further education;[18] the opportunity costs of further education are, therefore, quite high.

The second alternative, that of seeking employment after progressing from further into higher education, is attractive in that those completing higher education can expect a significant income gain.[19] However, because entry into higher education in the UK is highly restricted, there is a genuine risk that the move from further into higher education may not be possible which would leave the aspirant, as the previous discussion has indicated, in the worst possible situation. Until 1988, the participation rate in higher education of 18 year olds was under 15 per cent. In the wake of the subsequent expansion in higher education, this rate rose to nearly 30 per cent by 1993. The fact that the UK Government, in response to high levels of public borrowing, intends reducing the number of entrants into higher education in 1994 by 3.5 per cent raises legitimate fears that this expansion may be reversed. Such anxieties, in turn, do nothing to reassure young people that their ambitions to undertake higher education will not be thwarted by the exigencies of the economic cycle.

In terms of the demand for skilled workers, the problem is that employers in the UK are not convinced of the value of training. They accord it a low priority in their budgets and a low status within their organisations: pay and career advancement are determined by seniority not skill levels and worker skills are not broadened through job rotation and work teams; moreover, lack of skills and qualifications afflict managers as much as workers. One reason for this state of affairs is that industry in the UK is concentrated in the manufacture of products that are the least demanding in terms of skills. The shift in the structure of UK industry from manufacturing to services has not helped. The largest growth in employment in the UK has been in the part-time service sector where little or no training is required.[20]

The conjunction, in the UK, of employer attitudes to training and low staying-on rates in full-time, post-compulsory education means that the demand for and supply of well-trained workers are both stifled. Consequently, a majority of enterprises in the UK, get trapped in what David Finegold and David Soskice[21] termed a 'low-skills equilibrium'. A dearth of well-trained managers and workers leads to poor quality goods and services being produced and the fact that production is concentrated in such products means, in turn, that there is little demand for (or status attached to) well-trained personnel. A low skills base becomes, therefore, both the cause and the consequence of poor economic performance.

In order to break free from the vicious circle of poor training and poor performance, into which UK industry finds itself locked, the active intervention of the government is needed. What form should such intervention take? Most fundamentally, government should construct (or assist in the construction of) bridges between the end of compulsory schooling and entry into the jobs market. These bridges, when crossed, should equip school-leavers with the appropriate educational and vocational skills for employment. How should such bridges be built? The UK Government has sought to establish, for young people, two vocational paths into the world of work. The first is based upon full-time study at a further education institution and is aimed at obtaining General National Vocational Qualifications (GNVQs). Unlike the highly specific National Vocational Qualifications (NVQs) – discussed below – these are not intended to have occupational relevance and indeed they are viewed as the vocational alternative to (and equivalent of) the more academically oriented A-levels. The second and main path is part-time and work-based education and training and includes training provided by youth training and training sponsored and/or provided by employers. This work-based vocational path is aimed at obtaining National Vocational Qualifications (NVQs) which measure an individual's ability to perform a task at different levels of competence. Putting aside the low standards and attainments of work-based training in the UK[22] there is a more fundamental scepticism about whether the system of employer-led provision of education and training, adopted in the UK, is appropriate to its needs.

According to David Soskice[23] it is clear that, in the UK, the emphasis by the government on actively involving the private sector in the construction of such a bridge, has been misplaced. He argues that successful private sector involvement in the training of school-leavers requires certain institutional preconditions. First, companies need reassurance that workers trained by them will not be lured away by others through the promise of higher wages; this requires a system of managed wage competition between companies which makes poaching difficult. Secondly, companies need advice on setting up and running in-house training programmes; this needs powerful and influential employers' organisations – in which their members repose confidence – to advise on such matters. Thirdly, companies need access to long-term finance so that their financial position will not be jeopardised by long-term investments such as training; this requires close and long-term relationships between business and finance. Lastly, skilled workers, working with considerable autonomy, would possess considerable bargaining power and companies need reassurance that this power will not be misused; this requires the active involvement of unions in shaping the training policy of companies.

These conditions, which exist in all advanced economies in which the private sector plays a central role in training,[24] simply do not prevail in the UK. Nor would it be possible to develop such features easily since often they are embedded within, and stem from, the cultural traditions of the economies that possess them. Moreover, the nature of the training system adopted cannot be divorced from the type of economic role that a country wishes to play. The German system, which takes as its purpose the maintenance of German superiority in manufacturing, places considerable emphasis on teaching young workers about operating (and repairing) machines. The Japanese system, with its emphasis on lifetime association with a company, relies on company-based training, based on job rotation through the different departments, to acquaint employees with all aspects of the company's affairs.

The alternative to private sector initiative in the training of school-leavers would be to build educational and vocational bridges between school and employment, through an expansion of the further and higher education systems. In pursuing this alternative, the UK could learn many lessons from the USA. The USA's productive superiority is based largely upon its lead, over other countries, in services rather than in manufacturing. One explanation for this is the USA's superiority in terms of work organisation and in terms of customer interaction, both of which are central to a productive service sector. As a consequence, the worker qualities most in demand by employers, particularly in services, are social, organisational and computing skills.[25] It is precisely these qualities that a general system of education can deliver; the education system in the USA – in which most students are in school until they graduate at the age of 18 or 19 years and in which 55 per cent of high school graduates go on to another 2–4 years of general higher education – delivers these qualities in bulk. Mass participation in post-compulsory education therefore offers a route out of the 'low-skills equilibrium' trap discussed earlier.

However, for post-compulsory education to provide such a route certain changes must take place. Firstly and most fundamentally, there must occur a change in attitude towards vocational education. Technical and work-related subjects, in the UK's education system, have long suffered from a second-class status in relation to academic courses.[26] The result is that practical, technical and vocational skills tend to be undervalued and academic and theoretical knowledge to be overvalued. Given the low returns attached to vocational courses (discussed earlier) this may be understandable. This is a legacy of long years of neglect of technical and vocational courses in full-time further education. The remedy for that lies in improving the quality and status of such courses and the institutions that provide them.

Secondly, it is necessary to ensure that staying on in full-time education is financially more attractive than leaving after the age of 16 years. The UK, with fully funded places for all entrants, has a very generous higher education system,[27] but it also has a very niggardly further education system in which no financial support is available to those who, after compulsory schooling, either stay on in school or enrol in colleges of further education. Although financial support for students in higher education has over the past few years become less generous this has not been balanced by a loosening of the purse strings (through, for example, the payment of an education maintenance allowance) for those in the 16–18 years age group who are in full-time education.

Lastly, in order to make staying on in full-time education more attractive than leaving school at the age of 16 years, employers should stop recruiting mainly from the ranks of school-leavers.[28] To some extent this is already happening in the UK. There has been a collapse in the employment of unskilled males in the UK as many of the 'good jobs' that unskilled men used to do, in shipping and steel, have disappeared. Between 1977 and 1991 the proportion of low-skilled men with jobs fell from 88 to 67 per cent and, over the period, the proportion of low-skilled jobs in the economy fell from 60 to 35 per cent.[29] Paralleling this has been a dramatic rise, over the past 5 years, in the number of young people staying on in higher education. This has been in response to companies signalling both their need for social and organisational skills and also their belief that such skills are best acquired through higher education;[30] it has been made possible by the government allowing an expansion of the higher education system in the UK.

However, one niggling anxiety about the emphasis that most industrialised countries are coming to place on training, is that it may (quite wrongly) be seen as a panacea for all manner of economic ills. The problem with training, as *The Economist* newspaper noted,[31] is that it is easy to be seduced by its rhetoric: support for education and training sounds modern and caring and pro-market and pro-worker; it embraces the future by emphasising new technology and skills and it holds out the prospect of an abundant supply of well-paid jobs. Much of this rhetoric has strong foundations in reality.

However, it is appropriate, in concluding this chapter, to sound two notes of caution.

The first is that the benefits of an expensive and high-quality higher education system (which is almost an icon of faith in the UK) for economic performance may be overrated. On one estimate, 23 per cent of graduates were in jobs where a higher education degree was neither required nor helpful.[32] The other point of caution is that social pathologies are emerging, at least in the USA and, to a lesser extent, in Europe, as a problem that is as serious as a lack of job-specific skills.[33] Foisting training on people with low self-esteem, poor self-discipline and a lack of basic educational skills may not be very productive.[34] On this diagnosis, some of the problem of human capital formation may lie in family structures and in school rather than in universities and the work-place.

II Unemployment

5 The Measurement of Unemployment

Unemployment has emerged as the single most pressing problem facing the countries of the European Union (EU) in the 1990s.[1] The reasons why unemployment matters are that 'it generally reduces output and aggregate income; it increases inequality, since the unemployed lose more than the employed; it erodes human capital; and finally it involves psychic costs – people need to be needed'.[2] In 1992, 16 million people, one in ten of the EU's labour force, were unemployed. Of these, half had been unemployed for over a year. What makes the emergence of unemployment in the early 1990s particularly frustrating is that during 1986–90, which was one of strong job growth in the EU, the unemployment rate in the EU fell from 10.8 per cent in 1985 to 8.3 per cent in 1990. Since 1990, jobless totals in the EU have risen sharply. As Table 5.1 shows, between 1990 and 1992, unemployment rates rose in every country of the EU.

TABLE 5.1 *Standardised EC unemployment rates, December 1990–August 1992 (seasonally adjusted)*

	Total %		Male %		Female %		Under 25 %	
	1990	1992	1990	1992	1990	1992	1990	1992
Belgium	8.0	5.1	5.1	5.5	12.4	12.3	18.0	17.5
Denmark	8.1	7.3	7.3	8.6	8.9	11.0	10.5	11.5
Germany	4.4	4.7	3.8	4.2	5.4	5.5	3.9	4.2
Greece	n/a	n/a	n/a	n/a	n/a	n/a	n/a	n/a
Spain	15.9	17.1	11.8	13.3	23.5	24.3	31.3	30.3
France	9.2	10.0	6.9	8.1	12.1	12.5	19.5	21.5
Ireland	14.7	18.1	14.1	17.1	15.9	19.9	21.6	28.4
Italy	10.0	10.6	6.7	7.0	15.7	16.7	28.3	29.2
Luxembourg	1.8	2.0	1.3	1.4	2.8	2.9	4.3	3.6
The Netherlands	7.3	6.0	5.0	5.1	10.9	7.5	10.9	9.3
Portugal	4.0	4.6	2.6	3.4	5.8	6.0	8.9	9.6
UK	7.8	11.0	8.3	12.3	7.0	9.4	12.1	17.5
EC	8.4	9.5	6.7	8.1	11.6	16.5	16.5	18.2

SOURCE Employment Policy Institute, *Economic Report*, vol. 7 (December 1992).

A further sense of failure is due to the fact that the EU's sorry record on unemployment is in sharp contrast with the relative success that some other countries of the Organization for Economic Co-operation and Development (OECD) have had in keeping unemployment low. The unemployment rate in the EU was lower than that in the USA for every year of the period 1960–80 and, up to the first oil price shock of 1974, comparable to that of Japan. Table 5.2 below shows that the EU has had, since 1985, higher unemployment rates than non-EU Europe,[3] Japan and the USA and has also a much larger proportion of its unemployed in the form of long-term unemployed (that is, those unemployed for over a year). As the European Commission ruefully noted,[4] the USA and, to a lesser extent, Japan have managed to achieve a strong increase in employment creation. Where the two countries have differed is in the manner in which they have created jobs: the USA has created jobs by combining modest output growth with even more modest productivity growth; Japan, by contrast, has combined strong productivity growth with an even stronger output growth. Be that as it may, employment creation in North America and Japan has dwarfed that in the EU. Since 1974, both the EU and North America created a little over 5 million public sector jobs, but while North America created another 29.8 million private sector jobs, the EU was able to manage only another 3.1 million.[5]

TABLE 5.2   *Unemployment rates: EC, non-EC Europe, US and Japan, 1975–91*

	1975 %	1985 %	1990 %	1991 %	LTU* 1991 %
EC	4.1	10.8	8.3	8.8	50.0
Non-EC Europe	1.6	2.2	2.3	3.5	n/a
US	8.2	7.1	5.6	6.8	6.3
Japan	1.8	2.2	2.0	2.1	17.9

* Long-term unemployed
SOURCE   Employment Policy Institute, *op. cit.*

Against this background, the topic of unemployment forms the substance of this and the next three chapters. Naturally enough, the most urgent questions relate to the causes of, and policies for, reducing unemployment. The next chapter argues that the issue of unemployment cannot be separated from that of inflation. Therefore, the solution to unemployment lies not so much in creating jobs (which is easy) but in creating jobs *without generating inflationary pressures* (which is difficult). As a corollary, demand management policies, which emphasise job creation through an expansion of demand but which pay little attention to the inflationary consequences of such an expansion, are seen today as providing, at best, a temporary palliative for unemployment. A more permanent solution needs structural change through *supply-side policies*. A description of such policies and an analysis of their underlying logic is the subject of Chapter 7. Chapter 8 draws a distinction between unemployment and joblessness. Unemployment statistics understate the true extent of joblessness because many jobless persons, by virtue of the fact that they have stopped searching for jobs and, hence, dropped out of the labour market, are not included in the unemployment statistics. Why this has become an increasingly common phenomenon and what its social and economic consequences are, is discussed in Chapter 8. A major and the first port of call on this voyage of understanding the nature of unemployment, is the issue of how unemployment is (should be) *measured*. The measurement of unemployment is the subject of this chapter. Discussion of this issue clarifies the concept of unemployment, encompasses questions of whether some measures of unemployment are to be preferred to others and asks whether there exists a 'true' measure of unemployment.

There is no difficulty, in principle, in defining who are the unemployed: they are simply those persons who are out of work and who are seeking and are available for employment. Taken together, the unemployed and the employed constitute a country's (or region's) *labour force*. The labour force is typically less than the size of the 'working-age' population, defined as the number of persons between the ages of 16 and 64 years. This is because there are many persons between these ages who either do not wish to take paid employment (for example, housewives and students) or who are unable to do so (for example, the disabled and the sick). Thus, for example, the working-age population in the EU countries, in 1992, was 220 million (out of a total population of 330 million) of whom 148 million or 68 per cent, were in the labour force.

That fraction of the working-age population that is in the labour force is called the 'participation rate'. Obviously, the participation rate varies both by sex and by age group. For example, 'prime-age' males (those between 25 and 50 years) would typically have participation rates in excess of 95 per cent; for women the rate is lower, though it should be added, the outstanding feature of labour markets in the industrialised countries, over the past 20 years, has been the spectacular rise in female participation rates. For example, in the UK, women's participation in the labour force went up from around 50 per cent in 1973 to over 60 per cent in 1992, while the average for the EU countries increased, over the same period, from 32 to 40 per cent. Overall, averaging across the sexes and the different age groups, in 1992, approximately three-quarters of the working-age population, in OECD countries, was in the labour force, as compared to 68 per cent for the EU.

The problem of *measuring* unemployment arises when the term 'seeking and available for work' is sought to be made explicit. The International Labour Office (ILO) provides an internationally agreed definition of unemployment. According to the ILO, to be classed as unemployed an individual has to be jobless, available to start work within a fortnight and to have either sought work[6] at some time within the past 4 weeks or be waiting to take up a job. The ILO approach to measuring unemployment is dependent on a fairly detailed knowledge of an individual's circumstances and can, therefore, only be implemented through sampling methods.[7] The Labour Force Survey (LFS), involving detailed interviews with a sample of 60 000 households has, since 1984, provided (in addition to a wealth of labour market data) annual estimates, on the ILO definition, of the unemployment rate in Britain.[8] Such estimates are also available for other leading developed economies and this enables unemployment rates to be compared across countries on a standardised basis.[9]

Another method for measuring unemployment and one which does not rely on surveys, is to count the number of persons registered with government offices as claiming *unemployment-related benefits*. There are essentially two types of unemployment related benefits: *insurance-based* benefit (known in the UK as Unemployment Benefit) which is not means tested but which requires, for its receipt, on an adequate record of past contributions and which, in the UK, is not paid beyond 1 year and *means-tested* benefit (known in the UK as Income Support) which is not insurance related but which is only paid when the economic resources of an unemployed person are judged to be 'inadequate' and, in the UK, is paid for as long as the inadequacy persists. However, the income of most persons on Unemployment Benefit is often less than the Income Support level and so they would, in addition, also receive Income Support. After a year, when their entitlement to Unemployment Benefit had run out they would move entirely to Income Support.

This *claimant count* measure has the virtues of being inexpensive,[10] of being highly disaggregated[11] and of being available quickly and frequently.[12] However, it is open to two main criticisms. The first is that the claimant count measure is highly susceptible to changes in the rules and conditions governing eligibility to unemployment-related benefits. Since such changes determine who may or may not claim benefits, they could alter the unemployment total without any underlying change in the demand for and supply of labour. For example, the Unemployment Unit, pointing to 30 administrative or statistical changes that have altered eligibility to benefit in the UK since 1979, estimated that, in their absence, unemployment in 1992 would have been a million higher than the claimant count total of three million.[13] The second criticism of the claimant count measure is that the numbers claiming unemployment-related benefits may be significantly different from the numbers unemployed on the ILO/LFS measure. To reconcile the two measures one must *add to* the claimant count all those persons who are unemployed on the LFS definition but who are not claiming benefits (mainly because they are not eligible) and *subtract from* the claimant count all those claiming benefits but who are not unemployed on the ILO definition.[14] In 1991, 890000 persons were counted as unemployed by the LFS but excluded from the claimant count.[15] However, in the same year the claimant count included 660000 persons who were not deemed to be unemployed on the LFS definition either because the LFS regarded them as employed[16] or because they failed the LFS job search/availability criteria. Netting out the gross figures meant that the LFS reported a total of 2.3 million unemployed in the UK in 1991, while the claimant count figure was 2.08 million.

The progressive moves since 1986, to tighten the criterion of availability of work for the receipt of benefits in the UK, may have narrowed the gap between the claimant count and the LFS measures. The most important programme has been the Restart programme,[17] introduced in 1986, which requires every benefit claimant in the UK to be interviewed every 6 months by a Restart counsellor. The purpose of the Restart interview is, firstly, to provide assistance with finding a job. This help takes the form of Employment Training (targeted at persons unemployed for over 6 months), the Enterprise Allowance Scheme (which is a temporary subsidy to the self-employed), a Restart/Options course (which provides training in work attitudes and in applying for jobs) and membership of a Job Club (where people spend 3 hours a day gathering information and making job applications). The second purpose of the interview is to put pressure on unemployed persons to help themselves by using this assistance to find work. The carrot of the Restart programme was reinforced by the stick of the Social Security Act 1989 which, from October 1989, required claimants to provide detailed evidence of actively seeking work.

However, the ILO/LFS definition of unemployment could also be regarded as being flawed. All measures of unemployment, which have as their conceptual basis jobless persons seeking and available for work, are, in calculating the total number of persons who are unemployed, critically dependent on the definitions adopted for 'jobless', 'seeking' and 'available'. The ILO/LFS definition of being jobless, which is that the person had not worked for more than an hour in the week prior to interview, could be viewed as unduly restrictive since even the most casual experience of work would be enough to exclude a person from the unemployment count. Equally, it is also possible to regard the ILO/LFS definition of 'seeking', which is that some form of search had taken place in the 4 weeks prior to interview, as being restrictive since it would exclude those who, while genuinely wanting employment, were sufficiently discouraged to regard job search as futile. Adding the number of 'employed' claimants (that is, those claimants who were excluded from the LFS unemployment count because they were deemed to be 'employed'), the number of 'inactive' claimants (that is, those claimants who wanted a job but who were excluded from the LFS unemployment count because they failed its search/availability test) and the number of 'discouraged' workers[18] (that is, those who were not searching for jobs in the belief that none were available) to the LFS figures, it was estimated that the number of persons 'unemployed' in the UK, in the summer of 1993, was a million more than the LFS estimate of 2.9 million.[19]

The conclusion that emerges from the above discussion is that there is no single 'true' measure of unemployment. The appropriate measure of unemployment depends very much upon the purpose which it is required to serve. Reflecting this view, three measures of unemployment have been suggested.[20] The first is a count of those jobless persons who are actively searching for employment; such 'search-based' measures, such as that adopted by the LFS, are a measure of excess supply in the labour market. The second measure, which would subsume the first measure, would include 'discouraged workers', that is, jobless persons wanting but not searching for employment; this measure would then quantify the unfulfilled demand for employment. The third measure would attempt to quantify the social distress from unemployment and would contain all those persons living in households where the unemployment of one of its members was resulting in 'low' household income; by juxtaposition, it would exclude persons living in households with an unemployed member but which were 'well-off'. An alternative to these three measures would be to publish a spectrum of measures which would progressively broaden the definition of unemployment, starting, for example, with the long-term unemployed and progressing to the adult unemployed and then to the unemployed seeking full-time jobs, and so on. This is the practice adopted by the US Bureau of Labour Statistics which, as shown in Table 5.3, publishes seven measures – termed U1–U7 – of unemployment.

More generally, preoccupation with the measurement of unemployment is indicative of the fact that the halcyon days of full employment are seen as belonging firmly to the past. For 30 years after the Second World War, full-employment was associated with unemployment rates of 3 per cent or less and such unemployment as did exist was associated with *seasonal* (construction workers unemployed over winter) and *frictional* (workers changing jobs and, as a consequence, spending some time in unemployment) factors.

Today, with unemployment rates far in excess of this economists also make reference to cyclical and structural unemployment. Cyclical unemployment refers to variations in the unemployment rate caused by the business cycle. Unemployment rates are low in a boom, when demand is buoyant and are high in recession, when demand is depressed. On the other hand, structural unemployment refers to the persistence of high unemployment irrespective of the state of the business cycle. The next chapter traces the consequences of regarding unemployment as a cyclical phenomenon and attempting to combat it through changes in the level of demand. The chapter following that discusses the consequences of regarding unemployment as a structural phenomenon and attempting to combat it through policies which address the supply side of the economy.

TABLE 5.3   *Alternative unemployment measures (UK spring 1989)*

	Definition	Rate %
U1	Long-duration unemployment rate: persons unemployed 13 weeks or longer, as percentage of labour force	5.2
U2	Job loser rate: job losers as a percentage of labour force	1.5
U3	Adult unemployment rate: unemployed persons aged 25 years and over; as percentage labour force aged 25 years and over	6.6
U4	Full-time unemployment rate: unemployed full-time job seekers as percentage of full-time labour force	8.0
U5	Conventional unemployment rate: total unemployed as a percentage of civilian labour force	7.4
U6	Rate encompassing persons working part-time for economic reasons: total full-time job seekers, plus half part-time job seekers plus half of total number of persons working part-time for economic reasons, as percentage of the labour force less half of the part-time labour force	8.7
U7	Rate adding discouraged workers: U6 plus discouraged workers in the numerator and denominator	9.3

SOURCE   Employment Policy Institute, *Economic Report*, vol.8 (March 1994).

6 The Inflation–Unemployment Trade-off

It is a truth universally acknowledged that a country in possession of a low unemployment rate must be in search of an anti-inflationary policy. And, one could add, vice versa. This chapter reflects on the truth of this statement by examining the nature of the 'trade-off' between inflation and unemployment.

The ability of governments to deliver a 'good performance' with respect to these two variables is often regarded as a litmus test of their economic policies. Indeed, it would not be an exaggeration to say that full employment, in conjunction with a zero (or near zero) inflation rate, is the holy grail of macroeconomic policy. At the other extreme, the nightmare scenario is that of 'stagflation' when the economy stagnates at a low level of employment with the inflation rate continuing to rise. It is against this background that this chapter examines how inflation and unemployment are related.

Inflation is the rate of change in the *general* level of prices, expressed usually as an annualised percentage. It may be measured by a number of price indices[1] but it is usually measured (and reported in the media) by movements in the retail price index (RPI). The RPI is the price of a 'representative basket' of goods and services, calculated as a weighted average of the prices of the individual goods and services in the basket, the weights being the budgetary share of the individual items in the total of consumers expenditure. The RPI is a 'cost of living' index because it measures the change in gross income that would be required to allow a household to continue purchasing a representative basket of goods following an increase in the general price level.[2] Included in the RPI calculations for the UK are mortgage interest payments. Their inclusion rests on the argument that just as rent is the price paid by tenants for their housing services, payment of mortgage interest represents the price that owner–occupiers pay for equivalent services. However, others would argue that the inclusion of mortgage interest payments in the RPI basket is perverse because such payments are high precisely when governments are trying to lower inflation by raising interest rates.[3] Consequently in addition to the *headline* rate of inflation (which is the annualised rate of increase in the RPI) the UK also reports an *underlying* rate of inflation which is the rate of increase in the RPI excluding mortgage interest payments (RPIX).

Inflation may be *anticipated*, in the sense that prices rise at a rate at which all economic agents expect them to rise or it may be *unanticipated*, in the sense that the rate of price increase catches some (or all) economic agents by surprise. The most typical instance of anticipated inflation is one in which prices, year after year, rise at the same rate (whether this rate is high or low). On the other hand, if the annual rate of price increase is different (usually rising) from year to year, then inflation is likely to be unanticipated. When inflation is regarded as a 'problem' it could be interpreted to mean that the inflation rate is too high (though possibly steady) or that it is rising (though possibly from fairly low levels) or, as is usually the case, that it is both too high and rising. Whatever its causes (and these are discussed below), most of the costs that inflation imposes on society stem from its unanticipated nature or from the degree to which economic agents are 'surprised' by price increases.

Unanticipated inflation imposes costs by generating a sense of uncertainty. People are unable to make plans for the future with any degree of confidence because they do not know what the economic environment will be like in a few years time. A wide spectrum of decisions (when to retire, how much to invest in a pension, whether to buy a house, whether to start a business and whether to invest in new markets or products), embracing a broad range of persons and organisations, is affected by uncertainty about future inflation rates. Both businesses and households can make mistakes in their planning when inflation is unanticipated and, as a consequence, economic decision making becomes inefficient.[4] It is therefore important to control inflation and since there is a strong connection between low rates of inflation and an absence of volatility in their movement, this means keeping the rate of inflation both low and constant.[5]

When discussing the causes of inflation, economists often refer to 'demand-pull' and 'cost-push' factors. The basic idea behind *demand-pull inflation* is that the price level rises when demand in the economy exceeds its productive capacity. The origin of the term lies in the view of the economy propounded by John Maynard Keynes.[6] The Keynesian world was one of spare capacity, in which both men and machines were idle and the cause of their idleness was an insufficient demand for the output that capital and labour combined to produce. An expansion of demand would increase employment but would not affect wages and prices. However, once full employment had been reached (that is, the economy had reached its productive capacity) any further expansion of demand would mean that more money was chasing a fixed quantity of goods and services and, hence, would only serve to *pull up* prices. In contrast to demand-pull inflation, *cost-push inflation* raises prices by raising the costs of production. One could in turn distinguish between two types of cost-push inflation:[7] that resulting from wages pushing up prices even before the productive capacity of an economy had been reached (wage-push inflation) and that resulting from (non-labour) input price increases causing costs and prices to go up (supply-shock inflation).

Much of the inflation that occurred in the 1970s had its *origins* in supply-side shocks. The two inflationary periods beginning in 1974 and 1979 respectively, were connected with large increases in the price of crude oil. Thus, the 1973–5 rise in crude oil prices, from $4.00 to $13.90 per barrel, raised costs and prices in the economy of the USA by almost 4 per cent; the Iranian revolution of 1978 led to a second wave of oil price increases, with the price of a barrel of crude rising from $14.50 in 1978 to $37.00 in 1981 and this raised overall costs in the USA by approximately 5.5 per cent.[8] In general, the prices of imported goods and services (be they raw materials or finished products) are, for most countries, a major source of inflationary supply-side shocks. Import prices may rise either because supply prices rise or, more generally, because depreciation of the importing country's currency, *vis-à-vis* other currencies, makes imports more expensive.

However, in the absence of any other changes, a supply-side shock (for example, a sudden rise in the price of oil) should lead to only a single, sudden, jump in the general price level and thereafter, provided there were no further shocks, the inflation rate should return to its usual, pre-shock value. The fact that supply-side shocks often lead to a permanent (instead of a 'one-off') rise in the inflation rate is due to the repercussions that they have on wage-push inflation. Supply-side shocks lead to increases in the cost of living and these increases, as discussed in some detail below, are translated into higher wage settlements as workers seek to protect living standards; higher wages then push up prices and generate expectations about further price increases.

The idea behind wage-push inflation is that an expansion of demand will be divided between an increase in output (and, hence, in employment) and a rise in wages (and, hence, in prices). The precise division of the demand expansion between higher employment and higher prices would depend upon the state of the labour market. When the demand for labour was strong (that is, unemployment was low) most of the demand expansion would be reflected in wage and price rises; when the demand for labour was weak (that is, unemployment was high) most of it would go towards increasing output and employment. These ideas are captured in the Phillips curve[9] which postulates an inverse relationship between inflation and unemployment: other things being equal, high rates of inflation would be associated with low unemployment rates and low rates of inflation would be associated with high unemployment rates. The curve would also be steeper at lower, and flatter at higher, rates of unemployment showing, for example, that inflation would increase by only a small amount when unemployment was reduced from 10 to 9 per cent, whereas a reduction in the unemployment rate from 3 to 2 per cent would be associated with a sharp rise in the inflation rate. The state of the labour market is, therefore, an important influence on the magnitude of wage (and, hence, price) increases.[10]

The other important influence on wage increases is changes in the cost of living. If workers expect the cost of living to go up sharply, then these expectations will be reflected in appropriately high wage demands; conversely, if only modest rises in the cost of living are expected then wage demands will be suitably muted.[11] Combining the two influences on wage demands and the state of the labour market and expectations about inflation leads to the concept of an 'expectations-augmented' Phillips curve (see Figure 6.1). Inflation and unemployment continue to be traded off along a given Phillips curve but the size of the trade-off now depends on the inflationary expectations embodied in that curve: a Phillips curve embodying expectations of a 4 per cent inflation rate will have a lower rate of inflation associated with a given unemployment rate than a curve embodying inflationary expectations of 6 per cent.

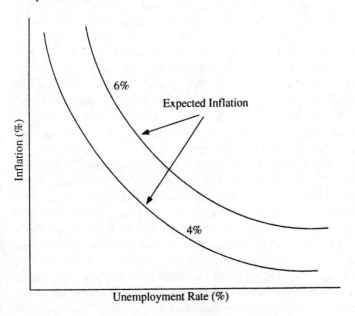

Figure 6.1 Expectations-augmented Phillips curves

Expectations about the future rate of inflation, in conjunction with the current state of the labour market, thus play a central role in determining the current rate of inflation. An understanding of how expectations are formed is therefore central to understanding the determination of the inflation rate. One approach to explaining the process of expectations formation, states that past values of the inflation rate determine expectations about its future values. In this backward looking or *adaptive expectations (AE)* approach, expectations are formed as a weighted sum of past values, with the largest weight being assigned to the most recent value, the weights declining as the values recede into the past. The problem with the AE approach is that when the inflation rate is rising, the expected rate for a particular year will be systematically below the actual rate for that year and, therefore, the inflation rate would consistently be underpredicted. (A special case of AE is one in which the next year's inflation rate is expected to be the rate that currently prevails and, in this case, expectations will trail behind the actual outcome by a year.) As a corollary, no rational agent would form expectations using adaptive expectations.

How would rational people form expectations? The theory of *rational expectations (RE)* says that rational people would form expectations by taking account of all relevant information. Some of this information would pertain to the stance of government policy and, in particular, to the *credibility* and the *consequences* of such policy. For example, if the government announced that it intended, over the next 5 years, to follow restrictive fiscal and monetary policies[12] then people, provided they believed that such a policy was credible, would anticipate that regardless of past inflationary experience, the inflation rate in the coming years would fall. Thus, in a RE framework while people might make mistakes in predicting the inflation rate for particular years these, unlike the systematic mistakes of AE, would be random errors. Do people actually form expectations using RE? Very possibly not. Most persons do not have the knowledge of economics to link outcomes with policies, nor might they be able (or indeed wish) to acquire such knowledge since there are considerable costs associated with such acquisition. The cutting edge of RE derives from the extension of the assumption of rationality, which is the behavioural bedrock upon which economics is based, to the process of expectations formation. Thus, the relevant question for RE is not whether it is true, but what would be the consequences for economic outcomes if it were to be true?

The most important feature about the inflationary process is that demand changes and changes in unit labour costs are not independent; often the former is the cause of the latter and the causal link is provided by the process of expectations formation. To see this, consider a situation in which prices rise, year after year, by 10 per cent. Then, in such a situation, the expectation that the inflation rate would be 10 per cent would always be realised and, hence, annual wage increases of 10 per cent, by generating price increases of the same magnitude,[13] would ensure that the real wage[14] would remain constant. Since the demand for labour depends upon the level of real wages, the constancy of real wages would mean that employment (and, hence, unemployment) would remain unchanged year after year.[15]

Suppose that there now occurs (say in 1990) a sudden increase in demand, for example through higher government spending not matched by a tax increase. The initial reaction of firms to this increased demand would be to raise prices by more than the usual 10 per cent: if workers, not realising that prices had gone up by more than 10 per cent, continued to demand wage increases of 10 per cent then the real wage would fall and employment, in 1990, would increase; in terms of Figure 6.2 the economy would move from point A to point B. In time however, workers would realise that the inflation rate had gone up and, accordingly, would demand higher wages so that the real wage (and therefore employment) would return to its original level. In terms of Figure 6.2 the economy would move from point B to C and if the process of adjustment took a year, then C would represent the position in 1991. At C real wages, employment and unemployment would be the same as that at A (that is, at pre-shock levels) but the steady-state rate of inflation would now be higher than 10 per cent. This is because the demand increase in 1990 raised the inflation rate (A to B in Figure 6.2) and, in turn, this raised inflationary expectations (B to C in Figure 6.2).

The time taken for expectations to adjust to the higher inflation rate would determine how long the economy could enjoy the 'benefits' of the demand injection in terms of higher employment.[16] If expectations were formed by RE, then this adjustment would be instantaneous, since the very *announcement* of the expansionary policy would lead to inflationary expectations being raised and hence to the rate of wage growth being increased. Expectations formed by AE would rise only after higher rates of inflation had been *observed* and, hence, some time would pass before the adjustment was made. However, once the adjustment was complete the benefits of higher employment would have been dissipated, leaving the economy with an unchanged rate of unemployment but with a permanently higher rate of inflation.

If, in 1991, there was a *further* injection of demand then this would lead to a *further* rise in the inflation rate as shown by the movement from C to D in Figure 6.2. If every year (say from 1990 onwards) the government injected extra demand into the economy then this would lead to higher and higher rates of inflation as the economy moved from D to E in Figure 6.2.

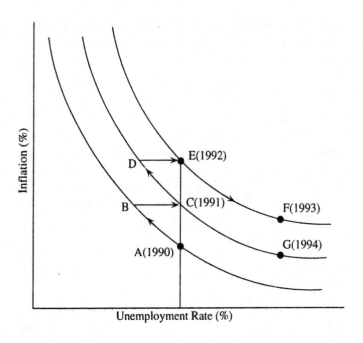

Figure 6.2 The wage-price spiral

The only way to stabilise the inflation rate would be to stop injecting extra demand into the economy; if this was done in 1992 (that is, when the economy was at point E in Figure 6.2) then the inflation rate would stabilise at, say, 20 per cent. To bring the inflation down from this stable (but high) rate would require the government to reverse the policies that, in the first place, caused the inflation rate to rise. This would mean not just eliminating the extra dose of demand but taking out demand – through some combination of tax increases, reductions in public expenditure and higher interest rates – in excess of the original increase. This would cause the economy to move from E to F in the first instance; as wage growth fell, in response to lower inflationary expectations, the economy would move from F to C and, if the government persisted every year with its contractionary policies, it would continue to descend the 'inflationary tree' (C to G and G to A) until at A there was no further demand withdrawal because the inflation rate had stabilised at an acceptably low level.

The nature of the inflation–unemployment trade-off in a modern economy is that periods of expansionary or contractionary policies move the economy from one inflation rate to another but that, in the long-run, regardless of the inflation rate, the economy returns to its underlying rate of unemployment. This underlying rate is referred to by a variety of names – the 'equilibrium' rate of unemployment and the rate of 'structural' unemployment are two – but perhaps the most accurate (if inelegant) is the *non-accelerating inflation rate of unemployment* (NAIRU). An economy cannot purchase a *permanent* reduction in the rate of unemployment below its NAIRU at the cost of a higher, *but stable*, inflation rate. Any attempt to do so would only lead to accelerating inflation.

The important question for policy makers is whether it is worth exchanging a *temporary* fall (or rise) in the unemployment rate (relative to the NAIRU) for a *permanent* rise (or fall) in the inflation rate. In part, the answer to this depends upon how far or close are the next major elections. It is alleged that governments formulate policies with a view to also maximising their electoral impact. Such behaviour generates a *political business cycle*[17] where, before an election, expansionary policies reduce unemployment (and, hence, win votes), leaving it until after the election for unemployment to return to its underlying, higher rate.

However, in part, the answer depends on the rate of exchange between these items. This rate is known as the *sacrifice ratio*. *The Economist*[18] recently argued that between 1980 and 1984, under the influence of tight monetary policy, the inflation rate in the USA fell from 10 to 3 per cent; over this period the NAIRU in the USA was estimated as 6 per cent and the cumulative excess of the unemployment rate over NAIRU during 1980–4 was approximately 11 percentage points. The implied sacrifice ratio was therefore approximately 1.5, that is 11 divided by 7. Every permanent fall in the inflation rate of 1 percentage point, in a given year, would require the unemployment rate to be 1.5 percentage points above the NAIRU for that year.

Much of the economic events in the UK, since Mrs Thatcher's accession as Prime Minister in 1979, can be explained in terms of the government attempting to exchange unemployment for inflation. Geoffrey Howe, the Chancellor of the Exchequer in Mrs Thatcher's first government, implemented a recessionary policy with a view to bringing down the inflation rate. By 1981, unemployment in the UK had doubled over its 1979 value to reach 3 million. In 1987, when it looked like the war against inflation had been won, the government shifted its attention to 'doing something' about unemployment. The then Chancellor, Nigel Lawson, pumped additional demand into the economy with a 2p cut in income tax and in 1988 there was a further 2p cut to reach the magic figure of a 25 per cent tax (basic) rate. As a consequence the unemployment rate fell from 10.3 per cent in 1987 to 5.8 per cent in 1990. Paralleling this fall, the inflation rate rose from 4.2 per cent in 1987 to 9.5

per cent in 1990. Anxiety over rising inflation prompted the government to take some demand out of the economy and this they did by raising interest rates. The high interest rates of 1991 triggered a recession, the effects of which are still with us: in January 1994 unemployment stood at 10 per cent and the inflation rate at 2.5 per cent. *Plus ça change, plus c'est la même chose.*

7 Unemployment and Labour Market (In)Flexibility

Although high rates of unemployment have emerged over the past decade as a pressing problem for the countries of the European Union there has been a marked shift in opinion as to the appropriate policies that should be followed in order to combat unemployment. In particular, the cosy certainties of the 1950s and 1960s that demand management policies could deliver full employment have (as the previous chapter showed) given way to the realisation that such policies are only able to purchase *temporary* improvements in the unemployment rate (relative to the economy's 'equilibrium' rate of unemployment, that is, to its NAIRU) at the expense of *permanent* increases in the inflation rate.

Hence, in dealing with unemployment, the challenge to policy makers today is not so much to create new jobs, but to create new jobs *without generating inflationary pressures* and, for meeting this challenge, emphasis is placed on *supply-side policies.* Such policies attempt to deliver permanent and non-inflationary decreases in unemployment by adopting measures to reduce the NAIRU itself. Because they address the structural aspects of unemployment, these policies take longer to work and are difficult to implement, not least because governments are reluctant to grasp the nettle of structural change. The analysis and description of supply-side policies, both in terms of their underlying logic and in terms of their likely shape, is the subject of this chapter.

A central issue in designing supply-side policies towards unemployment is that of *labour market flexibility.* The basic idea here is that while a country cannot insulate itself from economic shocks (for example, a rise in energy prices, a poor harvest or a weakening of demand in export markets), it can determine its response to such shocks and, in turn, the employment consequences of these shocks will depend upon the nature of this response. Given a particular shock, employment will fall by less in countries whose labour markets are 'flexible'. One aspect of labour market flexibility relates to how the burden of adjustment (to, for example, a sudden fall in demand for a particular country's products) is shared between the unemployed (through job losses) and the employed (through the acceptance of real wage reductions). In countries with labour markets that are *inflexible*, reductions in demand are fully reflected in job losses and, consequently, in higher unemployment;

real wages remain largely intact, so that the standard of living of those fortunate enough to retain their jobs is undisturbed. In countries with *flexible* labour markets, on the other hand, part of the fall in demand is reflected in job losses (and, hence, in higher unemployment) but a significant part is also reflected in a reduction in real wages (and, hence, in a lower standard of living for the employed) which then serves to arrest the fall in employment associated with the initial demand shock.

Much of the blame for wage inflexibility is routinely ascribed to trade unions. In the 1950s and 1960s the conventional wisdom was that union bargaining power combined with labour market shortages was mainly responsible for the tendency for pay to outstrip productivity growth. A major argument for incomes policies during this period was that government-imposed restraint on pay was the only way that the full employment that this period enjoyed could be made to co-exist with acceptable rates of inflation.

In recent years, when levels of employment have fallen considerably short of full employment, unions are viewed as monopoly suppliers of labour who price workers out of jobs. According to this view, the market for labour is like that for any other commodity. Just as an excess supply of, for example, fish should cause its price to fall to a level which equalised its demand and supply, so should an excess supply of labour lead wage rates to fall until unemployment was eliminated. The fact that the market for labour, unlike the market for fish, did not clear was due to market imperfections. These took the form of trade unions who, as monopoly suppliers of labour, caused unemployment by ensuring that wages stayed above competitive, market-clearing, levels. Hence, the solution to unemployment lay in making labour markets more competitive by eliminating (or at least weakening) union power. Supporters of such a hypothesis typically point to the fact that countries such as the USA, in which only a small fraction of the work-force belong to a trade union, have substantially lower rates of unemployment than countries in Europe, where labour is more unionised.[1] Furthermore, from this view, the success of the USA in creating new jobs has had much to do with real wage cuts: 30 million new jobs have been created since 1974, during which period real wages stagnated and between 1972 and 1982, actually fell by 10 per cent.

The problem with this 'monopoly supplier' hypothesis is that it cannot explain why certain countries (for example, the Nordic countries of Denmark, Finland, Norway and Sweden) in which trade unions are very powerful and command the membership of most of the work-force, have, nevertheless, highly flexible labour markets. Nor can it explain why, in the 1980s, when union membership declined and union powers were severely curtailed in the UK, wage inflation continued unabated.[2] The failure of the hypothesis that trade unions price workers out of jobs to satisfactorily account for these anomalies stems from two fundamental defects in its assumptions.

The first defective assumption is that trade unions represent, always and everywhere, a force that ensures real wage rigidity. This assumption was questioned by (among others) Lars Calmfors and John Driffill.[3] They pointed to the variety of wage-setting institutions that existed in the countries of the Organization for Economic Co-operation and Development (OECD). In the Nordic countries, centralised wage agreements between powerful national employer associations and union confederations were the norm; at the other extreme, in Canada, Japan, Switzerland, the USA, the UK, France and Italy, wage bargaining was decentralised and took place at the level of the enterprise. Lying between these poles were Germany, The Netherlands and Belgium where wage negotiations took place at the level of the industry. After studying these different institutional arrangements, Calmfors and Driffill concluded that *both* heavy centralisation and far-reaching decentralisation were conducive to real wage restraint, while intermediate levels of centralisation were least conducive. Centralisation meant that both parties to the process of wage negotiations took account of wider national interests; on the other hand, decentralisation assigned a greater role to market forces in determining wage outcomes. It was only when unions were powerful enough to thwart market forces, but not far-sighted enough to take account of wider interests, that real wage inflexibility would be greatest.

The second defective assumption is that the market for labour is, in nearly all respects, like the market for any other commodity. Robert Solow[4] has argued that since, in practical matters, the labour market is dominated by issues of equity and fairness (a characteristic not shared by say, the market for fish), it might be more sensible to regard it as different from all other markets in that the market for labour is, uniquely, a *social institution*. Two theories of labour market behaviour, which take account of the uniqueness of labour as a commodity, are the *efficiency–wage* and the *insider–outsider* hypotheses. Both are able to explain facts that the 'labour is just another commodity' approach cannot.

The *efficiency–wage* hypothesis argues that the effort that a worker expends on a job is, to some extent, within his (or her) control. In that sense, workers can 'choose' their productivity levels. Employers, being aware of this, believe that higher wages will elicit more effort (and, hence, higher productivity) from their work-force; conversely, low wages will simply result in lower productivity. Because the wage rate is both the price of labour and also an incentive to higher productivity, it is not simply an instrument to balance demand and supply. Nor can the existence of wages higher than market-clearing levels be blamed on trade unions. If wages do not clear the market it is because of the actions of employers.

The *insider–outsider* hypothesis (due to Assar Lindbeck and Dennis Snower[5]) argues that, unlike fillets of fish, workers are not perfectly substitutable in the eyes of employers. Older, more experienced, better trained workers ('insiders'), in whom the firm has invested trust and responsibility and who as a consequence are doing core jobs are likely to be more valuable than either inexperienced, less-trained workers or potential workers in the form of the unemployed (both of whom may be regarded as 'outsiders'). Faced with, for example, a sudden fall in demand, insiders will use their market power to resist real wage cuts and require that the entire burden of adjustment be met through job losses for the outsiders.

The market power of insiders derives from two sources. First, it may be expensive to sack such workers both because they are valuable workers who would be difficult to replace and also because legislation on job security may make parting with such workers an expensive affair. Second, insiders may refuse to cooperate with (and even harass) workers that they consider to have been employed at the expense of their (the insiders) real wage. In all this they could be aided and abetted by unions who might be more protective of the interests of insiders than of outsiders. On this hypothesis, therefore, wage setting would mainly reflect the interests of the employed insiders. David Blanchflower and Richard Freeman[6] have argued that in the 1980s the UK Government enacted a wide range of laws and programmes, a major objective of which was to weaken the power of trade unions.[7] However, these reforms, which succeeded in their objective of reducing union power, did not improve the response of real wages to unemployment because 'the reform package failed to recognise the power of insider pressures'.

The actions of government, through minimum wage legislation, may also directly contribute to wage inflexibility. However, the effect of such legislation on increased unemployment may not be very great. For example, costing the Labour Party's plans to introduce a national minimum wage in the UK of 50 per cent of median male earnings, the National Institute of Economic and Social Research (NIESR) concluded that the proposals would add approximately 60000 to the unemployed total over 5 years and 3.5 per cent to prices over 3 years.[8] This is because the benefits of minimum wages would mainly accrue to part-time workers (3.5 million employees or 15 per cent of total employees) and although their wages would rise by nearly 15 per cent, the knock-on effect on the national wage bill would be only 1 per cent.

Wage rigidities are just one (albeit, important) source of labour market inflexibility. However, there are also other sources of inflexibility and many of these stem from government policies. The fact that governments, on the one hand, tax the earnings of workers and, on the other, impose payroll taxes on employers drives a wedge between what workers receive as 'take-home' income and what employers pay as labour costs. The larger this tax wedge, the lower will be the incentives for employers to take on workers and for workers to seek out employment. Consequently, the volume of employment offered and accepted would be lower the larger the tax wedge. The size of the tax wedge (defined as the sum of income taxes and employees' and employers' social security taxes expressed as a percentage of the cost of employing workers) varies between countries: in 1992, it was 16 per cent in Japan, 24 per cent in the USA, 28 per cent in the UK, around 40 per cent in Germany and Japan and 51 per cent in Italy.[9]

Another source of inflexibility is the constraint imposed by hiring and firing rules and by the regulation of work practices. Limitations on working time, restrictions on using temporary and part-time workers and inflexibility in redundancy laws all act as disincentives to hire workers.[10] Improvements in labour market flexibility are often cited as the reason for the considerable fall that occurred, over 1993, in the unemployment total in the UK. This total (on a claimant count measure) peaked in January 1993, after which it fell fairly steadily, with the result that, in March 1994, the unemployment total was 200000 below its peak. The surprising feature of this fall was that it coincided with the recovery in output that was taking place. In the past, reductions in unemployment had tended to lag behind improvements in output.[11] The reason for the lag was ascribed to inflexible redundancy laws[12] because of which labour tended to be 'hoarded' in the initial phase of an economic downturn. It was only when it was clear to employers that recession was, as it were, here to stay, that job losses would occur. Conversely, when a recovery began it would not be immediately accompanied by increased employment since employers, conscious of the difficulty of ridding themselves of unwanted workers, would prefer to wait for signs of a more durable improvement in economic prospects before commencing to hire. However, because of labour market reforms in the UK in the 1980s, firing has become easier and employers have, as a result, become more willing to shed and to hire labour, in the initial phases of, respectively, recession and recovery.

A variant of this view suggests that the labour market, in the UK, has become more flexible but that this flexibility is manifested in the increasing use of part-time workers. However, in this regard, the catalyst for change has not been the legislative and financial incentives to take on part-time workers, much of which have remained largely unchanged over the past 25 years.[13] It has instead been the impact of global competition, which has led companies to look for ways of reducing costs and changing attitudes to work, which has led to the growing demand for work from married women.[14] From another argument, it is not that the labour market *per se* has become more flexible in the UK but that the structure of industry in the UK has changed in favour of industries with flexible labour markets. The growth of the service sector (and the parallel decline of the manufacturing sector) has led to a more flexible relationship between output and employment, since employers in the service sector are able to adjust employment in line with output much more easily than their counterparts in production industries.[15]

The previous paragraphs discussed the issue of labour market flexibility from the perspective of employers who were unwilling to reduce real wages (efficiency–wage hypothesis) or who willingly acceded to the demands of core workers that real wages should not be reduced (insider–outsider hypothesis) or who were inhibited from expanding employment by the government's fiscal or employment policies. The upshot of this discussion was that the greater the strength of these forces, the smaller the number of jobs that would exist in a given economic context. However, given a certain number of jobs, whether people would be hired to fill them would depend upon two things: whether the attributes of unemployed persons were suited to the requirements of the job vacancies (that is, the degree of '*mismatch*' between the unemployed and vacancies) and the *effectiveness* with which unemployed persons searched for jobs.

Mismatch between job seekers and available jobs may take a number of forms. It may be regional, with unemployment in certain regions being higher than in others, it may be occupational or industrial, with certain occupations or industries having markedly higher unemployment rates than others and, finally, it may span issues of race, gender and age. Whatever the nature of the mismatch, a common feature is that vacancies exist in certain spheres of activity (for example, in the North or in managerial or professional occupations) but unemployed persons inhabit different spheres (for example, they live in the South or are unskilled) and, furthermore, there are barriers to mobility between these disparate spheres, be they regions, occupations or industries. A useful way of measuring the degree of mismatch in a particular area is by the *variance of relative unemployment rates*.[16] For example, in 1987, the variance of relative unemployment rates across the regions of Britain was only 6.3 per cent and this, when compared to a variance across Italian regions of 19.6 per cent, indicated a much lower degree of regional mismatch in Britain than in Italy; similarly, in 1985, the variance of relative unemployment rates across occupations, in Britain, was 22 per cent compared to a variance across regions of 6 per cent, thus indicating a much higher degree of occupational, as compared to regional, mismatch in Britain.[17]

Effective job search, as Richard Layard, Stephen Nickell and Richard Jackman[18] observe, is about the speed with which the unemployed find jobs. The reason that effectiveness in job search is important is that the pool of unemployed persons provides a supply of labour to the economy. If the pool is 'too small' then labour shortages could develop and this would generate inflationary pressures by bidding up wages and prices. On the other hand, if the pool is 'too large' then wages and prices would tend to fall. It is only when unemployment is at the NAIRU that wage and price growth would be steady. Ever since the 1970s, the UK has needed at least 2 million unemployed to keep inflation stable and today this figure is closer to 3 million. The reason why the NAIRU for the UK is so large (and rising) is that those among the unemployed who have been out of work for over 1 year (approximately 38 per cent of the unemployed) are not regarded by employers as suitable candidates for employment. If one adds to this the unemployed persons who are 'unemployable' (because they have no relevant skills) then approximately *half the unemployed in the UK do not count*, in the sense that, by not constituting an effective supply of labour, they make no contribution to the process of holding inflation down.[19] Research suggests that, in the main, two factors influence the effectiveness of an unemployed person's job-search: how long he (or she) has been unemployed and the nature of the unemployment benefit system.[20]

The basic fact about the duration of unemployment is that the chances of a unemployed person finding a job decline in relation to the length of time that person has been unemployed. Approximately 3 million persons lose their jobs every year in the UK. Of this, most are able to find alternative employment within 6 months and approximately 80 per cent leave unemployment within 1 year.[21] Nevertheless, a significant proportion of job losers are still unemployed after 1 year. The problem is that the chances of a person who has been unemployed for 1 year of finding a job are less than 20 per cent, as compared to a nearly 60 per cent chance for someone who has only recently become unemployed.[22] Countries which have a higher proportion of their unemployed in long-term unemployment (12 months or more), would therefore need a larger stock of unemployed persons to keep inflation steady (that is the NAIRU) than would countries where the duration of unemployment is generally short. That, in a nutshell, is the problem posed by long-term unemployment. In 1991, only 6 per cent of the unemployed in Sweden and the USA had been out of work for 1 year or more while; by way of contrast, the comparable figures for France, the UK and Germany were 44, 38 and 31 per cent, respectively.[23]

One possible reason why the long-term unemployed find it difficult to find jobs is that it is the more able of unemployed job seekers who are the first to find employment; from that argument, the group of persons who are long-term unemployed selects itself by containing a disproportionate share of less able persons. However, there is also clear evidence that long-term unemployment adversely effects the chances of *any* unemployed individual escaping unemployment by first eroding his (or her) motivation to find a job and, second, through the fact that employers interpret a protracted spell of unemployment as an adverse comment upon a person's employability.

On motivation, the basic fact is that the extent and nature of search activity declines with unemployment duration. On stigmatisation, the basic fact is that many employers discriminate against the long-term unemployed by routinely rejecting applications on the basis of unemployment duration; others, who may consider such applications, believe that the long-term unemployed are 'inferior' workers and this view is confirmed when, at interviews, such persons appear 'unduly' anxious and depressed.[24] The relevant question is whether long-term unemployment demotivates and deskills otherwise perfectly good workers or whether the long-term unemployed were, to begin with, less able and energetic than those among the unemployed who were successful at finding jobs relatively quickly. It is difficult to disentangle the answers to these separate questions. The evidence is that becoming unemployed caused psychological ill-health (and this, in turn, rebounded on motivation and morale), but that this state of ill-health attained a plateau after about 6 months of unemployment and did not decline further as the period of joblessness lengthened.[25] It was also the case that finding employment, after a period of unemployment, did much to restore a person's (pre-unemployment) state of well-being.[26] However, it is more difficult to predict, on the basis of a person's characteristics, whether he (or she) would suffer long-term unemployment.

Most countries of the OECD operate an unemployment benefit system which, in effect, provides a source of income (subject to the relevant rules and regulations, which vary from country to country) to jobless persons.[27] The system of unemployment benefits affects the numbers in unemployment, by influencing the effectiveness with which the unemployed search for jobs. It does so in three ways. First, through the *level* of benefits relative to wages. The ratio of benefits to wages is called the 'replacement ratio' since it is the fraction of employment income that is 'replaced' through the benefit system. This ratio differs between countries depending upon the relative generosity of their benefit systems. Second, through the *duration* of benefit availability. In some countries benefits can be collected indefinitely, while other countries limit the period for which benefits are available. Third, through the *treatment* of those claiming unemployment benefit. In some countries the benefit system plays an active role (through the parallel provision of employment services, training and so on) in helping the unemployed to find jobs, while in other countries the benefit system plays a passive role by simply providing financial support to the unemployed.

Although most popular discussions about the effects of benefits on unemployment (as a result of the stereotypical image of 'scroungers on the dole') focus on the level of unemployment benefits, of the three aspects cited above it is the generosity of benefits that has the least predictable influence on unemployment. Indeed, several countries with very high replacement ratios (for example, Sweden with 80 per cent and Norway with 65 per cent) have low rates of unemployment while a country like Italy, where the basic unemployment benefit for most of the 1970s and the 1980s was around 800 lira (40 pence) per day,[28] has a very high unemployment rate.

The duration of unemployment benefits is of more relevance to determining search effectiveness. Those countries which limit the period for which unemployment (and unemployment-related) benefits are available (the USA 26 weeks, Japan 30 weeks and Sweden 60 weeks) are also the countries, as noted earlier, with the smallest fraction of the unemployed in long-term unemployment. By contrast, in countries where the benefit system is open-ended (France, Germany, The Netherlands and the UK) the long-term unemployed constitute a significant part of the total unemployed. Limiting the duration of benefits concentrates the search activity of unemployed persons and is an important factor in preventing the build up of long-term unemployment.

However, the effectiveness of search can be greatly improved by providing the unemployed with assistance in finding jobs. Labour market policies, designed to provide such help, can take a number of forms.[29] First, it could involve *employment services and administration*. This covers all expenditure connected with informing unemployed persons about vacancies and providing them with guidance and help in preparing job applications. Such assistance is usually provided through employment exchanges. Second, it could involve *labour market training*. This involves providing training for persons whose job prospects are poor usually because they are young workers who are entering the world of work with little training or skills, they are workers with experience of employment but for whose skills demand has declined or they are long-term unemployed whose motivation and skills have eroded. Third, it could involve *direct job creation and employment subsidies*. This covers public sector jobs for unemployed persons and subsidies to private sector employers to hire unemployed people.

Thus, a good benefit system should be generous, it should be time limited and it should be accompanied by labour market policies designed to help the unemployed to find jobs.[30] In this regard Sweden provides a model. Unemployment benefits are generous, with a replacement ratio of 80 per cent but the duration of benefits is limited to 60 weeks. The distinguishing feature of the Swedish system is, however, its emphasis on providing the unemployed with assistance in finding employment, rather than just with financial help. Active labour market policies ensure that long before entitlement to benefit has expired, the unemployed have been found work, if necessary after training. Thus, after 60 weeks, only 3 per cent of the unemployed are still without jobs. This pattern is totally different from say, the USA, where benefits are also time-limited but where (except to single mothers) no assistance is provided to the unemployed with finding jobs.

In summary, therefore, non-inflationary solutions to the problem of unemployment requires policies to reduce the 'equilibrium' unemployment rate or, in other words, to reduces the unemployment rate (NAIRU) required to keep the inflation rate steady. Such policies take the form of improving labour market flexibility. Labour market flexibility may be improved by increasing wage flexibility (so that the burden of adjustment to adverse economic shocks is shared between reductions in real wage and reductions in employment), by reducing the mismatch between job vacancies and the unemployed and by improving the effectiveness of job search by the unemployed. The latter involves reducing the fraction of the long-term unemployed in the unemployed total and also improving the efficacy of the unemployment benefit system.

8 Jobless Men and Working Women

The discussion in the preceding chapter, on search-based measures of unemployment, pointed to two routes out of unemployment. The first, the 'high' road, was to escape unemployment by securing a job and the second, the 'low' road, was to leave the labour force by ceasing to search for jobs (that is, to transfer from unemployment into inactivity). A journey down either of these ways would lead to an improvement in the unemployment statistics. By the same token, the pool of unemployed persons is *fed* from two sources: job losses, which cause people to transfer from employment into unemployment (provided, of course, that this is accompanied by job search) and renewed job search, which results in jobless persons rejoining the labour force by transferring from inactivity into unemployment. The previous chapter emphasised the employment creation route out of unemployment. This chapter discusses the effect on unemployment of withdrawals from the labour market.

These two forces – job gains or losses, on the one hand and entry into or withdrawal from the labour market, on the other – which serve to determine the unemployment total are linked by the fact that they often work in opposite directions. The optimism generated through jobs being created, which causes the unemployment total to fall, could lead 'discouraged' workers, who had given up searching for jobs, to re-enter the labour market and push up the unemployment total; conversely, the pessimism generated by job losses could induce withdrawals from the labour market by discouraging unemployed workers from searching for jobs. An example of these offsetting forces is provided by the fact that the *employment rate* of working-age males (that is, the percentage of men between the ages 16 and 64 years[1] who were employed) fell from 92.0 per cent in 1975 to 77 per cent in 1993 in Britain or, equivalently, the *non-employment rate* for this group rose from 8 to 23 per cent. However, the rise in the *unemployment rate* (that is, the percentage of the labour force that is jobless) for this subgroup, from 5 per cent in 1975 to 12 per cent in 1993, underestimated the scale of male job loss since there was a parallel in a rise in the male *inactivity rate* (that is, the percentage of working-age males who are jobless and not searching for work and, therefore, not in the labour force) from 3 per cent in 1975 to 12 per cent in 1993.[2] By 1993, in addition to the 2 million working-age men classed as unemployed, a further 2 million jobless were no longer actively seeking employment. Thus, according to John Schmitt and Jonathan Wadsworth,[3] the extent of labour market slack in Britain is seriously understated when it is measured by the unemployment rate.

The poor representation of excess supply in the labour market by the unemployment rate is a feature which many developed countries have come to share and the feeling has, therefore, grown among some economists that excess supply is better measured by the rate of non-employment (rather than by the unemployment rate). As Edward Balls and Paul Gregg[4] have pointed out, non-employment rates for prime-age males[5] (that is, the percentage of males, between the ages of 25 and 54 years, without a job) rose over the 1980s in almost every country of the OECD.[6] The differences between the countries lay in the accuracy with which this rise was represented by the unemployment statistics. In the countries of Continental Europe, the unemployment statistics were a true reflection of this rise. On the other hand, in Australia, Canada, Sweden and the UK, the rise in inactivity was at least as important as the rise in unemployment and, hence, the rise in non-employment was understated by the unemployment statistics.

The high rate of non-employment among (non-student) working-age males – which at 23 per cent in 1993, in Britain, was nearly twice the unemployment rate for this group – is worrying for a number of reasons. First, in a group which is traditionally characterised by high participation rates (in 1975, less than 3 per cent of working-age males in the UK were inactive, that is, jobless and not seeking work), joblessness, as reflected in a withdrawal from the labour market, is no less worrying than that reflected in unsuccessful, but continuing, job search. Indeed, the latter may, often, be the cause of the former since a lack of success in finding a job could discourage further search.

The second cause of anxiety about high non-employment rates for working-age males is that much of the fall in activity is concentrated among unskilled men. The unemployment rate among men with low qualifications[7] in Britain rose by almost 14 percentage points between 1979 and 1993, while inactivity rates (that is, the percentage not in the labour force) for this group rose by almost 15 percentage points so that, by 1993, 38 per cent of poorly qualified men were without a job.[8] The fact that a job not sought is a job not found only serves to increase anxiety about the large contribution that inactivity makes to the non-employment of unskilled men. Such worries are compounded when conventional economic explanations fail to account for the steady rise in inactivity rates that has occurred over the last 15 years. The rise was not cyclical, since the Keynesian style expansion in Britain, in 1987, failed to shift it: it was not the result of an open-ended benefit system, since once unemployment rates are replaced by non-employment rates, the simple correlation between benefit duration and joblessness breaks down, nor was it the result of excessively high wages choking off demand for labour, since relative earnings of low-skilled workers were at their lowest level in 1993 in Britain for over a decade and in the USA (which has a prime-age, male, non-employment rate comparable to Britain[9]), real wages of the unskilled had actually fallen by one-third over the past two decades.[10]

The fall in male activity rates, with which a rise in male non-employment rates was associated, was largely associated with a collapse in the demand for unskilled male labour that occurred in the 1980s in most countries of the OECD. This fall reduced the number of unskilled jobs available and also depressed the real wages associated with such jobs. As a consequence, unskilled workers left the labour market, either because they were discouraged about the prospects of finding employment or because they did not find employment to be sufficiently rewarding. The point at issue is why the demand for unskilled male workers has fallen.

From one argument,[11] much of this fall was due to the changing pattern of trade – which, in turn, could be largely ascribed to a progressive dismantling of trade barriers – between developed (the North) and developing countries (the South). This pattern has changed, from one where the North exported manufactured products to the South and received in exchange primary products, to one where, today, the North exports skill-intensive manufactured goods to the South in exchange for (unskilled) labour-intensive manufactured products from the South.[12] These changes have had profound consequences for the structure of Northern industry.[13] Firstly, the North has reduced the scale of its labour-intensive activities, either by stopping production of certain products, preferring instead to import them from the South or by splitting the production process so that only the skill-intensive parts are located in the North, with the other parts being located in the South.[14] Secondly, in response to Southern competition in labour-intensive products, the North has intensified its search for new ways of production that would use less unskilled labour. The totality of the two effects has been to reduce the demand for unskilled, relative to skilled, labour in the North by approximately 20 per cent.[15]

However, the reason that the collapse in the demand for unskilled labour in the developed countries has had such a disproportionate effect on *male* joblessness is that much of the job creation in the 1980s has been in part-time, service sector jobs which men are unwilling to take. The proportion of part-time jobs in Australia and France doubled between 1973 and 1992. Between January and September 1993, according to the Labour Force Survey (LFS), the number of full-time jobs in the UK fell by 40000 and part-time jobs rose by 100000, with the lion's share of the new jobs being accounted for by the retailing and the hotel and catering sectors. In 1993, the 5.9 million part-time employees in the UK constituted almost one-quarter of its work-force but of such employees, only 15 per cent were men. Nor was the UK alone in having such a large share of part-time jobs. The proportion of part-time jobs in total employment was nearly 30 per cent in Australia and Sweden and just under just 20 per cent in Japan, the USA and Germany. On average, approximately three-quarters of these part-time jobs were held by women.[16]

Part-time workers offer several advantages to employers: they are cheaper than full-time workers because their hourly rates and also their non-wage costs[17] are lower and they are also the archetypal 'flexible' workers in that their numbers can be easily adjusted to meet the changing needs of employers. Many of these financial and legislative incentives to employ part-time workers have existed in the UK for the past 25 years. It was, however, the combination of such advantages, with the growing demand from married women for part-time employment, together with the increasing pressure of competition from developing countries in the production of labour-intensive products, that led, in the 1980s, not just to *new* jobs being concentrated in part-time appointments but also to the repackaging of *existing* full-time jobs into part-time positions.[18]

The main reason why men shun such jobs is that low-skilled men who are jobless do not want low-paid,[19] part-time, service sector employment.[20] This, in turn, is due to several factors: the income from part-time jobs is not enough to support a family, such jobs are seen as 'women's' jobs and the capabilities that unskilled men possess are not those that employers seek. Men with industry-specific experience are, therefore, likely to wait for re-employment in jobs similar to the ones they used to have, rather than accept a less well-paid job in another industry.[21]

Part-time jobs are very attractive to women married to men who hold full-time jobs. For such women, part-time jobs offer flexibility – for example, they allow women to return to the labour market as soon as the youngest child is at school – and also a useful supplement to the family finances. On the other hand, part-time employment, particularly in the UK, is financially unattractive to women whose husbands are unemployed since, after a very low threshold,[22] the wife's earnings only serve to reduce the husband's social security benefits. Indeed, in the UK, since April 1992, a married man who was unemployed would lose entitlement to Income Support if his wife worked more than 16 hours per week.[23] A major consequence of the asymmetric attraction of part-time jobs for married women with employed and unemployed husbands is the growing gap between 'work-rich' (two earner) and 'work-poor' (no-earner) households. The full-time jobs that have been created in the UK have been taken by men and the part-time jobs by their wives who want (and are able) to combine paid employment with looking after their children.[24]

An unfortunate consequence of the concentration of joblessness in particular families and the further concentration of such families into particular neighbourhoods and housing estates, is the rise of what has come to be termed the *underclass*. This is a group comprising persons who lack (or, at least, do not display) the social and cultural skills and values of mainstream working-class and middle-class persons and, indeed, who adopt a lifestyle that normal society would regard as 'undesirable'. Failure to work regularly, to postpone childbirth until marriage, to refrain from violence and to cope with school and with social situations are all characteristics of the underclass.[25] The rise in male joblessness is seen as a *cause* of the growth of such an underclass, not least because the low wages associated with unskilled labour increase the attractiveness of illegal and even criminal activities.[26] However, the rise in male joblessness is also seen as a *consequence* of the growth of an underclass, since this group is composed of persons whose persistent poverty and chronic joblessness can be attributed to their own, seemingly perverse, behaviour. The view that the real problem of joblessness lies not in a lack of demand or of appropriate skills, but in a social pathology which leads a significant proportion of the unemployed, through a perversion of values and attitudes, to be unsuited to the world of work with its requirements of self-discipline and self-respect, itself contains distinct strands, each of which stems from a particular explanation for the existence of a underclass.[27]

The first strand regards persons comprising the underclass as being rational, in the sense that they pursue, what they perceive to be, their self-interest. Unfortunately, the situation in which such persons find themselves, means that their self-interest requires them not to work and to be dependent for their income on welfare payments. This explanation for the existence of an underclass implies that changing such behaviour requires a change in people's situations, not a change in their nature. The most articulate proponent of this view is Charles Murray,[28] who argued that the nature of the US welfare system provided incentives for people to pursue, out of rational self-interest, behaviour that normal persons would regard as aberrant. Thus, according to Murray, poverty and dependency resulted from people 'making decisions that maximised their quality of life under the welfare system' and, the welfare system made 'it profitable for the poor to behave in the short-term in ways that were destructive in the long-term'.[29]

A central concern, among those who believe that the welfare system provides malign incentives, is the rise in male joblessness and female-headed families in the USA since 1965, when the Great Society programmes were initiated. These programmes, which had the overall effect of greatly increasing the generosity of the welfare system, created a structure of incentives in which not working was a perfectly rational response to an economic environment (created through government policy) in which having a job was no longer necessary for survival. This environment, by increasing welfare payments to single mothers, also ensured that having children outside marriage made better economic sense than raising a family within the context of a two-parent family. Although the causal links, outlined above, have been challenged from several quarters,[30] it is the pervasive and persistent nature of such anxieties that have discouraged the successful East Asian economies – which in terms of industrial structure and performance are very similar to those of Western Europe and North America – from adopting Western style welfare systems.

Another strand is provided by those who believe in a 'culture of poverty', whereby lifestyles of the chronically poor are not conducive to holding down a job and also are self-perpetuating and self-reinforcing. As Paul Peterson[31] graphically puts it, 'street life in the ghetto is exhilarating ... in a world where jobs are dull, arduous, or difficult to obtain and hold, it is more fun to hang out, make love ... and exhibit one's many purchases or conquests'. Referring to teenage pregnancy in the USA, Elijah Anderson[32] observes that two lifestyles tug at people in underclass neighbourhoods. The stable family with its emphasis on education, marriage and work is one; the other is 'the culture of the street'. A young girl, whose life is dominated by street culture, may be so isolated from the wider world, that she actually thinks she is doing well by becoming pregnant and receiving welfare, since her role models are other girls who too have become single mothers. At the same time, the pregnancy is an important proof of sexual prowess for the presumed father while a loose relationship with the mother allows him to maintain a free lifestyle.

The sociologist William Julius Wilson[33] has provided a penetrating analysis of how deviant norms come to be adopted. One feature of poverty and unemployment is its concentration in certain 'black spots'. The poor and non-poor, in many instances, do not live as neighbours. Rather, there are several areas where most of the residents are poor and unemployed. The difficulty of securing employment is compounded by the fact that employment opportunities are usually located some distance away from such areas. Moreover, as the concentration of poverty in these areas increases, these areas come to be seen as undesirable places in which to live. Thus, anybody who can leave, does leave. Typically the leavers are persons with jobs and who may be more dynamic and ambitious than the people who do not (or are unable to) leave. With this migration, the social buffers – in the form of mainstream values – that surround and protect such areas erode over time and ultimately collapse. Neighbourhoods that have no role models and that have few legitimate employment opportunities, will result in their residents possessing only a weak attachment to the labour market. Such persons will aimlessly drift in and out of low-wage, low-skilled employment and, indeed, may turn to illegal activities for income thus further weakening their ties to and respect for the legitimate labour market.

Lastly, a view that tries to steer a middle path between the one which holds that the underclass phenomenon is a rational response to the incentives embedded in the social security system and that which sees the underclass as embodying a perversion of mainstream values and culture, has been put forward by Lawrence Mead.[34] He argues that the idea of an underclass holding 'deviant' values does not stand up to scrutiny. Survey data shows that the poor consistently reaffirm their attachment to 'middle-class' norms such as the importance of work, stable families, completing school and being law abiding. The problem is that they live less often by these norms than, say, middle-class persons.

The reason for this, according to Mead, is not that the poor are insincere in their affirmation of mainstream values, but that their competence to live consistently by these values is limited. The poor do not face great obstacles to finding employment if one assumes a normal level of competence, namely the confident competence of affluent persons. Given this assumption, the behaviour of the chronically poor and perpetually unemployed does appear perverse. However, it is precisely this competence assumption – the ability to live one's life as one chooses – that Mead questions. He sees the poor as being '*dutiful but defeated*'. Their being 'dutiful' leads them to desire the same lifestyle as the rest of society. In that sense, an underclass does not exist. However, the harshness and humiliation that is inseparably a part of the lives of the poor, leads them to perceive as insurmountable difficulties and obstacles that a 'normal' person would easily overcome. They are thus 'defeated' and in that sense, from a middle-class perspective, an underclass appears to exist.

The anxiety for Europe is that it is beginning to develop its own underclass.[35] With the long-term unemployed constituting nearly half of the total unemployed in many European countries, social marginalisation and alienation is driven by the persistence of mass unemployment. As a consequence of such alienation, Europe is beginning to develop urban ghettoes possessing all the frightening characteristics – crime, drugs, poverty and unemployment – of those in the USA. Unfortunately, the measures – education, skills and jobs – required to reverse this trend are extremely difficult to implement.

III Distribution

9 Inequality

Macroeconomic policy has essentially two main preoccupations: stabilisation and growth. Stabilisation involves smoothing out fluctuations in the time-path of national income so that periods of boom do not alternate with periods of slump. Of course such fluctuations can never be entirely eliminated and so the purpose of stabilisation policy is to reduce the amplitude of the business cycle – that is to say, to reduce the differences between the peaks and the troughs of national income. Growth involves the increase over time of national income and this requires expansion of a country's productive capacity. This, in turn, requires new investment in either physical or human capital.

To these preoccupations is sometimes added a third – distribution. This involves a consideration of how the national cake is (or should be) divided. The division considered may be between capitalists and workers (reflected in the shares going to profits and wages) or it may be between different families (or households), as reflected in the share of national income accruing to, for example, the richest (or the poorest) 20 per cent of households. The use of the word 'sometimes' in the opening sentence of this paragraph implies that distribution is the Cinderella of the macroeconomics – it is important only insofar as it aids (or hinders) the attainment of the objectives of stabilisation or growth.

Indeed it is fashionable, among those who believe in giving free rein to the 'invisible hand' of the market mechanism, to argue that attempts through the egalitarian public policies of the post-war decades to override market-determined levels of inequality were responsible for many of the economic ills that, in the 1980s, beset countries that had adopted such policies. The catalogue of such ills includes low levels of work effort, absence of entrepreneurial incentives, militant trade unions and high rates of strike activity and absenteeism. A different argument for inequality 'not mattering' ties the issue of income inequality to that of income mobility. From this argument, income mobility would ensure that as some families were moving up the income ladder, others were moving down. Hence, the precise rung that a particular family occupied in a particular year was of not much relevance since its occupation would be purely temporary.[1]

As a counter-weight to such views, there are instances of successful industrialised economies – of which the Scandinavian countries are a prime example – which are strongly egalitarian. Furthermore, it could be that it was precisely the high levels of equality in these countries that were responsible for their impressive rates of economic growth. Such a view would acknowledge that wages and productivity must be in harmony but it would argue, in contrast to the conventional view that productivity determines wages, that under certain circumstances wages can, instead, determine productivity. Thus, for example, a policy which compressed wage differentials and paid, say, welders more than their marginal product, would offer an incentive to producers to undertake the necessary investment to raise the productivity of welders. If the state offered to subsidise such investment then the chances are that it would be undertaken. As a consequence higher levels of productivity would follow higher levels of equality.

Those who favour greater equality also point out that high levels of economic inequality can, by generating social and political discontent, disrupt (and perhaps destroy) the economic and political system that generates such inequality. For that reason, equality being good for economic and political stability, is also good for growth. For example, the fact that, in Poland, the Democratic Left Alliance – which emerged from the ruins of the Communist Party – was able to return to power in the elections of 1993 was widely credited to its promise of a 'just allocation of sacrifice'. This was designed to appeal to those – low-paid state employees, pensioners and industrial workers – who had lost out in the market-led economic successes of the previous 4 years.

The study of distribution therefore is important because there is an intimate connection between equality and well-being. This connection may be direct, in that one might find the presence of glaring inequalities to be morally repugnant. Or it may be indirect, in the sense that, without passing any moral judgement on the prevailing level of inequality, one might deplore its effects on something else that one valued, such as economic and political stability.

The overlap between equality and well-being raises, in turn, the question *equality of what?* Some persons may, for example, associate well-being with equality of opportunity, while others may believe in equality of outcomes. The two objectives are not necessarily compatible. In the USA, attempts to ensure that the ethnic balance in universities is representative of the regions in which the universities are located (that is, to bring about equality of outcome) have led to differential admission standards being applied to different ethnic groups (that is, to inequality of opportunities).[2]

Even within the respective domains of opportunities and outcomes, disagreement may persist about what should be the focus of equality. Some might favour equality of income, others might favour wealth and still others might emphasise equality of civil liberties. Amartya Sen[3] argues that the major ethical theories of social arrangement all share an endorsement of equality in terms of some 'focal variable'.[4] Consequently, the essential difference is not between those who are 'for equality' and those who are 'against it' but between proponents of different focal variables. The endorsement of equality in terms of one variable may co-exist with or it may require the rejection of another variable. For example, equality in the distribution of incomes may co-exist with grave inequalities in the distribution of wealth; the equal guarantee of extensive liberties requires the rejection of, for example, equal distribution of incomes.

In the analysis of economic inequality the focus of attention is usually income, though inequality in the distribution of wealth also receives some attention. One question that is central to the analysis of economic inequality is how it should be measured, since without reliable measurement, one cannot arrive at informed conclusions and make policy recommendations for distribution.

In measuring inequality the basic aim is to be able to represent the distribution, for example of household incomes in Britain in 1994, in terms of a single number. Then if this number is greater than the corresponding number derived for British household incomes in 1993 (or for French household incomes in 1994) one can, meaningfully, say that inequality in Britain increased between 1993 and 1994 (or that, in 1994, there was more income inequality in Britain than in France). Any measure that is capable of performing this role is referred to as an *inequality index or measure.*

In order to ensure that the chosen inequality index is capable of giving sensible results economists require that it should satisfy certain properties. First, it should satisfy the *principle of transfers:* if income is transferred from a richer to a poorer person then the value recorded by the index should fall.[5] Second, it should satisfy the property of *scale invariance:* the value of the index should not change if all incomes are increased (or decreased) by the same proportion.[6] Third, it should satisfy the *principle of anonymity:* the value of the index should depend only on the incomes and not on the persons associated with these incomes. Lastly, it should satisfy the property of *population homogeneity:* if the population is replicated (for example, by combining the British distribution with itself and obtaining a distribution with twice as many households as the original but otherwise identical) then the value of the index should not change.

Any inequality index satisfying the above properties belongs to the family of *relative inequality indices.* The term 'relative' refers to the fact that the value of such indices is invariant to changes in income which leave the positions of the persons, relative to each other, unaltered. Equi-proportionate increases (or decreases) in all incomes have this effect.[7] The conceptual basis of this family of indices is provided by the *Lorenz curve* depicted in Figure 9.1. To derive the Lorenz curve, the population under study is first ordered by ascending magnitude of income (that is, starting with the person with the lowest income). Then the cumulative proportion of the population (measured along the horizontal axis and taking values from 0 to 1) is plotted against the cumulative proportion of income received by such persons (measured along the vertical axis and also taking values between 0 and 1) to yield the Lorenz curve. Any point on the curve depicts the share of income, *y* per cent, accruing to the poorest *x* per cent of the population. The broken, diagonal line in Figure 1 represents the *line of perfect equality:* the share of income cumulates at the same rate as the population so that the poorest *x* per cent also receive the same (*x*) percentage of income.

The fact that inequality exists means that the Lorenz curve will lie inside the perfect equality line and, intuitively, the further away from the line that it lies the greater will be degree of inequality. Relative inequality indices reflect 'Lorenz curve inequality' because every such index will record a higher value as the curve shifts away from the diagonal. Thus, in Figure 9.1 the distribution represented by curve B is more unequal than that represented by curve A since curve B lies completely inside curve A and, therefore, the poorest *x* per cent of persons in A receive a greater share in total income than do the corresponding group in B. This greater 'Lorenz curve inequality' will be reflected in the higher values recorded for B over A by all relative inequality indices.

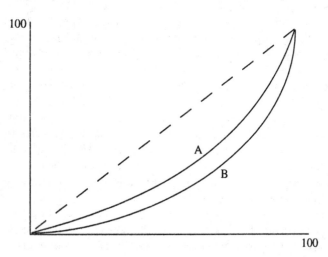

Figure 9.1 A hypothetical Lorenz curve configuration

A problem arises when, as depicted in Figure 9.2, Lorenz curves intersect. Then it is no longer possible to say that one distribution is unambiguously more or less equal than the other. For example, Figure 9.2 shows the Lorenz curves crossing at a point, Z; B has a more equal distribution of income for low levels of income (that is, to the left of Z), but A has a more equal distribution for higher levels of income (that is, to the right of Z). Any judgement on the relative degree of inequality between A and B would be influenced by one's social values: attaching greater weight to the inequality at the lower end of the income scale would favour B, while valuing equality if it occurred at higher incomes would reverse this judgement. In such situations, where Lorenz curves intersect, using different indices of relative inequality to say whether one distribution was more unequal than another could lead to contradictory results. That is because social values, reflecting one's preference for equality at different points in the income scale, are built into the different indices and different indices embody different values.[8]

One of the most commonly used measures of inequality is the Gini coefficient. It belongs to the family of relative inequality indices and, hence, its value would rise or fall as the Lorenz curve moved away from or closer to the diagonal. It is not surprising that the Gini coefficient has this property since it is derived directly from the Lorenz curve: it is defined as the ratio of the *area between the Lorenz curve and the diagonal* and the *total area under the diagonal*. Thus, as the distribution becomes more equal and the

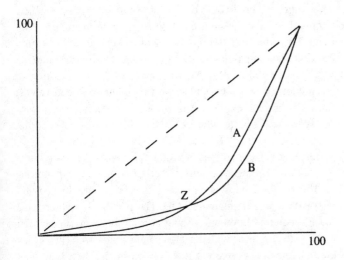

Figure 9.2 A hypothetical Lorenz curve configuration

Lorenz curve shifts closer to the diagonal, the area between the curve and the diagonal decreases leading to a fall in the value of the Gini coefficient.[9]

The properties of inequality indices constitute the major *conceptual* problem in the measurement of inequality. There are, also, a number of other, more practical, problems. The most important of these problems is the choice of income unit. Although the analysis of inequality should be about the welfare of individuals, one is effectively restricted to considering individuals grouped as families or households. This is so because while one can observe the incomes earned by individuals through their dealings with the outside world, one cannot observe the sharing of income that takes place between them in their familial dealings with one another which is the final arbiter of their welfare.

The main problem about measuring inequality in the context of family income is that families differ in size. A weekly income of £400 for a family consisting of husband, wife and child would lead to a lower level of welfare than the same income accruing to a single-person family. Economists attempt to solve this problem by expressing the size of a family in terms of its 'adult equivalents' and then adjusting the family's income accordingly. There are two ideas here. First, that there are economies of scale in living together: two persons living separately would in aggregate, require more income to maintain a certain standard of living than if they lived together, for example, £200 as against £175. Second, because of differences in age, different family members have differing needs; most notably, children have different needs from adults, for example the consumption needs of children are half that of adults. From this logic, one could define a husband and wife living together as 1.75 adult equivalents and define each child living with them as half an adult equivalent. Then the first family (husband, wife and child) would consist of 2.25 adult equivalents and the income of this family, *adjusted for size*, would be £178 (or £400/2.25) per adult equivalent. This could then be compared to the income (£400) of the single-person (or one adult-equivalent) family.[10] Such adjustments, expressed in terms of per adult-equivalent income, are likely to yield a better idea of welfare differences between the families.

These ideas can be given concrete expression by considering some international comparisons of income inequality.[11] Table 9.1 shows computations of the Gini coefficient for a number of countries using both adjusted and unadjusted personal disposable income (PDI). The countries are presented according to their inequality rankings (shown in parentheses) with the high inequality countries, that is, those with the largest Gini coefficients, preceding the low inequality ones. The greatest inequalities in the distribution of (unadjusted) PDI are to be found in the 'newer' countries – Australia, the

USA and Canada – while the Scandinavian countries – Norway and Sweden – show the least inequality.

TABLE 9.1   *International comparisons of inequality: 1979–83*
Gini × 100 (rank)

	PDI		Adjusted PDI	
US	330	(1)	315	(1)
Australia	314	(2)	292	(2)
Canada	306	(3)	290	(4)
The Netherlands	303	(4)	291	(3)
UK	303	(4)	275	(6)
Switzerland	292	(6)	275	(6)
Israel	292	(6)	276	(5)
Germany	280	(8)	249	(8)
Sweden	264	(9)	197	(10)
Norway	255	(10)	222	(9)

SOURCE   T.M. Smeeding, 'Cross-national Comparisons of Inequality and Poverty Position', in L. Osberg (ed.), *Economic Inequality and Poverty: International Perspectives* (Armonk: M.E. Sharpe, 1991), p. 45.

Adjusting PDI for family size reduces the measured level of inequality for every country, except Israel. This indicates that family size and income are positively correlated[12] so that expressing a family's income in terms of its income per adult equivalent serves to reduce inequality. The rankings, too, alter as a consequence of the adjustments – The Netherlands and Israel join Australia and Canada as among the most unequal of countries. However, as Smeeding notes (see Table 9.1), in many cases the Lorenz curves for the countries intersect. Hence, a comparison of inequality between the countries on the basis of Gini coefficient values obscures important differences between families in different parts of the income distribution. To draw out such differences would, however, require one to go beyond the inequality indices and to examine directly the Lorenz curves on which they are based.

Recent work done on income inequality in the UK by the Institute of Fiscal Studies,[13] concluded that the increase in income inequality during the 1980s dwarfed movements in inequality in the previous decades. Much of this growth in inequality was due to the emergence, in the 1980s, of mass unemployment: the growth in inequality over the 1980s was in large part due to growing earnings inequality. The correlation of unemployment and inequality also meant that in 1991, families with children constituted more than half of the families in the lowest income decile; in 1960, when levels of unemployment were much lower, this proportion was less than one-third.

Given that inequality exists what are the economic policies that can reduce it? As observed above, the amount of inequality depends upon the state of the economy. Recessionary conditions, when unemployment is high and wages of low-paid workers are increasing relatively slowly to other incomes, will result in greater inequality. Hence, macroeconomic policies that affect the state of the economy, in terms of boom or slump, will also affect the distribution of national income. These general effects must be borne in mind in any discussion of policies that affect inequality.

Inequality is influenced by a government's tax and transfer policies. Progressive taxes (which impose higher rates of tax on those with higher incomes) and income support programmes (which direct government transfer payments towards the needy) both serve to reduce inequality. Table 9.2 shows the extent to which taxes and transfers have reduced inequality in the UK. Without these, in 1986, the richest and the poorest 20 per cent of households would have received, respectively, 51 and 0.3 per cent of income. The value of the Gini coefficient for the distribution of 'original' income[14] would have been 0.52. With taxes and transfers these proportions were, in fact, 42 and 6 per cent, respectively and the value of the Gini coefficient for the distribution of 'final' income was reduced to 0.36.

TABLE 9.2   *Quintile shares of original and final income, 1986*

Quintile group	Original income	Final income
Top	51	42
Fourth	27	24
Third	16	17
Second	6	11
Bottom	0.3	6.3

SOURCE   *Economic Trends*, Central Statistical Office (London: HMSO, December 1988), p. 114.

However, calculations such as those shown in Table 9.2 do not provide information about the effects of specific changes in tax and benefit rates on different types of families. How many families were affected by a particular policy change? Who were the main beneficiaries and how much did they gain? Who were the main losers and how much did they lose? In evaluating the distributive effect of any budgetary changes these are the important questions that need to be answered.

In attempting to answer such questions most commentators reach for their pocket calculators to work out the effect of these changes on a range of hypothetical families. However, the diversity of families in the population is so great that it is difficult to see how it can be adequately captured by consideration of a small number of hypothetical families.[15] For example, in the UK, the Department of Health and Social Security's Tax/Benefit tables relate to eight different family types; however, 30 per cent of families in the UK population do not have even approximately the age/size composition of one of these family types.[16]

An alternative, more fruitful approach is to base answers to the above questions on an analysis of a representative sample of families drawn from regular household surveys[17] and not on hypothetical family types.[18] Such an approach should also take into account the *responses* of families to changes in tax and benefit rates and not confine itself to the first round cash impact of the changes in tax/benefit rates. For example, the effect of changes in tax and benefit rates on incentives to work is the subject of extensive (and often vigorous) discussion involving expressions such as 'the poverty trap' and the 'unemployment trap'.[19] A first step towards taking account of such responses would be to identify the families who might fall into such traps.[20] However, unless one goes down this alternative and admittedly more difficult path, based on representative samples of families and taking cognisance of their behavioural responses, any attempt to evaluate the effects of distributive policies must remain a shot in the dark.

10   Poverty

Most people have an intuitive appreciation of what constitutes poverty. The pensioner relying on the heat of a single electric bar to see him/her through the winter or the lone parent unable to afford a television licence are some of the images of poverty. However, in order to analyse poverty, rather than to simply describe it in a particular situation, one needs some criteria which can be applied to individuals and families living in a variety of circumstances, on the basis of which they can be judged to be poor or not. This is the problem of *identification.*

Having identified the poor, one needs a device by means of which the information on the poor can be encapsulated into an index of poverty. Such an index would measure the amount of poverty in a given society. This is the problem of *measurement.* An important reason for measuring poverty is to enable comparisons of economic well-being across time and also across different population subgroups. If the measurement problem can be 'solved' then, using such a poverty index, one can say, for example, that while poor persons exist in both Britain and India, there is in some well-defined sense, more poverty in the latter than in the former. Measurement is also important because it enables the effectiveness of public policy to be assessed and the groups towards which policy should be targeted to be identified. Thus, for example, using a poverty index one could arrive at an assessment of whether poverty in Britain increased during the period of Conservative Government in the 1980s and, furthermore, which were the groups most affected.

These two issues – identification and measurement – lie at the heart of the study of poverty and this chapter discusses how each of these issues have been addressed by economists. The analysis of poverty, concerned as it is with the identification and measurement of deprivation, may lead to policy recommendations[1] to alleviate poverty. This chapter therefore also looks at some of the practical issues surrounding the study of poverty and, in particular, it examines some of the policies put forward for 'doing something' about poverty.

The simplest and most commonly employed solution to identifying the poor is to specify a 'cut-off' income level, called the *poverty line* and to regard someone as poor if their income does not exceed (or alternatively, falls below) this poverty line. The poverty line is therefore an expression of the resources needed to meet 'basic needs'. Although there can be disagreement about what these needs might be, it is generally conceded that they should reflect prevailing social standards: basic needs in British society will not be the same as basic needs in an Indian context and a person with a particular level of resources may be regarded as poor in one society but not in another. Since social standards also change over time, it follows that one might regard a person as being poor in Britain in 1990, while recognising that a similar person would not have been regarded as poor in the Britain of, say, the 1930s. Thus, in a very real sense, the analysis of poverty begins with judgements about social norms. This view was articulated more than 200 years ago by Adam Smith when he wrote about those necessities which 'the custom of the country renders it indecent for creditable people, even of the lowest orders, to be without'.[2]

The poverty line approach to identifying the poor, though simple, raises a host of problems, some conceptual and others of a more practical nature. At a conceptual level, the problem is that the 'lowness' of income can only be judged in the context of the actual possibilities of converting income into the ability to function adequately. For example, a disabled person may need more income to be able to function at the level of capability of a healthy person. Thus, what matters for inadequacy of income is not some externally given poverty line but the inability of income (perhaps because of the social environment or perhaps because of the personal characteristics of the income recipient) to generate an adequate level of capabilities.[3] The general problem is, as Martha Nussbaum and Amartya Sen[4] write, that to really know about our fellow citizens 'we need to know not only about the money they do or do not have, but a great deal about how they are able to conduct their lives'.

In addition to the conceptual problems touched upon above, there are several practical problems associated with identifying the poor by means of a poverty line. The first of these is the specification of the poverty line. Here there are several alternative approaches. One might specify the minimum 'basket' of goods and services and specify the poverty line as the cost of buying that basket; the composition and size of the basket would (hopefully) reflect prevailing social standards. Yet another approach might be to seek a poverty line which most people agreed was reasonable – a 'consensual' poverty line; in this approach respondents are asked, through surveys, what they consider to be an adequate minimum income and from these answers a 'social consensus' may be derived. A third approach, usual in countries with well-developed welfare systems, would be to take the government's income support level and to regard some percentage of this as the relevant poverty line. A fourth approach would be to specify the poverty line purely in terms of the prevailing income distribution; for example, a person might be regarded as poor if he (or she) had an income less than half that of the average income, regardless of how high the average might be.

Each of these methods for specifying a poverty line has its drawbacks. The minimum basket of goods and services cannot be drawn up in a purely scientific manner; consequently, different investigators may specify different baskets and, hence, come to different conclusions about poverty. The consensual level of income represents a majority view, across all types of people, of the minimum income needed to avoid poverty and may not therefore reflect the reality of the lives of the deprived. A poverty line based on the government's minimum income level leads to the contradiction that attempts to help the poor, by raising this level, only increases the number of poor. Lastly, poverty lines specified in terms of the distribution of income mean that improvements in the living standards of low-income groups which are shared with the remainder of the population will be discounted; conversely, a general decline in prosperity will not reveal itself as an increase in poverty as the relative picture remains unchanged.

The second problem with identifying the poor *via* a poverty line is one of choosing the appropriate income unit.[5] The choice is essentially between household and family. A household consists of people living at a common address and sharing common housekeeping, while a family is a single adult or a couple either childless or with dependent children. Since the implicit assumption made is that the unit's resources are shared equally among all its members, in terms of identifying the poor it could make a great deal of difference whether a family or household was chosen as the unit of analysis. For example, a household consisting of a married couple and their 20 year old comprises two 'families'; the 20 year old living with his parents might be regarded as poor on the basis of his income, that is when assessment was on a 'family' basis, but might not be regarded as poor when the income of the parents and of the son were pooled, that is when assessment was on a household basis.

In 1985, the basis on which 'poverty' statistics were collected in Britain was altered. One change was that the unit of assessment was no longer the family but the household. Another change was that the poverty line[6] was no longer defined in terms of the government's income support levels but in terms of the average level of income.[7] The new statistics showed that, in 1985, 4.3 million persons lived in *households* whose incomes were less than half the national average. The Institute of Fiscal Studies[8] estimated that if the change in the income unit from the family to the household had not been effected, the number of persons living in *families* whose incomes were below average would have been 5.5 million. If persons whose incomes are below average are regarded as poor, then the move from assessing poverty on the basis of family income to assessing it on the basis of household income succeeded in 'reducing' the number of poor persons in Britain by over 1 million.

Assuming that all the above problems relating to identification can be satisfactorily resolved,[9] the next step is to aggregate the diversity of information on the poor into an index of poverty such that the value of the index would rise if poverty increased and would fall if poverty decreased. Paralleling the construction of inequality indices (discussed in the previous chapter), economists require that a chosen poverty index should satisfy certain properties, in order to ensure that it is capable of giving sensible results. Amartya Sen[10] set out three basic properties that any poverty index should satisfy. The first was that the measurement of poverty should *focus on the incomes of the poor* and should exclude information on incomes of the non-poor. The second property was that the value of the poverty index would *rise (fall)* if the income of any poor person was *reduced (increased)*. The third property was that the value of the poverty index would *rise (fall)* if income was transferred from a poor person to one who was *less (more)* poor.

The first property set the framework within which poverty was to be measured (that is, only incomes of the poor were to be considered) and the second and third properties were useful in exposing the limitations of traditional poverty indices such as the *head count ratio* and the *poverty gap ratio*. The head count ratio, which measures the proportion of poor persons in the total population, does not alter if incomes of poor persons fall because such a change does not affect the number of poor persons. As a corollary, the head count ratio pays no attention to how *far* poor incomes are below the poverty line. The poverty gap ratio attempts to address this question by expressing the average income shortfall of the poor (that is, the average gap between poor incomes and the poverty line) as a proportion of the poverty line income. The value taken by the poverty gap ratio, in a particular context, would therefore reveal that, on average, poor incomes were x per cent below the poverty line.[11] However, in terms of the second of the desirable properties, noted above, this index suffers from the defect that a transfer of income from a poor person to one more (or less) poor would leave the average poverty gap and, hence, the value of the index, unchanged.

Consequently the 'ideal' poverty index would have three dimensions. First, like the head count ratio, it would take account of the number of poor persons relative to the population as a whole and rise or fall in value depending upon whether these numbers increased or decreased. Second, like the poverty gap ratio, it would take account of the depth of poverty and rise or fall in value as the average income shortfall increased or decreased. Third, it would, in addition, also take account of the amount of *inequality among the poor* in such a way that its value would rise (fall) when the amount of inequality among the poor increased (decreased), possibly through an income transfer from a poor person to one less (more) poor. The *Sen poverty index* (and other distribution-sensitive poverty indices) incorporates all three dimensions. The Sen index thus has embedded within it the head count ratio, the poverty gap ratio and a measure of inequality[12] among the poor such that the value of the index would rise if there was an increase in any of the following: the number of poor relative to the population, their average income gap and their relative deprivation.

Timothy Smeeding[13] has estimated poverty levels, using the head count ratio, for a number of countries (and for a range of population subgroups within each country) using as the poverty line, half of median per adult-equivalent disposable income of families (that is, family disposable income adjusted for size and composition using equivalence scales). His results (see Table 10.1), which yielded an average poverty rate of 9.4 per cent across the countries, show the following progression in terms of poverty rates. The countries with the lowest poverty rates (around 5 per cent[14]) were the Scandinavian countries and (West) Germany, the next group were the Swiss and the Dutch with poverty rates of around 8 per cent, Canada, Australia and the UK all had above-average poverty rates in the 11–13 per cent range and the USA, at 16.6 per cent, had the highest poverty rate of the countries shown in Table 10.1. In all the countries single-parent families had the highest poverty rates and these were at least twice that of married couple families.

In terms of what should be done to alleviate poverty, Isabel Sawhill[15] has argued that any anti-poverty strategy must have the following components: substituting, whenever possible, work for welfare and improving job opportunities, strengthening family responsibilities so that child support is the responsibility of both parents, not just that of the custodial parent, breaking the cycle of poverty and welfare dependency for those locked into 'dysfunctional' lifestyles[16] and providing income support for those who still remain poor. An effective strategy to combat poverty would not seek universal remedies, based on regarding the poor as a homogenous group, but would seek instead to tailor policy to the differing circumstances of poor persons. Thus, one needs to know who the poor are and the causes of their poverty, before one can suggest what to do about their poverty. Table 10.1 suggests that poverty is particularly acute in single-parent families – over half of persons living in such families in the USA and Australia and nearly one-third in the UK, were poor. Other studies suggest that there is a strong overlap between unemployment and poverty – in one estimate, the unemployed in 1985 contributed nearly 40 per cent to total poverty in the UK.[17] This indicates that policies to combat poverty should emphasise the first two components noted above.

Both the issues of lone-parent poverty and employment for the poor are not without controversy. In the UK, the 38 per cent rise between 1992 and

TABLE 10.1 *Proportion of poor persons living in various demographic groups**

| | | Non-elderly[†] | | | | | Elderly[†] | | | |
| | Total of all persons | Single persons | Lone parent with children | Couples | | | Couples | | Single persons | |
				0 children	2 children	2+ children	65–74 years	75+ years	65–74 year	75+ years
US	16.6	19.6	54.0	3.9	6.1	12.1	15.0	22.5	39.6	43.4
Australia	11.4	17.8	55.4	2.3	6.9	10.3	7.3	3.5	30.1	35.4
Canada	12.3	19.9	46.3	3.9	5.7	11.5	12.0	9.4	32.0	40.1
The Netherlands	7.5	18.6	21.0	0.9	3.2	3.7	2.3	3.9	2.0	7.1
Switzerland	8.2	15.1	21.2	1.9	2.1	6.0	4.0	6.8	16.9	23.9
UK	11.7	12.6	29.3	1.1	2.5	7.5	23.6	32.1	51.5	59.7
Israel	11.0	9.3	22.6	2.6	2.6	9.8	13.2	24.1	23.4	35.1
Germany	4.9	9.9	7.2	1.4	1.1	1.3	8.6	11.0	12.9	22.4
Sweden	5.0	14.0	9.8	2.3	2.5	4.6	0.6	0.0	0.9	1.3
Norway	4.8	12.9	8.1	1.7	2.0	1.9	2.9	5.8	4.9	11.3
Average[‡]	9.4	15.4	28.6	2.2	3.6	6.7	8.9	11.6	21.4	28.0

* Poor are persons in families with adjusted incomes below half median-adjusted income.

[†] Non-elderly are families headed by a person age 64 years or younger; elderly heads are 65 years or older.

[‡] Average is unweighted mean of each column.

SOURCE T.M. Smeeding, 'Cross-national Comparisons of Inequality and Poverty Position', in L. Osberg (ed), *Economic Inequality and Poverty: International Perspectives* (Armonk: M.E. Sharpe Inc., 1991), p. 48.

1993 in the number of Income Support claimants who were lone parents led to the government drafting proposals for addressing the 'problem' of single parenthood. Such proposals[18] focus on reducing the incentives to become a single parent by reducing amounts paid to separated couples both of whom are on Income Support and restricting benefits to lone parents who continue to have children on Income Support, providing incentives to single parents to support themselves through work through improved child care provision, increasing the responsibility of the lone parent's own parents in situations where the lone parent is a teenager and obtaining more child support maintenance from the absent parent.[19] Not surprisingly, these benefits have met with some hostility. There is little evidence that women become pregnant to gain economic benefits, either through jumping council house queues or through gaining eligibility for income support. Indeed lone parenthood is mostly associated with substantial income losses: recent research found that Income Support was £23 a week less for single parents than was needed for basic necessities.[20]

The issue of employment opportunities for the poor has two aspects – one uncontentious, the other controversial. No one would dispute that an improvement in macroeconomic conditions, leading to an expansion of employment and a consequent reduction in poverty rates is a good thing. What is contentious is whether, in the absence of genuine job opportunities, the poor should be obliged to move from welfare to 'workfare', that is, obliged to work as a condition for receiving income support.[21] There are two arguments for workfare. At a philosophical level, there is the argument that it demeans the poor to absolve them from the responsibilities and obligations that others – who are not poor – assume without question.[22] At a pragmatic level the potential contribution to national output (as previously idle persons begin to 'work') and the potential saving in social security payments (as earnings are substituted for income support) are attractive features of workfare. Critics of workfare say that the returns from such schemes, in terms of increased earnings and employment are either small[23] or require large public investment to be successful.[24] While not denying the duty of a citizen to work, such critics emphasise the importance of ensuring that jobs be at regular work-places[25] and have associated with them a sense of purpose and permanence. In the absence of such jobs, workfare may, ironically, end up demeaning the poor by punishing them for their poverty.

11 The Welfare State

The term 'Welfare State' or 'welfare system' usually refers to the activities of the state in five areas: social security, health, education, housing and personal social services. The size of a country's welfare system is measured by the total amount that the government spends on these areas ('welfare spending'[1]) expressed as a percentage of its gross domestic product (GDP). Most countries spend on welfare in order to achieve certain common objectives. Differences between countries in the size of their welfare systems, in the arrangements for administering such a system and in the manner by which welfare services are provided, then reflect differences in the extent to which (and the manner in which) they wish to pursue such objectives, not to differences in the objectives *per se*.

Figure 11.1 shows how welfare spending in the UK was allocated between the main areas of welfare activity. Almost half of the total welfare spending of £160 billion was on social security payments (pensions plus other social security). Because social security payments play such a large role in the welfare budget and also because issues of health, education and housing involve problems too specific and too complex to be dealt with in a single essay, this chapter focuses on social security.

The primary objective of the Welfare State is to *support living standards.*[2] This may be subdivided into four narrower objectives. The first of these is the provision of a safety net in the form of a guaranteed minimum level of income: no one's living standard should, particularly over an extended period of time, be allowed to fall below some socially acceptable minimum. The second is the support, in the face of unforeseen and foreseen contingencies (for example, unemployment, sickness, disability and retirement), of living standards to which people are accustomed. The third is the support of living standards over the lifecycle of individuals; in pursuing this objective the Welfare State acts as a 'savings bank', extracting contributions during periods of high earnings and paying out benefits during periods of low earnings (for example, when retired or engaged in full-time education) and thereby smoothing out levels of income over the lifetime of individuals. The last objective is the support of living standards when traditional family provision of certain services (for example, caring for the elderly) is no longer possible.

These objectives are realised through a government-induced transfer of resources from some (richer) sections of society to other (poorer) sections.

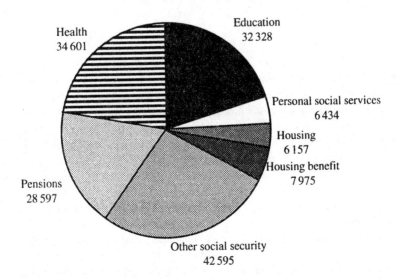

SOURCE   John Hills, *The future of Welfare: a guide to the debate* (York: Joseph Rowntree Foundation, 1993), p. 8.

Figure 11.1 UK government welfare spending 1992–3

In most industrialised countries the bulk of these transfers take the form of cash transfers, where the beneficiary directly receives more resources[3] through, for example, the payment of unemployment or sickness benefit.[4] The other form of transfer is an indirect transfer where goods and services are made available, at subsidised prices (through, for example, the provision of publicly funded schools, housing, personal social services and hospitals and other medical services) to people who, in the absence of such public provision, would be unable to buy adequate quantities (of the appropriate quality) of such goods and services. However, the extent of resource transfer (and, hence, the size of the Welfare State) differs between countries and depends upon different degrees of commitment to the objectives of the Welfare State. The degree of commitment, in turn, is a product of the cultural, social and political traditions of a country and these traditions shape a country's outlook on what the size of its welfare system should be and the form that it should take.

    In terms of size, at the one extreme, is the *residual* welfare system,[5] the objective of which is solely to provide a safety net for the poor and in which the receipt of welfare benefits, whether in the form of cash or in the form of publicly provided goods and services, is subject to means testing. The welfare system in the USA is the prime example of such a minimal system though the Australian system, in which most benefits are means tested, could also be placed in this category. It is no accident therefore that, as Figure 11.2 shows, welfare spending as a percentage of GDP is, in the context of the Organization for Economic Co-operation and Development (OECD), among the smallest for Australia and the USA. The polar opposite of the residual welfare system is the *universal (or institutional)* welfare system (for example, Austria, France, Germany and the countries of Scandinavia) in which benefits and services are intended for all members of society. Again it is no accident that the percentage of GDP devoted to welfare spending is highest for such countries.

Cash transfers are effected through *social security payments*. As observed, *inter alia*, by A.B. Atkinson and John Hills,[6] such payments in industrialised countries combine three different elements: *social insurance* designed to provide security against adverse contingencies, both anticipated and unanticipated, *social assistance* designed to alleviate poverty by providing a safety net in the form of a minimum income level and *categorical transfers* targeted towards particular categories of persons (for example, the disabled, war widows, families with children and so on). The receipt of social insurance benefits is conditional on the occurrence of some contingency (unemployment or sickness) and is linked to past contributions paid by the recipient; in general, however, their payment is not conditional upon the recipients' income and in that sense they are *universal* benefits. Social assistance, on the other hand, is *means tested* and payments are conditional on a recipient's resources[7] being below a prescribed level though it could, additionally, be linked to other factors.[8] Categorical payments (for example, Child Benefit in the UK) are universal benefits (that is, payable to all in the category) without regard to past contributions.

Different countries combine these elements in different proportions. As Figure 11.3 below shows, half of the total social security spending of £74 billion in the UK, in 1992–3, was social insurance benefits. In the same year, means-tested benefits constituted one-third of total social security spending, while categorical payments (mainly Child Benefit, paid to families with children) constituted approximately 16 per cent of total social security payments. In the French social security system, insurance against life's hazards is the primary objective and the alleviation of poverty a subsidiary objective. In contrast to the system in the UK, social insurance is the rule and social assistance is the exception, with universal (that is, non-means tested) benefits being much more common than means-tested ones.[9] Consequently, social assistance in France, through the *Revenue Minimum d'Insertion*, was

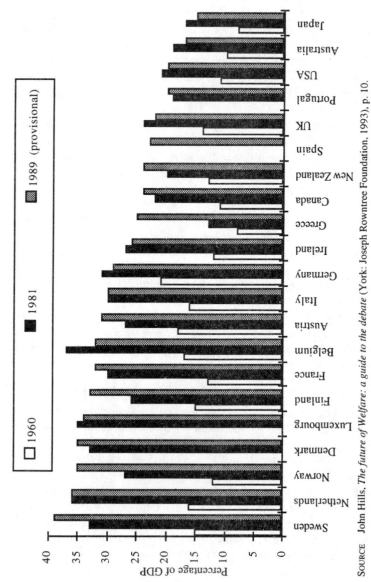

SOURCE   John Hills, *The future of Welfare: a guide to the debate* (York: Joseph Rowntree Foundation, 1993), p. 10.

Figure 11.2 Government social spending in industrialised countries 1960–89

received by only 0.6 million recipients in 1991 while, in the UK, there were nearly 5 million recipients of its main means-tested benefit, *Income Support*.[10]

With the breakdown, in the 1980s, of the post-war consensus on the desirability of the Welfare State, the issue of the efficiency of the welfare system has become very important. This issue has many facets. The first relates to the efficiency of welfare provision, particularly with regard to the nature of benefits (means-tested versus universal benefits) and the mode of provision (private versus social insurance). The second issue is that of microeconomic efficiency and relates to the disincentives to work and to save embodied within the Welfare State. The third is that of macroeconomic efficiency and asks whether the Welfare State is too large, in the sense that too great a proportion of national income is being spent on welfare.[11]

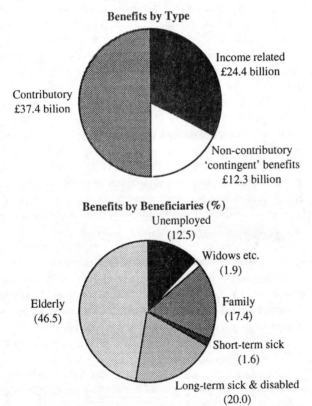

Benefits by Type

Income related
£24.4 billion

Contributory
£37.4 bilion

Non-contributory
'contingent' benefits
£12.3 billion

Benefits by Beneficiaries (%)

Unemployed
(12.5)

Widows etc.
(1.9)

Elderly
(46.5)

Family
(17.4)

Short-term sick
(1.6)

Long-term sick & disabled
(20.0)

SOURCE   John Hills, *The future of Welfare: a guide to the debate* (York: Joseph Rowntree Foundation, 1993), p. 39.

Figure 11.3 UK cash benefits 1992–3

Turning first to the issue of efficient welfare provision, a basic question with respect to the Welfare State is why the state should involve itself in activities (the relief of poverty excepted) which could be (perhaps better) carried out by the private sector? In particular, it might be argued that state involvement in education and health is unnecessary since these goods could be supplied privately, nor is the need for social insurance obvious since private insurance could provide security against contingencies such as unemployment, sickness and retirement. In the face of these arguments, a welfare system in which the government plays a larger role in supporting living standards than simply providing a safety net, can be justified on two counts. First, education and health are often regarded as 'merit goods' in the sense that when consumption of these goods is increased there is a social gain, over and above the gain that accrues to the individuals. Consequently, from a social perspective, market supply of such goods, which focuses entirely on private gain, will, unless supplemented by state provision, lead to an underprovision of merit goods. Second, problems with the insurance of certain contingencies mean that private insurance may not be a viable substitute for social insurance.

In particular, the existence of two problems, *adverse selection* and *moral hazard* (both of which arise from the insurer possessing imperfect information about the insured) means, that for several contingencies, private insurance cannot be an adequate substitute for social insurance.[12] Adverse selection arises when bad-risk individuals are able to conceal the fact from the insurer. When the insurer cannot distinguish high- from low-risk individuals he (or she) may charge a premium based upon average risk; in that case low-risk individuals may not consider it worthwhile to insure and the insurer would be left with a majority of high-risk customers. Moral hazard is due to the fact that individuals, who are insured against a particular contingency (for example, theft of a bicycle), lack the incentive to exercise the degree of care (unfailingly locking one's bicycle) that they would have exercised had they not been insured. The fundamental problem arising from moral hazard is that the insured party, through his (or her) actions can influence the probability of the event occurring, against which insurance has been taken out. The greater the cover, the less the incentive to take due and proper care and greater the chances of the contingency occurring.

Problems associated with adverse selection and moral hazard are particularly acute with respect to contingencies covered by social insurance. For example, with respect to unemployment it is not possible to assess accurately the risk that different individuals face of losing their jobs. Moreover, moral hazard would mean that individuals could, in the presence of unemployment insurance, contribute to their own joblessness. Thirdly, since unemployment is a continuing event, monitoring the fact that the unemployed are genuinely seeking work could be a costly business. Finally, individuals for whom the probability of unemployment was very high (for example, workers in declining industries) would find it impossible to obtain insurance. Problems of a similar nature arise with respect to insurance against sickness, though the monitoring problems are easier than with unemployment. Retirement pensions pose a different set of problems. Here the problem is one of evaluating uncertainty rather than risk. While actuarial calculations allow risk to be quantified accurately, the uncertainty attached to future inflation rates cannot be quantified. This means that private pensions cannot offer a hedge against the real value of the pension being eroded through unanticipated inflation. Protection against inflation can only come through the state, either through an indexation of private pensions or through social insurance against retirement.

For all these contingencies, the state can, through social insurance, provide a comprehensive level of security in a way that, for reasons discussed above, private insurance cannot. This is because social insurance does not embody the principle of actuarial fairness, involving the careful matching of contributions and benefits, which is the *sine qua non* of private insurance. The hallmark of social insurance is flexibility, with governments being able to vary the terms under which different benefits[13] are paid or even to introduce new benefits and to abolish existing benefits. The other characteristic by which social insurance differs fundamentally from private insurance is its compulsory nature. This permits risk to be pooled, eliminating the danger of low-risk individuals refusing to insure and thus offering a solution to the adverse selection problem noted above. For all these reasons private insurance does not offer a viable alternative to social insurance.

Nevertheless, discontent continues to grow towards social insurance being the primary form of income maintenance, as it is in most OECD countries. It is felt that the social and economic assumptions which underlie the effective use of social insurance (stable families with full-time male breadwinners coupled with low rates of unemployment and a population in which fewer than 10 per cent are over 65 years of age) as a means of income maintenance are no longer valid today. High divorce rates and the rapid increase in the number of single-parent families, mass unemployment and the growing incidence of long-term unemployment, increases in life expectancy and a concomitant ageing of the population and the co-existence, through low-paid work, of poverty and employment, have all meant that the level of contributions have been insufficient for social insurance benefits to provide an adequate level of income maintenance. Instead, in the UK, such benefits have increasingly had to be supplemented by non-insurance means-tested benefits.[14]

The argument is, therefore, increasingly being made that there should be even greater means testing of benefits than there is at present.[15]

The problem with greater means testing of benefits is that they exacerbate the disincentive effects of the welfare system which, as noted earlier, cause concern about its microeconomic efficiency. These disincentives affect individual choice in three main areas of economic activity: choice between employment and joblessness, choice of hours worked and choice between saving and consumption. If the proportion of earnings replaced by unemployment and unemployment-related, benefits (termed the 'replacement ratio') is sufficiently high then some people may actually be better off out of work than in work – this is known as the *unemployment trap*.[16] The choice of hours worked is affected by the fact that the higher earnings that result from longer hours worked could lead to withdrawal of means-tested benefits;[17] the loss of benefits combined with the higher taxes to be paid on increased earnings might mean that working more hours might make a person only marginally better off – this is known as the *poverty trap*.[18] Means-tested benefits for retired persons might mean that they would be penalised, through withdrawal of benefit, from having income from savings and occupational pensions; this then acts as a disincentive to save and to join occupational schemes unless the sums are large enough to make dependence on means-tested benefits unnecessary – this is known as the *savings trap*.[19] In addition to these areas, the social security system is alleged to affect family structure by increasing marital break up and illegitimacy.[20]

The evidence on the disincentive effects of the US welfare system has been reviewed by Robert Moffitt.[21] Studies of Aid to Families with Dependent Children (AFDC) recipients – mostly poor, single mothers[22] showed that the programme generated work disincentives that were not trivial: in the absence of the programme, recipients would, on average, have worked 14.4 hours per week instead of the 9 hours per week that they worked while on the programme. Assuming that these hours were worked at the minimum wage, of every dollar transferred to AFDC recipients in 1989, 37 cents were lost through reduced earnings. By way of contrast, there is no evidence of a strong relationship between AFDC benefit levels and the probability of marital breakdown or the growth of illegitimacy. Such case study evidence, as has been cited, to show that the AFDC programme acts as strong disincentive to marriage,[23] has also been strongly contested.[24] On this issue therefore, the jury must be regarded as still being out.

The last issue of concern about the Welfare State is the size to which it has grown. In the 3 years up to 1992–3, welfare spending in the UK rose, as a percentage of GDP, from 21.4 to 26.4 per cent; in the same year such spending, at £160 billion, accounted for over two-thirds of government expenditure.[25] Although the USA spends, relative to the UK, a smaller proportion of its GDP on welfare,[26] it too worries about a 'welfare explosion': between 1970 and 1987, real expenditure, in the USA, on means-tested programmes increased by 224 per cent.[27] Indeed, between 1960 and 1981, there was a rapid growth of welfare spending in most OECD countries with the unweighted average of the proportion of GDP taken by such spending rising from 14 to 26 per cent. This raises fears that the Welfare State, as it exists in many industrialised countries, may no longer be affordable and, indeed, by diverting resources from more productive purposes, may be acting as a brake on economic growth and rising living standards.[28]

These fears are aggravated by the worry that the expansion of welfare spending may have no upper limit since a major force behind such expansion is the higher expenditure associated with an ageing population. In every country of the OECD, the ratio of working-age persons to those 65 years or older (known as the 'support' ratio) will be considerably smaller in the year 2040 than it was in 1980. The UK support ratio, which in 1980 was approximately 4.2 (the lowest, after Germany, in the OECD) is projected to fall to approximately 3.1 by 2040. An increase in the proportion of older persons in the population has two implications. First, there will be upward pressure on health expenditure: HM Treasury has estimated that, compared to a person of working age, health care costs for the over-75s are nine times as great and for those aged 65–75 years four times as great. Second, on a pay-as-you-go system of state pensions (such as that exists in the UK), where each generation effectively meets the pension needs of the preceding generation, an increasingly smaller number of persons of working age will be contributing to the pensions of an increasingly larger number of retired persons and may reach the point where the existing system of state pensions becomes unsustainable.

It is no accident, therefore, that many of the proposals for welfare reform, in the UK, have emphasised pensions: raising the retirement age,[29] means testing the basic pension,[30] abolition of the earnings-related component of the state pension and continuing to link the growth of pensions to price (rather than income) increases are some of the proposals that have been put forward, in the recent past. All these proposals, as A.B. Atkinson[31] notes, are predicated on the belief that 'welfare spending is out of control ... [and that] pension provision is a burden on the economy and a threat to our future'. However, according to John Hills,[32] the 'demographic time bomb' has been exaggerated.[33] Even if benefits became income linked, the total net effect on public finances in the UK, over the next 50 years, would not amount to more than 5 per cent of GDP. Thus, the real question, according to him, is not whether the Welfare State is affordable (it is), but rather whether it is worth paying for. In this connection it would be as well to remember that the Welfare State is not just an instrument of redistribution. As discussed earlier, because of imperfections in incentives and information, it also plays a role in promoting economic efficiency. It is in its ability to improve social welfare, by promoting both equality and efficiency, that the justification for the Welfare State ultimately rests.

12   Health Care

Sickness is a contingency against which people need to be protected. This protection should take two forms. The first is protection from the loss of income that occurs when people are unable to work because of ill-health. The second and arguably more important form of protection is through the availability of medical and hospital services that will alleviate the condition of the sick. Protection from income loss is provided through income maintenance policies – discussed in the previous chapter – which pay out sickness and invalidity benefits. Protection, in terms of restoration to health, takes the form of health care provision[1] and the provision and finance of such care is the subject of this chapter.

Since sickness is a contingency it can be insured against, just as one might, for example, insure the contents of one's home against theft. Furthermore, this insurance can be supplied by private insurance companies, who can purchase health care services, on behalf of the insured persons, from private doctors and hospitals. In principle, therefore, there is no need for government involvement in the field of health care. In practice however, governments in most industrialised countries play a major role in the provision and finance of health care. Table 12.1 shows that the share of public spending in medical care in 1987, across a number of the Organization for Economic Co-operation and Development (OECD) countries was (the USA excepted) greater than 70 per cent. Moreover, for every country in Table 12.1, this share rose steadily during 1960–87. Even in the USA, where health care is closest to the free-market model of private health insurance coupled with private ownership of health care facilities, public expenditure accounted for over 40 per cent of total expenditure on health care.[2]

The reason for heavy government involvement in the field of health care is that a system entirely reliant on private insurance and private provision would contain grave defects. Since good health plays an important part in determining personal welfare, such defects cannot be ignored. The first and most obvious defect is that persons with existing medical problems would not be able to obtain insurance (and therefore care) for such problems. For that reason alone, there would be gaps in coverage.

The second defect arises from the fact that insurers, typically, would not know the 'true' risk of an individual seeking health cover. If such a risk was known, then the insured person could be charged an *actuarially fair* premium. However, when insurers cannot distinguish between customers in terms of their degree of risk, they may charge a premium based upon average risk. In such an event, some individuals who regard themselves as being 'low risk', would not consider it worthwhile to take out insurance cover and insurers would be left with a majority of high-risk customers. As a consequence, insurers would end up with an *adverse selection* of customers comprising mainly of persons in the high-risk category.[3]

TABLE 12.1   *Public and private expenditure on medical care, 1960–87*

	Public spending as percentage of total
Australia	
1960	52.6
1970	52.6
1980	61.7
1987	70.5
Canada	
1960	42.7
1970	70.2
1980	75.0
1987	73.9
Germany	
1960	67.5
1970	74.2
1980	79.4
1987	77.8
Japan	
1960	60.4
1970	69.8
1980	70.8
1987	73.0
The Netherlands	
1960	33.3
1970	84.3
1980	75.8
1987	73.9
New Zealand	
1960	80.7
1970	80.3
1980	83.6
1987	82.5

TABLE 12.1   *continued*

	Public spending as percentage of total
Sweden	
1960	72.6
1970	86.0
1980	92.1
1987	90.8
Switzerland	
1960	61.3
1970	63.9
1980	67.5
1987	NA
UK	
1960	85.3
1970	87.0
1980	89.6
1987	86.4
USA	
1960	24.7
1970	37.0
1980	42.4
1987	41.4

SOURCE   N. Barr, 'Economic Theory and Welfare State', *Journal of Economic Literature*, vol. xxx (1992), pp. 741–803.

It is important to emphasise that the self-assessment by customers of their 'risk status' may be based upon a subjective rather than an objective evaluation of their state of health and that the two may sometimes be in conflict.[4] Given self-assessment of health risk, whether a person chooses to take out health insurance or not would then depend on his or her attitude to risk. For example, the fact that 35 million people in the USA have no insurance has much to do with the fact that small companies do not offer health insurance to their employees, because such companies attract workers who 'place relatively low value on health insurance and prefer [instead] a higher take-home pay'.[5]

As long as insurance is voluntary, the fundamental consequence of adverse selection is that coverage will not be universal. However, eliminating adverse selection requires more than removing the asymmetry of information between insurers and the insured. It requires, in addition, an absence of the mismatch between what an individual's degree of risk actually is and what he or she perceives it to be. Hence, if actuarially fair premiums could conceivably be charged, they should also be perceived as such by persons contemplating taking out cover. The other additional requirement for the elimination of adverse selection and, hence, for universal (but voluntary) cover, is that all persons be risk averse, that is to say, prefer to avoid, rather than be indifferent towards (or even embrace) risk.[6]

However, a common premium policy, based upon charging the same premium for different risk categories, is unlikely to be a stable outcome since rival insurers could woo away persons in the low-risk groups by offering them better terms than those they are presently getting. This realisation (or experience) will force insurance firms to discriminate between customers in terms of the premiums charged. For example, Blue Cross/Blue Shield, the largest non-profit health insurer in the USA, was forced by competitive pressures to drop a common premium in favour of differential premiums.[7] This discrimination is usually on the basis of information culled from people's medical histories. Assessment of risk based on such information is known as *experience rating*. Experience rating has its firmest adherents in the USA. The USA is unique in the extent to which individuals and groups are charged widely differing rates, on the basis of characteristics (age, gender, area of residence, industry and occupational group and present and past medical conditions) that are regarded as useful predictors of the likely demands that they will make on health care in the future.[8] In contrast, most countries which operate a single-payer system (that is, a health insurance system under which a single agency pays medical bills) use *community rating*, by which everyone is charged the same premium regardless of their current health condition.

The reason for the unpopularity (outside the USA) of experience rating is that it raises more problems than it solves. The main argument for experience rating is that it is 'efficient', in the sense that it relates individual premiums to expected consumption of health care. However, this efficiency is purely illusory and, as a consequence, premiums based on experience rating can give rise to grave iniquities. Health care costs can be divided into three types: costs arising from actions within an individual's control (such as smoking), costs related to individual characteristics (such as age or genetic history) and costs which relate to purely random factors.[9] Efficiency requires that everyone should bear that part of their health care costs that arise from actions within their control, though an attempt to extend this proposition to make persons liable for all the sources of their risk can be highly iniquitous.[10] However, that is precisely the problem with experience rating: insurers do not distinguish between the different sources of risk and simply charge a premium based on current and past health status.

In summary, if universal cover for health risks is the aim of government policy then a system of voluntary health insurance will not deliver this. This is because the premiums charged (either on the basis of community rating involving a pooling of risk or on the basis of individual premiums based on experience rating) would not reflect the 'true' risk of ill-health and could also mask, particularly with experience rating, grave iniquities. Hence, the only effective way to secure universal coverage without (unjustifiable) inequalities in premiums, is to have a system of *compulsory coverage based on community rating*. Needless to say, this would mark a significant departure from a purely market-provided system based on voluntary cover.

The second danger of relying on purely private health insurance and private provision of health care arises from *moral hazard,* which takes the form of overconsumption of health care services. This overconsumption arises because, once the premium is paid, health care is a free good to the person insured; hence there is no incentive to economise on consumption.[11] On the supply side, if providers of health care were reimbursed for all their costs by the insurer, then they too would have no incentive to limit the amount of medical and hospital services provided.

As Table 12.2 shows, several countries have experienced a rapid escalation in the percentage of their GDP taken up by health care expenditure. Improvements in technology and the ageing of populations means that some of this cost increase is unavoidable. However, the concern in many countries (particularly the USA) is that health care costs are higher (and rising faster) than what would be justified by purely technological and demographic considerations. Indeed, this concern has become so great, that control of health care costs has become the major objective of health care policy in many industrialised countries,[12] with the USA seeking, in addition, universal access to health care.

Proposals to restrict health care expenditure focus on methods to provide incentives both for reducing consumption and for restraining provision.[13] Providing incentives to reduce consumption is achieved by making people liable for a certain percentage or amount of the costs of their health care, usually subject to a ceiling. The USA has large co-payments (generally, 20 per cent) even for the fully insured. In continental Europe, out of pocket charges, paid by patients, often contribute approximately 15 per cent to health spending: in France and Italy, patients pay 25–30 per cent of the costs of seeing a general practitioner, while Belgium, Germany, France and Italy impose charges (typically £5–£10 per day) for stays in hospitals. Only in the UK are co-payments a trivial proportion (3–4 per cent) of health-care expenditure.[14]

TABLE 12.2   *Public and private expenditure on medical care, 1960–87*

	Total spending as percentage of GDP
Australia	
1960	4.7
1970	5.1
1980	6.9
1987	7.9
Canada	
1960	5.5
1970	7.2
1980	7.5
1987	8.8
Germany	
1960	4.7
1970	5.5
1980	7.9
1987	8.1
Japan	
1960	2.9
1970	4.4
1980	6.4
1987	6.8
The Netherlands	
1960	3.9
1970	6.0
1980	8.2
1987	8.5
New Zealand	
1960	4.4
1970	5.1
1980	7.2
1987	6.9
Sweden	
1960	4.7
1970	7.2
1980	9.5
1987	9.2
Switzerland	
1960	3.3
1970	5.2
1980	7.3
1987	7.7

TABLE 12.2 *continued*

	Total spending as percentage of GDP
UK	
1960	3.9
1970	4.5
1980	5.8
1987	6.1
USA	
1960	5.3
1970	8.0
1980	9.5
1987	11.2

SOURCE Nicholas Barr, *op. cit.*

Providing incentives to reduce the supply of health care may take several forms. First, instead of being based on *retrospective* payment (where fees are paid after the treatment, at the rate quoted by the provider), the payment system for health care services may be based on *prospective* payment, where charges for different treatments are agreed in advance through *fee schedules* which apply, with limited exceptions, to all buyers and providers in an area. A worry frequently expressed about fee schedules is that the medical profession may attempt to recoup income losses by providing a greater volume of health care and that, therefore, fee schedules might not have any effect on the total health care costs. The evidence, however, is that volume increases do not (and indeed, cannot) match fee restrictions. Doctors may be able to justify a few additional tests in response to fee restrictions, but it is highly unlikely that they would carry out unnecessary (and perhaps painful) procedures on a scale large enough to compensate fully for such restrictions. Consequently, Medicare in the USA, for example, has a standard assumption that volume increases will make up only up to half of any fee constraint imposed by Medicare.[15]

Fee limits operate in most countries – Australia, Canada, France, Germany and Japan – that fund health care through payment on a fee for service basis.[16] Consequently, a chest X-ray with two views, for example, costs $45 in the USA (where restrictions, except on the publicly funded schemes, Medicare and Medicaid, do not apply) but only $19 in Germany (where they do).[17] One means of implementing fee schedules is to classify patients into one of 467 diagnostic related groups (DRGs) and pay hospitals a fixed prospective fee per patient, determined primarily by the DRG to which the patient was assigned.[18]

The second method of controlling health care costs is to have, instead of a fee for service payment system (whether subject to fee schedules or not), a payment system under which for a fixed, annual fee, paid to a health management organisation (HMO), a person is provided with the necessary medical services. A HMO thus incorporates the functions of both insurer and provider – it guarantees to provide medical services (some of which may be supplied by the HMO itself) and the fixed payment that it receives in return offers it an incentive to economise on health care provision.[19]

The third method for controlling health care costs is to limit patient choice by allowing only certain (low-cost) providers to supply health care to insured patients. Such providers secure this position by tendering competitively to become Preferred Provider Organisations (PPOs) and only the lowest tenders (consistent, of course, with acceptable levels of health care) obtain the business of the insurance company and its patients. For example, most private health plans in the UK contain a 'low-cost' option which restricts the hospitals from which one may obtain treatment. The last method is for governments to impose constraints on the overall budget of organisations that supply health care, thus placing the onus of worrying about prices and volumes on their managers. This is the logic of hospital care in Australia, Canada, Germany, France and the UK.

The foregoing discussion has indicated that there are two criteria that a good health care system should satisfy. First, it should provide universal coverage so that no one is without health insurance. Second, it should provide health care of an acceptably high standard at a reasonable cost. Neither of these objectives can be achieved by a system of purely private provision. Nicholas Barr[20] categorises health care systems into three types. The first is a *market-based approach,* characterised by private purchase of insurance and private provision of health care, of which the USA is the best example. The second type is based on *compulsory social insurance* financed by earnings-related contributions, with some supplemental role for private insurance and provision. This is the type of system that prevails in Australia, Canada, Germany and Japan. The third type is one where health care is *tax financed,* with state ownership (or, at least, regulation) of the factors of production. This is the type that prevails in New Zealand, Sweden and the UK. As Table 12.3 shows, in both the second and third types, the percentage of the population covered by public health schemes is very high, reaching full coverage in countries where health care is tax financed. In contrast to countries that have adopted such systems, only 25 per cent of the population in the USA is covered by the two main public insurance schemes, Medicare and Medicaid.

TABLE 12.3   *Percentage of population eligible for public health schemes and average percent of bill paid by public insurance, selected countries, 1987*

	Hospital care	Ambulatory care	Medical goods
Percentage of population covered			
Germany	92	92	97
The Netherlands	77	72	80
Sweden	100	100	100
Switzerland	98	98	100
UK	100	100	99
USA	40	25	NA
Percentage of bill paid			
Germany	97	85	56
The Netherlands	80	67	58
Sweden	100	90	75
Switzerland	100	86	90
UK	99	88	93
USA	55	56	NA

SOURCE   Nicholas Barr, *op. cit.*

Given the limitations of a market-based system of health care, it is no accident that, in 1992, 35 million people, constituting 14 per cent of its population, were uninsured against health care risks in the USA. It was this fact, along with the rapid growth in health care costs, that underpinned President Clinton's health care reforms. Under these reforms, by 1998, everyone would have been entitled to health insurance through the *guaranteed* acceptance/renewal of a health plan, on a *community rating* basis, offered by the regional or corporate health alliance to which a person would have belonged by virtue of residence or employment. Furthermore, everyone would have been *required* to have health insurance, with this universal coverage being largely financed by mandating firms to pay 80 per cent of average premiums, albeit with a cap of 7.9 per cent of payroll costs. Subsidies, financed through general revenues, would have been available for funding premiums in excess of the cap and also been available to low-income families.

In addition to providing universal coverage, the other major purpose of the reforms was to control health care costs. This was to have been achieved by coverage through health alliances which, in the main would be organised on a regional basis.[21] Each alliance would offer a choice between three health care plans: HMOs, PPOs or fee for service. Each plan would incorporate a particular form of co-payment by the insured and, within each alliance, the same premium would be charged to all who sought coverage under a particular plan, that is to say each plan, within an alliance, would be community rated.

The other country, apart from the USA, which is attempting a major reform of its health care system is the UK. However, unlike the USA, where President Clinton's reform proposals were predicated on dissatisfaction – mainly with escalating costs and less than universal coverage – with market-based provision of health care, the reforms in the UK sprang from the view that the monopoly position of the government, in its embodiment as both purchaser and provider of health care (through the National Health Service (NHS)), bred inefficiency. The UK health care reforms have, therefore, emphasised a greater role for market forces and competition (but within the existing context of tax-financed health care) through the creation of *internal (or quasi) markets*. The fundamental step towards achieving this was by separating the purchasers from the providers of health care. Under the new system there were to be two types of purchasers – district health authorities (DHAs) and budget-holding general practitioners (GPs) – and two types of providers – 'self-managed' NHS Trusts which would be run as independent businesses[22] and the more traditional hospitals that remained under DHA control. It was envisaged that, over time, the purchaser and provider sides would be dominated by fund-holding GPs and NHS Trusts.

NHS Trusts, which were to be run (like any company) by a board of directors, would enter into contractual arrangements with purchasers. These contracts could be of the fee for service type, with a detailed fee schedule specified in advance or they could take the form of broadly defined services provided for an annual fee. In the context of the latter type of contract, the NHS Trusts would operate as HMOs; in the context of the former type of contract they would be subject to detailed price controls with all the attendant implications (described earlier) of such controls. Fund-holding GPs, who would receive budgets on a capitation basis, could use their funds to provide and purchase medical services for their patients. In effect, fund-holding GPs too would function as HMOs.

Thus, in both the UK and USA, the objective of health care reform, has been to push their systems, from diametrically opposing directions, towards the middle ground of 'managed competition'. In the USA, President Clinton's aborted reforms sought to 'socialise' a system which essentially relies on private finance and provision; in the UK, reforms have sought to 'privatise' a system which was built on the monolith of state finance and provision. Both sets of reforms spring from the belief that the best forms of health care should temper the efficiency that markets provide with the equity of government-sponsored regulation. It is this consensus about the desirability of managed competition that is the common thread that runs through the different health care systems of the industrialised world.

IV Government

13 The Economic Role of Government

Much of economic theory of the textbook variety is a celebration of the free market system. This celebration has two parts. First, the operation of the price system, in the context of competitive markets, leads to a balance between the demand and supply of the different goods and services traded. In other words, flexible prices results in competitive market clearing. Second, the market-clearing equilibrium – brought about through flexible prices and competitive markets – is a 'good thing' in the sense that it is also a point of economic efficiency.[1] In other words, competitive outcomes are also efficient ones.[2]

These results – which are, of course, a vindication of Adam Smith's intuition about the existence of an 'invisible hand' bringing consistency and order to the chaos of individual actions – would be remarkable in themselves. But there is more. The efficient outcome will have been brought about through parsimony in the use of information; the only things that individuals, in making their supply–demand decisions, need to know are the prices of the different commodities. Furthermore, since the efficient outcome is the result of firms and consumers acting 'selfishly', by looking only to their own interests, it is 'incentive compatible' in the sense that its existence does not depend upon altruistic behaviour. Lastly, not only will competitive markets lead to an efficient outcome, but *any* efficient outcome that one might desire can be attained through the operation of competitive markets.[3] This last statement is a very powerful result for it says that if one does not like the particular efficient outcome (perhaps because there were great inequalities associated with it) that resulted from the operation of competitive markets in a specific context, then all is not lost. In such a situation all that is required is to specify a different, more desirable, outcome and to modify the context suitably; competitive markets operating in the new context would then lead to that outcome.

Against the background of these results the government does not have much of a role. If economic outcomes were not socially desirable then one role for government would be to change the context within which markets operated. This context is provided by the initial endowments with which individuals are equipped for trade in the market. For example, persons who were wealthy or who possessed skills and education would be better equipped for trade than the poor and the unskilled and, hence, would benefit disproportionately from market outcomes. If endowments were unfairly distributed then market outcomes, notwithstanding the fact that they were efficient, would also be unfair. Thus, within the framework of market sovereignty, redistribution – whereby the government altered initial endowments to prevent grossly inequitable outcomes – would be an acceptable role for government. Even here, its role would be limited by the injunction, that in the pursuit of redistributive objectives, the government should not, by distorting incentives, pervert the free functioning of markets. Since this injunction could only be satisfied through the highly infeasible instrument of 'lump-sum' taxes and transfers (that is, all 'rich' persons pay, for example, £100 each and all 'poor' persons receive the same, irrespective of their wealth or poverty), in practice the redistributive role for government would be non-existent.

Although proponents of free markets concede that government might legitimately have a say, however circumscribed, in the sphere of distribution (that is, in terms of who receives how much) it would deny government any role, other than a purely facilitating one, in the spheres of *production* and of *allocation* (that is, in terms of deciding how commodities are to be produced and what and how much is to be produced). In terms of production, the basic choice is between production by the private sector and production by the public sector. Economists who believe in the free functioning of markets would argue that the most useful role that government could play in this regard would be to abdicate its productive responsibilities in favour of the private sector – a process known as *privatisation*. Given the central role that privatisation has, in the recent past, played (and continues to play) in the economic life of the UK, of Germany and of the countries of Eastern Europe, a separate chapter is devoted to this topic and it is not addressed here. Such economists would, in similar vein, argue that the most useful contribution that governments could make to allocative decisions (relating to what and how much to produce) would be to remove 'market imperfections'. These imperfections, which prevent markets from functioning properly, are associated with an absence of competition (for example, through the existence of monopolies) or with the presence of barriers to price flexibility (for example, through price-support mechanisms such as minimum wage legislation). The task of government would then be to take the necessary steps to ensure that all impediments to the proper functioning of markets were removed.

Economists who are not content with this purely passive role for public policy, point to numerous real-world instances where, notwithstanding the existence of competition and price flexibility, markets fail to deliver on efficiency. (Indeed as the Nobel-laureate Robert Solow[4] has pointed out, many of the young stars of economics, of the past 20 years, made their mark by going beyond the simple competitive model and considering the consequences of dropping some of its restrictive assumptions.) In the presence of such cases of *market failure*, they would argue, governments have no alternative but to intervene actively to help markets overcome these difficulties. Indeed Joseph Stiglitz[5] argues, contrary to the traditional view that market failures are the exception, that such failures may be so pervasive as to be the norm. However, it is not at all obvious that government will necessarily succeed where markets have failed. Consequently, not all cases of market failure will be amenable to correction through government action. The key to effective government intervention, therefore, lies not in demonstrating the existence of market failures (and thereby establishing a rationale for government intervention) but rather identifying situations where such failures are of the kind that would make intervention worthwhile.

There are essentially three sources of market failure: monopoly, particularly natural monopoly, public goods and externalities. Each of these types of market failure offers potential scope for government economic intervention, over and above the purely passive role described earlier. The existence of a monopoly invites governments to break up the monopoly through appropriate legislation. Where this is not possible (as, for example, with natural monopolies) it can either take responsibility for production by nationalising the industry or it can regulate the private sector monopoly. These issues are discussed in the chapter on privatisation.

Public goods are those goods which are consumed collectively by a group of persons so that members of the group who do not wish to pay for such goods cannot[6] be excluded from their consumption. Therefore, left to itself the market would not provide public goods since the essence of market provision is the exclusion from enjoying the benefits of goods and services for which no payment is made. Defence is a classic example of a public good, the provision of police and fire services is another, while street lighting and public television are further examples of public goods. In all these examples, social welfare is obviously increased by the provision of public goods. Since such goods would not be supplied by the market the responsibility for their provision then falls upon the government which extracts, from individuals and households, mandatory payments (in the form of taxes) for the public goods provided. It is important to emphasise that the government provision of public goods does not imply the government production of such goods: for example, the government provides defence goods in the form of tanks and aircraft but these could be produced by private firms.

The third type of market failure relies upon the notion of *externalities*. Actions by one party often contain, as a by-product, consequences (either beneficial or harmful) for the welfare of other parties. Such consequences which the person (or persons) taking the action imposes, *without incurring any cost*,[7] upon other persons are known as 'externalities'. For example, as a result of its production an upstream firm discharges effluent into a river which then affects a downstream firm which uses water from the river in its production process; a firm trains its labour force, part of which then leaves to take employment with other firms thereby benefiting the latter, and a noisy, late-night party disturbs the peace of a neighbourhood. The important point is that the imposition of an externality is costless. The firm discharging effluent does not pay for polluting the river and the revellers are not required to compensate their neighbours for disturbing them, while the firm providing trained labour to other firms in the industry is not recompensed by them for this service. Thus, left to themselves private agents will, in deciding their actions, ignore the existence of any externalities. Hence, in the presence of externalities, markets will either produce too much (if the externality is a 'bad', for example pollution or noise) or too little (if the externality is a 'good', for example trained labour) relative to the amount that is socially desirable. The role of government is then to get markets to produce the 'right' (that is, socially desirable) amounts of the 'commodities' (pollution, noise or trained labour) associated with the externalities.

The relevant question is, of course, how the government might achieve this. The basic reason for the existence of externalities is that markets, in which the commodities associated with externalities could be traded, do not exist. For example, a factory can costlessly pollute the atmosphere – and so deprive all of clean air – because there is no market in which pollution, as a commodity, may be bought and sold and, hence, be appropriately priced. The problem for government is therefore to create the conditions which would bring into existence these 'missing markets'. The most usual reason for missing markets is that legal entitlements are not well defined. In many instances these legal entitlements relate to property rights. Certain resources (called common property resources) do not belong to any specific party. Therefore, such resources are open to use by all and the result is over-exploitation. For example, since the fish in the North Sea may be harvested by fishermen from all countries, in the absence of government action the result would be overfishing. In other instances, legal entitlements in the presence of a nuisance may not be clear; thus in the example cited earlier, it may not be clear whether a particular household had the right to hold a noisy party or whether their neighbours had the right to a quiet night.

The economist A.C. Pigou[8] argued that markets for externalities should be created by taxing the externality-emitting activity.[9] Thus, an activity, for example steel production, which earlier polluted the atmosphere without the steel producers bearing any of the costs of pollution, would now be taxed.

This tax would have two effects: on the one hand, by reducing pollution (through reduced steel output) it would be welfare enhancing, while on the other hand, the fact that steel output was now lower, as a result of the tax, would be welfare reducing. The optimal tax rate would be the one which yielded a steel output that maximised social welfare, that is, which maximised the difference between the utility from a given output of steel and the disutility from the pollution generated by the production of that steel. More generally, the system of Pigovian taxes was an economic defence of the common law principle that the party causing a nuisance was required to pay damages.

In a celebrated paper Ronald Coase[10] attacked the idea that government action in the form of penalising the nuisance creator was necessary to achieve efficiency. In Coase's view the fact that someone caused a nuisance, as judged by common law principles, did not imply that holding them liable was necessary for attaining an efficient outcome. On Coase's analysis,[11] from an efficiency perspective, the initial allocation of legal entitlements did not matter provided such entitlements could be freely traded. It did not matter whether one party had the legal right to create a nuisance (as a by-product of its main activity) or whether the other party had the legal right to be free of the nuisance, provided the initial set of rights could be bought and sold freely. Thus if a polluter had the right to pollute, the parties adversely affected would pay the polluter to reduce pollution; if the affected parties had the right to clean air then the polluter would have to compensate them for the pollution and, as a consequence, would reduce pollution. Therefore, irrespective of the initial allocation of rights, trade in legal entitlements would produce the optimal amount of pollution[12] without any further need for government intervention.

The acid rain legislation in the USA, which is part of the 1990 amendments to the US Clean Air Act, is a good example of government working to create a market for pollution by allowing legal entitlements to pollute to be bought and sold.[13] Under this law, which took effect in 1995, a firm will receive permits to release an amount of sulphur dioxide where this amount is based on its industry's average emission rate. The possession by a firm of such a permit then establishes its legal right to pollute up to the amount specified. The fact that these permits may be bought and sold provides an incentive to invest in pollution-reducing technology since the earlier a firm meets or exceeds the standards set the more opportunity it will have to sell its surplus permits to other firms and thus realise a return on its investment. As a result of such 'emissions trading' it is expected that in the first 5 years of the programme, sulphur dioxide emissions will be 3–5 million tonnes below the ceiling set.

The existence of market failure thus provides the intellectual underpinning for government intervention in the economy. More recently, the concept of market failure has been extended to justify government involvement in the process of economic development.[14] Interest in the role of government as a catalyst for development is derived from the observation that, in many of the world's most successful economies, governments have played an active part in guiding the course of industrial performance. For example, no analysis of Japanese economic development would be complete without a discussion of the role of government in promoting development. As Masahiko Aoki,[15] points out, Japanese bureaucracy is often viewed as a far-sighted planner which, in partnership with the ruling Liberal Democratic Party, gives a clear growth-oriented boost to the market economy by means of promotional and protective industrial policies and by a system of fiscal and monetary incentives.

It has been argued[16] that the development task facing countries in the last decade of the twentieth century is different from that which faced today's developed countries in the nineteenth century. Then the development problem was one of invention and innovation; the problem today is one of imitation and adaptation. The process is one of transferring and applying 'best practice' techniques and this requires the commitment of current resources to uncertain future gains. Much of this uncertainty will be institutional – it arises because institutions to reduce this risk to acceptable levels either do not exist or, if they do, operate imperfectly. The problem of development is that the markets for future outputs and inputs do not exist or, in other words, it is one of *missing markets*. It is this *market failure* that provides both the rationale and the direction of government intervention. Governments must intervene in the economy to create such 'future oriented' institutions so as to compensate for the missing 'futures' markets for outputs and inputs.

Take financial markets as a specific example. As Lester Thurow[17] points out, by the standards of consumer satisfaction, British and American financial markets are the most 'efficient' in the world. To list but a few of their features, investors get the highest rate of return, companies publish quarterly accounts and pension funds are obliged to move funds between assets in search of maximum return. By contrast the German and Japanese financial systems are highly 'inefficient': profit information is difficult to obtain, the interests of shareholders are neglected, banks and industries are linked in close business alliances with the former providing a steady diet of capital to the latter in return for seats on the board and from time to time financial scandals surface. In such a 'producer-oriented' system the influence and power of impatient shareholders is minimised while in the Anglo-American 'consumer-oriented' system this same influence is maximised. The end result for industry may be summarised in Thurow's (*op. cit.*, p. 48) words 'anyone who is in a capital-intensive business and does not have a huge technological advantage over the Japanese should get out!'

The creation of 'future-oriented' institutions is, according to Newbery,[18] particularly important in the case of manufacturing. This importance stems from the nature of modern industry with its requirements of large-scale investment, of specialised and lengthy training for managers and workers, of access to competitively priced inputs both from home and abroad and of access to foreign markets for the sale of some of its output. Investment requires access to financial institutions that will lend long-term at internationally competitive interest rates. The requirements of training need the intervention of government to ensure that the reluctance of firms to train workers, in the face of uncertainty about whether such workers will not be poached by other firms, is not a barrier to the creation of a well-trained labour force. Access to competitively priced inputs has two aspects. First, on the domestic front, the machinery for wage negotiation should not be such that wage growth consistently outstrips productivity improvements. If competitiveness is being lost through the process of 'free' collective bargaining then the task of government is to carry out the necessary reforms and to send the appropriate signals to arrest and indeed reverse this process. Second, on the external front, the exchange rate should be both competitive and reasonably stable and the market for imports should not be distorted either through discriminatory quotas or tariffs. The role of government is to set up institutions or to enter into negotiations that will ensure this. Finally, the desirability of selling for export requires the setting up of arrangements, in which firms have confidence, to provide a structure of incentives for foreign sales.

The role of state intervention in economic development is one of the oldest issues in economics and debate on this topic has revolved around the question of when and to what extent governments should intervene. As we have seen such intervention can be justified on the grounds of market failure; in many instances markets do not provide the institutional framework needed to alleviate the risks of modern manufacturing and, hence, it becomes the responsibility of government to create such a framework. Thus, what is important is the quality rather than the quantity of intervention. It is differences in *quality*, not *quantity*, that explain why state intervention has proved disastrous for the economies of Latin America, Eastern Europe, Africa and the Indian subcontinent but has provided the foundation for growth and prosperity in successful economies such as Japan, Korea and Taiwan.

14 The Growth of Government

The past three decades have seen the emergence, in countries of the Organization of Economic Co-operation and Development (OECD), of a phenomenon which has been termed 'the growth of government'. This refers to the increasing importance that government activities have come to play in the economic affairs of the industrialised democracies. Many economic and political commentators regard this with some alarm. Indeed, since about 1980, most government thinking in the OECD countries has reflected the view that the economic frontiers of the state should be rolled back. Mrs Thatcher, on becoming prime minister in 1979, signalled the start of the 'Conservative revolution' in economic policy which, with the subsequent election of President Reagan and Chancellor Kohl, quickly spread beyond Britain and one of the ideological pillars of this revolution was that there was a need for less, not more, government.

TABLE 14.1   *Structure of expenditure as a percentage of GDP in seven OECD countries (selected years)*

	1960	1970	1980	1990
USA	27.7	32.4	33.7	37.0
				(9.3)
Germany	32.0	38.6	48.3	46.0
				(14.0)
France	35.7	38.9	46.1	50.4
				(14.7)
UK	32.4	39.0	44.6	42.9
				(10.5)
Italy	32.1	34.3	41.7	53.2
				(21.1)
Canada	28.9	35.7	40.5	46.4
				(17.5)
Sweden	31.1	43.7	61.6	61.5
				(30.4)
Unweighted Average	31.4	37.5	45.2	48.2
				(16.8)
Standard Deviation	2.6	3.7	9.1	7.8

SOURCE   OECD, *National Accounts.*

Table 14.1 shows total government expenditure as a percentage of gross domestic product (GDP) in seven OECD countries, for selected years of the period 1960–90. For all the countries shown in Table 14.1, government expenditure as a percentage of GDP was higher in 1990 than it was in 1970 and considerably greater than it was in 1960.

Table 14.2 shows the shares, in GDP, of the main economic categories of government expenditure for five countries (USA, Japan, Germany, France and the UK) of the OECD for the years 1979 and 1990. Two items dominated government expenditure: cash transfers to the personal sector, mainly in the form of pensions and other social security benefits and government consumption of goods and services expenditure, in which expenditure is dominated by the government's wage bill. The largest item in the government budgets of all the countries was expenditure on income transfers: this varied from 32 per cent of total government expenditure in the USA and the UK, to nearly 40 per cent in Germany. Income transfers were, in turn, dominated by transfers undertaken for income maintenance purposes and here the dominant item was retirement pensions.[1]

A rise in the proportion of GDP accounted for by government expenditure will be inevitable if growth of the latter outstrips that of the former.[2] However, even if real government expenditure and real GDP grew at the same rate, differential productivity growth between the public and private sectors of the economy would ensure that, in nominal terms, government expenditure as a percentage of GDP would rise. This 'relative price' or 'Baumol'[3] effect occurs because while rising productivity gains, to some extent, offset the rising cost of labour in the private sector, it is conventionally assumed that there are no such gains associated with the public provision of goods and services. Consequently, if workers in the public and private sectors of the economy enjoy the same rates of wage increase, then prices of publicly provided goods and services will rise relative to that of goods and services provided by the private sector. Hence, government expenditure as a proportion of GDP will rise. There is, of course, nothing inevitable about such a rise. The 'Baumol effect' relies on wage growth parity between public and private sector workers and the effect can be frustrated by a government deciding to hold public sector pay claims below private sector levels. Neither is there anything inevitable about the fact that productivity growth in the public provision of goods and services must always be zero; in the absence of reliable measures of government output this is simply a conventional assumption in national income accounting.

Although conventional wisdom has it that the growth rate of productivity in the public sector is less than in the private sector, this is based on studies conducted in the 1960s and 1970s.[4] It is not clear that such a consensus would

TABLE 14.2   Structure of government outlays by economic category (per cent of GDP)

	USA			Japan			Germany			France			UK		
	1979	1990	Change	1979	1990	Change	1979	1990	Change	1979	1990	Change	1979	1990	Change
Total current disbursements	30.4	35.2	4.8	23.9	24.7	0.8	42.4	42.3	0.0	41.4	46.6	5.2	39.2	38.1	-1.1
Government consumption	17.0	18.3	1.2	9.7	9.0	-0.7	19.6	18.5	-1.1	17.6	18.3	0.7	19.7	20.0	0.3
Subsidies	0.4	0.2	-0.2	1.3	0.7	-0.6	2.2	1.9	-0.3	2.0	1.6	-0.3	2.4	1.1	-1.3
Social security and other transfers	10.2	11.5	1.3	10.3	11.2	1.0	18.9	19.3	0.4	20.4	23.5	3.1	12.8	13.7	0.9
Debt interest payments	2.8	5.2	2.4	2.6	3.8	1.1	1.7	2.6	1.0	1.4	3.1	1.7	4.4	3.4	-1.0
Government investment	1.7	1.6	-0.1	6.3	5.0	-1.3	3.2	2.3	-1.0	3.1	3.3	0.2	2.6	2.1	-0.5
Capital transfers	-0.4	-0.2	0.1	0.5	0.0	-0.4	1.8	1.1	-0.6	0.4	0.2	-0.2	0.7	-2.9	-3.6
Other transfers	-0.1	0.4	0.5	0.9	1.0	0.1	0.2	0.1	-0.1	0.1	0.1	0.0	0.0	0.0	0.0
Total	31.7	37.0	5.2	31.6	30.7	-0.9	47.6	45.8	-1.8	45.0	50.2	5.2	42.5	42.9	0.3

SOURCE   H. Oxley and J.P. Martin, 'Controlling Government Spending and Deficits: trends in the 1980s and prospects for the 1990s, *OECD Economic Studies*, No. 17, 1991, p. 158.

survive in the changed economic climate of the 1980s and the 1990s. On the face of it, very little changed in the UK public sector during the 1980s.[5] However, as has been observed,[6] there occurred, over this period, a considerable change in attitudes to work practices whereby the private sector, with its emphasis on choice, standards and quality (achieved through flexibility, performance and local management), became the model for the public sector. These changes were particularly marked in four areas: pay determination, performance incentives, flexible working practices and local management.[7]

In terms of pay determination, the major change has been the breakdown in the monolithic structure of public sector wage negotiations, both in terms of occupations and in terms of regions. By 1991, approximately 1.4 million employees – covering teachers, dentists, doctors, nurses, paramedics and senior civil servants – had independent pay review bodies, senior health service and local authority staff were on individually negotiated contracts and local authorities in the South East of England had broken away from national negotiations. In terms of performance incentives, the practice of performance-related pay was beginning to spread downwards from senior management. The increase in female and part-time workers, particularly in local government and the civil service, meant that the culture of the 9a.m.–5p.m. working day was under attack. Lastly, the setting of objectives and targets and the devolution of management responsibilities was now widespread in the public sector. Taken together, these changes imply that the basic assumption underlying the 'Baumol' effect – namely, that productivity in the public sector grows more slowly than in the private sector, but that wages in both sectors grow at the same rate – should, in the changed climate of the past decade, be treated with some caution.

The 'Baumol' effect was designed to explain why there was likely to be a rise, over time, in the ratio of government expenditure to GDP. It did not, however, explain why government expenditure *per se* should increase over time. To understand this, one needs to examine the determinants of government expenditure. The idea that there was a long-run tendency for government expenditure to grow can be traced to the writings of Alfred Wagner[8] and is the basis of 'Wagner's Law'. Wagner ascribed three main reasons to the increase in government expenditure over time. Firstly, industrialisation and modernisation would lead public activity to grow at the expense of private activity since, in an increasingly complex society, the need for expenditure on regulatory activities would grow. Second, the demand for collective and quasi-collective goods – in particular for education and culture – was regarded by Wagner to be relatively income elastic. Finally, Wagner asserted that because of 'the fundamental inefficiency of private enterprise' economic growth would require the state to take over the operation and management of natural monopolies. Consequently, expenditure on administrative services (for the first of the above reasons) and on health, education and social services (for the second and third reasons) would, relative to private expenditure, grow over time.

Consistent with Wagner's Law, there is, at least in Britain, considerable public support for state-provided services. Some evidence for this assertion is provided in a survey carried out by National Opinion Poll (NOP)[9] which asked a sample of 1551 electors in Britain (in the period 23–25 November 1991) whether, if extra money became available as a result of economic growth, they preferred (as best for the country) a policy which cut taxes while maintaining public expenditure at the present level or a policy which increased public expenditure while maintaining the present level of taxation. Only 25 per cent of the sample favoured lower taxes, while higher public expenditure won the support of 71 per cent.[10] When respondents were asked which of the two options they preferred as 'best for you and your family', again a majority (by a margin of 36–55 per cent) favoured increased expenditure to reduced taxes and again this majority was maintained across supporters of the different political parties.

A variant on Wagner's Law was provided by George Stigler,[11] who argued that it was the middle and upper income groups that were the major beneficiaries of public expenditure programmes and, hence, it was from these sources that the demand for public services would be relatively strong. This was because upper/middle income groups were both major users and major suppliers of some public services. Julian Le Grand and David Winter[12] corroborated this for Britain: they showed that families of the professional and managerial class were, proportionate to the rest of the population, high users of health and educational services[13] and also major suppliers (through being doctors, teachers and so on) of such services. It is not surprising, therefore, that in the NOP survey cited above, the largest support for a policy of increasing public expenditure came from the middle and professional classes (ABC1 electors): 78 per cent of the respondents in these classes favoured more expenditure to less taxation.

Another argument, one that has a great deal of plausibility, is that there are broad demographic and social factors that tend continually to raise the level of public expenditure . Howard Glennerster[14] argued that, since the late 1950s, Britain had seen a growing political demand for social services arising from the increasing numbers in the different client groups (and indeed of the groups) and society's greater knowledge about their needs. In turn, these needs themselves had grown enormously in the post-war period. From a related view, the decline of kinship and neighbourhood groups – as a supportive socioeconomic system – had been particularly severe since 1945.

The high employment levels and high labour force participation rates of the post-war years, combined with increased personal mobility and spending power, reduced the claims of community and family life to levels that could be regarded as minimal. According to this view, therefore, the relationship between the social structure, the economic system and public expenditure was fundamental to understanding the 'growth of government': a large part of public expenditure has been absorbed in coping with the effects of social and economic change; in many cases the effort was to prevent a fall in welfare by setting up alternative social structures.[15]

Demographic pressures have perhaps been most strongly felt in expenditure on health and social services. This is a combination of two effects. First, the dependency ratio[16] for the elderly went up in most countries of the OECD in the 1970s and 1980s and, furthermore, demographic projections indicate that this ratio will continue to increase. Second, the needs of the very young and the elderly, in respect of health care, are considerably greater than the remainder of the population: it has been estimated that, compared to a person of working age, health care costs for the over-75s are nine times as great, for the 65–75 years age group approximately four times as great and for the 0–4 years age group approximately twice as great (HM Treasury, 1984). In one estimate,[17] average real spending[18] per head of population, across the OECD countries, covered by the public insurance health system grew at an annual rate of 5.3 per cent over the 1970s and at an annual rate of 1.9 per cent over the 1980s. The lower growth rates for the 1980s can be explained by attempts made by governments to control, during this period, the upward spiral of public expenditure in general and of expenditure on health in particular.

The other area in which demography plays an important role in determining expenditure is in the area of education. Here demographic changes have worked so as to reduce the pressure for public expenditure increases: falling fertility rates have ensured that, in most OECD countries, the dependency ratio of the young fell over the 1970s and the 1980s. The demographic factor has, however, been largely offset by increased participation rates in post-compulsory education and a characteristic of the past three decades in the OECD countries has been a rise in the numbers of men and women in adult education as well as a rise in the number of children in extended schooling. One consequence of this trend has been a rise in the level of formal educational qualifications of the population: between 1984 and 1992 the percentage of males without any educational qualifications fell from 34 to 23 per cent and that for women fell from 45 to 32 per cent.[19] To a large extent, this emphasis on education has been due to a realisation on the part of governments that greater education and training are essential for maintaining industrial competitiveness. Falling numbers in compulsory education, due to demographic factors, but increasing numbers in post-compulsory education has meant that real spending per student continued to grow over the past 20 years – the OECD average annual growth rate for real spending per student was 1.8 per cent for 1975–80 and 1.6 per cent for 1980–8.[20]

The third important component of public expenditure heavily influenced by demographic changes is retirement pensions. Unlike expenditure on health and on education – which are payments for final goods and services – expenditure on pensions constitutes a transfer payment from the working-age population to the retired population. For most countries of the OECD, payments of retirement pensions are a dominant part of total general government expenditure – in Britain, for example, in 1989 they constituted 23 per cent of total expenditure.

Labour market trends, particularly relating to higher participation by women, have also had profound consequences for payments of retirement pensions. Although the number of elderly people in Britain – between now and the turn of the century – will not increase by very much, the total number of pensioners will increase by 600000, largely because more women will be entitled to pensions in their own right. Lastly, the state of the economy has also a major influence in determining the level of social security payments. Typically, the loss of employment entails the payment of both insurance-related (but not means-tested) and means-tested (but not insurance-related) benefits. It was estimated by HM Treasury,[21] that every increase of 100000 in the numbers registered as unemployed, led to a rise (over the year) of £185 million in total benefits paid to the unemployed.

Thus, demographic, social and economic factors combine to generate a level of demand for publicly provided goods and services. Governments then decide the extent to which they are prepared to meet this demand. In taking this supply decision, governments may be influenced by considerations of social welfare. In terms of the analytical framework developed by Amartya Sen,[22] a collapse of the 'entitlements' of a particular group of persons[23] may trigger public action because the consequences of such a collapse offend one's norms of how society should properly function. An extreme example of such action is public expenditure for famine relief,[24] while another example might be government action to help the homeless who 'sleep rough' on the streets of cities.

Of course, public action may arise as the consequence of the call for public action (for example, through the media) since, under certain circumstances, inaction would threaten the very existence of a particular government. Thus Amartya Sen[25] noted that an achievement of democracy in India (with all its accompaniments such as a free press, vocal opposition parties, pressure groups and so on) was that large-scale famines were no longer possible since, long before things reached such a state, public pressure would force governments to act. By way of contrast, around 20 million died in the Chinese famine of 1958–61 and, remarkably, the famine – which was the largest ever, in terms of total excess mortality, in recorded history – continued over a number of years without public recognition and without any change in public policy.

One might, however, in assessing the motivation for decisions on government expenditure, take a narrower view of self-interest. This view relates to expenditure on activities where there is no obvious public perception of 'social welfare'; nevertheless these activities are funded because, in some well-defined sense, it is in a government's self-interest to do so. Such expenditure decisions may be termed 'political' and it is such decisions – motivated by narrower considerations of self-interest – that form the basis of 'public choice' explanations for the growth of public expenditure. Such politically motivated expenditure decisions may arise in a variety of ways.[26] First, the government may undertake expenditure in order to correct *market failure*. For example, publicly funded expenditure on training may be necessary because the fear of having their trained workers poached by others may make private firms reluctant to undertake such expenditure themselves.[27] Second, the government may act as a redistributor of income and wealth. For example, the expansion of suffrage has meant that less well-off persons (with incomes below the median level) have been given the vote and, in turn, they have exercised their electoral power by voting for more egalitarian policies. Third, the rise of interest groups (for example, the 'poverty lobby') has exerted pressure on governments to expand spending and this has not been helped by the fact that interest groups can be mutually reinforcing in exerting such pressure.[28] Lastly, the pressure for more expenditure may emanate from within government as ministers and bureaucrats attempt to expand their influence.[29]

In summary, therefore, a considerable part of the growth in government expenditure in the OECD countries might be explained by demographic and social factors. These factors generate a 'demand' for certain types of expenditure (both final and transfer). The sources of this demand are a larger number of claimants and also a desire for higher standards of per capita provision; overlaying this trend in government expenditure are counter-cyclical[30] movements in such expenditure generated by the income shortfall of those adversely affected by the state of the economy. In democratic societies, public expenditure decisions, no matter how well motivated, cannot be separated from what the public wants for, in its own interest, the government cannot ignore vociferous calls for action. Thus, governments choose to meet the demand for public expenditure because, in large part, it is in their political interest to do so.

15 Privatisation

The previous chapter discussed the growth of government, over the past three decades, in the countries of the Organization for Economic Co-operation and Development (OECD). One feature of the 1980s, common to several countries of the industrialised world, was an attempt to curb the growth of government by 'rolling back' the frontiers of the state, a feature that was sufficiently widespread and strong to be termed the 'Conservative Revolution'.[1] One aspect of this attempt by government to divest itself of some of its involvement in the economy was the transfer to the private sector of many of the economic activities that had earlier been carried out by the public sector, a process that was labelled *privatisation*. In 1992, across the world, $69 billion worth of state-owned firms passed into private hands and, if planned privatisations materialise, this figure could double by the year 2000.[2] Indeed, a policy that, in 1983, appeared heretical to all but the most radical believer in free markets, is today a part of conventional economic wisdom.

Privatisation policies were pioneered in the UK and pursued so vigorously by the successive Conservative Governments elected since 1979 that it is probably true to say that there is little left to privatise. The process began with the sale of shares in British Petroleum, though it was not until 1984, with the sale of British Telecom, that privatisation impinged itself on the public consciousness and became a matter of national debate. Today every public utility in England is privatised – gas in 1986, water in 1989 and electricity in 1990 – and the government has divested itself of ownership in several areas of industry.[3] As a result of this activity, between 1979 and 1987, half a million employees were transferred from the public to the private sector and the proportion of gross domestic product (GDP) that resulted from the activities of publicly owned enterprises fell from 11.5 to 7.5 per cent.[4] The French privatisation programme, legislation for which was passed in June 1993, expects revenues of $50 billion through the privatisation of 21 state-owned firms. The Italian Government hopes to raise $10–15 billion through its privatisation programme. However, in the past 5 years, the centre-stage for privatisation has shifted from Europe to Latin America: in 1992, this region accounted for 35 per cent (as compared to only 6 per cent in 1988) of the total value of privatisations in the world. Even this may be dwarfed by privatisation in Eastern Europe and the countries of the former Soviet Union: in 1992, with its privatisation programme still not fully under way, this region accounted for 32 per cent of the total world value of privatisations.[5]

Against this background the purpose of this chapter is to examine the economic logic that underlies what, today, has arguably become the *haute couture* of economic policy – the process of privatisation.

The term 'privatisation' has been used to describe four interrelated strands of policy:

(1) *Denationalisation (or divestiture).* This involves the sale of public sector assets, and can take two main forms. First, the entire assets of an enterprise or utility can be sold. This has happened, for example, in the case of Ferranti, International Computers and some of the subsidiaries of British Rail. Second, a new company can be created under the Companies Act and a proportion of the shares in the new company can be sold. This has occurred, for example, in the case of British Airways, the electricity and gas utilities in Britain and the water and sewerage services in England and Wales. A related question here is to whom the shares should be sold. If the sale takes the form of a sale to another firm within the industry (a 'trade sale') the buyer will typically be a foreign firm. For bigger enterprises, a stock market flotation may be the chosen method of sale. Lastly, lying diametrically opposite to the trade sale, is the sale of companies through voucher schemes; under such schemes all citizens receive vouchers (for example, Russian citizens received vouchers worth 10000 roubles) which can be either invested directly in firms or sold to other investors. Often the government retains a shareholding in the new company (called the 'golden share') to provide a bulwark against hostile take-overs and sometimes it also restricts the proportion of shares sold to foreigners.

(2) *Deregulation (or liberalisation).* This involves the relaxation or abolition of statutory monopoly powers and hence the opening of state activities to private sector competition. This occurred in the case of bus deregulation. Sometimes denationalisation and deregulation are achieved simultaneously, as was the case with the creation of British Telecom (BT), where Mercury was allowed to compete for services in at least some sectors of the market. The two forms of privatisation have also gone hand in hand in the case of electricity generation, although the amount of actual competition here is likely to be limited.

(3) *Contracting out (and market testing).* In this case private sector firms are allowed to tender for services which the public sector continues to finance. This has happened extensively in the NHS and in local government in Great Britain. In addition to contracting out, an increasing proportion of central government services are being subjected to market testing.

(4) *Franchising.* This is a hybrid form of privatisation which has elements
     of both denationalisation and contracting out. Under franchising
     agreements, the government sells the right to provide all or part of a
     service for a limited period of time. This has happened, for example,
     in the case of motorway service stations and features in the current dis-
     cussions surrounding the privatisation of British Rail. The right to
     provide independent television services is also now franchised, with the
     right to supply for a fixed period of time being sold through a process
     of competitive tendering (or in the case of Central TV, in which there
     was a single bidder, non-competitive tendering!).

When, in 1979, the privatisation ball was set rolling in the UK, government
ministers had little idea of its likely consequences.[6] In fact, the process of
privatisation helped the government to achieve several important objectives
that were only tangential to the main purpose of privatisation, which was to
improve the efficiency of enterprises by transferring them from public into
private ownership. The most important of these objectives were firstly, to
reduce the public sector borrowing requirement (PSBR) through the sale of
public sector assets[7] and, secondly, to reduce the power of public sector unions
by subjecting them to the discipline of the market.[8] However, the case for
privatisation depends ultimately upon the argument that the transfer of
ownership (and control) of enterprises from the public to the private sector
improves their efficiency and it is this argument that deserves greater
scrutiny.[9]

Economists distinguish between two notions of efficiency. *Productive
efficiency* asks whether the level of output that is being produced, whatever
that level might be, is – given the available technology – being produced at
least cost (that is, most efficiently). *Allocative efficiency* asks whether the
level of output that is being produced is indeed the level of output that ought
to be produced or, in other words, asks if the economy's resources are being
allocated efficiently between the production of the different goods and
services.[10] The conditions for allocative efficiency are established by
comparing the price of a commodity with the additional cost associated
with producing an extra unit of its output (marginal cost).[11] Marginal cost
represents the value of resources that have to be transferred from other uses
to produce the extra output; price represents the benefit that consumers
derive from the additional output. Consequently, allocative efficiency is
arrived at when the extra cost is exactly balanced by the additional gain or,
in other words, when the quantity of output produced is such as to equate
marginal cost with price.[12] At output levels greater than this 'efficient' level,
marginal cost would exceed price and, hence, additional output would

convey negative net benefit, while at output levels smaller than the efficient level, since marginal cost would be less than price, additional quantities would confer positive net benefit.

The maximization of social welfare requires, as a necessary condition, that both productive and allocative efficiency be achieved. If the market structure within which firms operate is truly competitive, then indeed both types of efficiency will be achieved. A competitive market structure is usually understood to mean a situation in which there are many sellers and buyers of a product so that no individual has 'market power', that is the power to influence price by selling (or buying) more or less. Such a market structure ensures that producers would produce efficiently since, if they did not, they would be driven out of the market by their more efficient competitors; it also ensures allocative efficiency since profit maximising firms will produce levels of output for which marginal cost equals price. Finally, free entry into the market will ensure that all 'excess' profits are competed away. It is this logic that leads such a market structure to be regarded as an ideal and an important objective of industrial policy has, traditionally, been to introduce a greater element of competition into existing market structures.

In recent years economists have considered a second type of competitive environment. This is a situation in which there is competition *for* the market, as distinct from the situation described above, of competition *in* the market. A competitive environment in this sense requires that it is easy for firms to enter a market and also that exit from the market does not result in firms incurring financial penalties. This type of competitive environment is known as *market contestability*.[13] The general idea is that although there may be only one or a few firms in a market, these firms will not be able to abuse their market position, for example by charging monopoly prices or by producing inefficiently, since such action would encourage other firms to enter the industry and to serve better the consumers' interest. A requirement for competition *for* the market to exist is that there should not be significant entry barriers. In order to encourage contestability, industrial policy should aim, therefore, to reduce entry barriers.[14] Either of the above types of competition would ensure that both productive and allocative efficiency are achieved and, hence, that the interests of consumers are served.

One justification for privatisation is, therefore, in terms of injecting more competition into existing market structures. For example, deregulation in the UK, in 1980, of express coaching services was intended to expose the publicly owned monopoly, National Express, to competition from independent coach operators. However, in many instances it is not always possible to create a competitive environment and this is particularly the case with *natural monopolies* such as electricity, gas and water. Because of economies of scale, the least cost production can only be achieved when production is carried out by a single supplier. For example, economies of scale arise in the case of utilities (electricity, gas and water) due to the high investment costs that are required to provide the distribution network. As more consumers are linked to the distribution network the capital costs can be spread more thinly.[15] In such cases the question arises as to whether the mere fact of change from public to private ownership, without any increase in the degree of competition, would lead to efficiency improvements.

Throughout the 1960s, successive governments in the UK developed pricing and investment guidelines to be followed by the managers of public sector organisations and, in general, these guidelines were set with a view to encouraging the achievement of allocative efficiency. Thus, public sector organisations were instructed to set prices to reflect marginal costs. However, the guidelines of the 1960s ignored the notion of productive efficiency and there was nothing, save the goodwill of public sector managers, to ensure that production costs were not higher than necessary.[16] The problem of attaining productive efficiency was made more difficult by the fact that the investment requirements of public organisations were often subordinated to the requirements of macroeconomic management (for example, the need to restrict public sector borrowing) and that, as a consequence, investment in such organisations suffered. Moreover, the view developed that given their ready access to the public purse, public sector managers were less likely to resist trade union wage demands and, hence, had larger wage bills than their private sector counterparts who faced more stringent and unyielding budget constraints.

As a consequence, there emerged a view in the UK that change of ownership alone (that is, without the concomitant introduction of competition) would lead to improvements in productive efficiency.[17] The basis for this view was that private sector organisations, unlike those in the public sector, would be subject to the discipline of capital markets. Failure to earn an adequate return on capital would lead to a reduction in share values and, ultimately, through take-over, to loss of control of the firm. The problem with this analysis was that although a private operator could be expected to produce efficiently, the non-competitive nature of markets could tempt firms to earn monopoly profits by raising prices above costs. Consequently, notwithstanding the fact that it was an efficient producer, a private firm in a non-competitive environment might not be allocative efficient.

Therefore, in the case of natural monopolies policy makers face the following dilemma. Price guidelines (set prices to reflect marginal costs) could encourage public firms to be allocative efficient, but there was little pressure on such firms to produce efficiently. The discipline of capital markets, reflected in the demands of shareholders for market rates of return on their investment, would encourage private firms to produce efficiently, but the lack of competition in or for the market for the service would mean that firms would not be allocatively efficient. In both cases the consumer would be the loser. In the first case, costs would be higher than they needed to be and this would be reflected in prices. In the second case, costs would be lower but, in the search for monopoly profits, prices would be set above costs.

In line with their ideological belief in small government, Conservative Governments in the UK, since 1979, have sought to resolve this problem by preferring private (to public) sector provision but, at the same time, setting up regulatory bodies to protect consumers from monopoly exploitation.[18] Regulation, in the UK, has taken the form of *price* regulation.[19] These arrangements can be viewed as creating 'contracts' between the privatised companies, on the one hand and consumers, represented by the regulator, on the other.[20] This contract specifies the range of services that will be provided at the prescribed price. The performance of the privatised firms is monitored by the regulator who periodically revises the contract. However, once a regulated price has been established and until it is next reviewed, any subsequent cost increases cannot be passed on to consumers, but instead must be met out of reduced profits. Similarly any cost reductions will not be reflected in lower prices but, instead, will result in improved profits.[21] Since the level at which the regulated price is set should reflect marginal costs, price regulation provides incentives for the regulated firms to produce the optimal quantity at the lowest cost or, in other words, to be both allocative and productive efficient.

The novelty of the price regulatory framework used in the UK, for all privatised utilities,[22] was to link the regulated price to movements in the retail price index (RPI). The $RPI - X$ formula required that the percentage increase in the prices of the products of privatised utilities should be, at least, X percentage points below the rate of increase in the RPI. It is then for the regulator, perhaps through a process of negotiation with the regulated firms, to set a value for X.[23]

Price regulation has two major weaknesses.[24] The first is that of *regulatory capture*. The idea here is that the regulatory body will rely on the regulated firm for much of its information, particularly with regard to the cost structure and the investment requirements of the firm. Through time, a close working relationship may be established between the regulator and the regulated firm with the danger that the regulator will begin to see things from the point of view of the regulated firm. Once this happens the regulatory framework has failed. Thus, it is important for the regulators to maintain their independence, both from the regulated firm, and also from other interest groups such as consumer groups, trade unions and the government.

The second major weakness of price regulation arises with respect to the quality of the service provided. In the face of price regulation, there is an incentive for regulated firms to either dilute the quality of service provided[25] or to press for higher prices on the grounds that the quality of service has improved. Moreover, when faced with a single supplier consumers will be unable to register their dissatisfaction with, as the case may be, poor quality or high prices, by turning to a rival supplier. Thus, a further aspect of the regulatory framework in the UK is concerned with consultation with consumers, both through discussions with consumer groups and through surveys of consumers, about the desired level of quality. For example, a major source of controversy in the UK concerns the impact of European Community (EC) environmental standards upon the water industry. These standards have led to improvements in the quality of water and sewerage services at considerably increased costs and the privatisation of the industry has meant that this increase is passed on to consumers in the form of higher prices. The Office of Water Services (OFWAT) – the regulatory body for the UK water industry – has made efforts to determine consumer preferences regarding the quality they want at prices they are prepared to pay.[26]

John Vickers and George Yarrow[27] have argued, in the context of the UK, that when privatisation was applied to industries that operated in reasonably competitive markets, the policy was a success.[28] It was, however, less successful when applied to firms with monopoly power.[29] Firstly, the existing obstacles to entry into these industries continued even after privatisation. Secondly, problems of access by the regulator to good quality information, meant that the regulated firms had considerable influence on the outcome of the $RPI - X$ formula. Thirdly, the focus of regulation has been entirely on price and has ignored regulatory incentives for investment behaviour.[30] The last point has particular force with respect to the water industry in the UK. As Dieter Helm and Najma Rajah[31] observe, the economic attribute of the water industry that has set it apart from most of the other privatised utilities is the high level of investment needed to bring standards of water and sewerage standards up to those required by EC environmental regulations. The scale of this investment, in conjunction with the government's requirement that water companies earn a competitive rate of return on this investment, has therefore, led to rapidly escalating water prices.[32] Consequently, the regulatory body has had to not just regulate price but has had also to express its views on the amount of investment (and the rate of return) that it thinks is appropriate for the industry to undertake.

In comparing the privatisation experience of the industrialised countries with that of the 'transition' economies of Eastern Europe, the most significant difference is that the scale and speed of the privatisation process in the countries of the former Soviet bloc – particularly in Czechoslovakia, East Germany, Hungary and Poland – has dwarfed anything attempted in the West. In these countries, the sale of state enterprises is the cornerstone of the attempt to create a market economy out of the debris of a command economy. Czechoslovakia and Poland, in emphasising speed, have opted for a strategy of mass privatisation with give-away schemes. This has met with approval from those who argue that the speed of transition, from a command to a market economy, is of the essence[33] and that conventional Western standards for judging the success of privatisation are of much less importance than the fact of privatisation. On the other hand, Germany and Hungary have opted for a more gradual sale of state assets. This has met with approval from those[34] who argue that setting too quick a pace can jeopardise a country's budgetary and macroeconomic position and, thereby, endanger the process of transition itself. Both sides of the argument invoke considerations of microeconomic efficiency, public finance, macroeconomic stability, fairness and political acceptability[35] but as to which side is right remains to be seen.

In contrast to Eastern Europe, where the main purpose of privatisation is to create a market economy, countries of Asia and Latin America have pursued privatisation for more conventional reasons: to promote efficiency, to raise finances and to break the power of public sector unions. Here, unlike in Eastern Europe, where one might legitimately suspend disbelief about the efficiency of the newly created enterprises, it is legitimate to enquire about whether any efficiency gains have followed from privatisation. The World Bank[36] has conducted 12 case studies in four countries – Chile, Malaysia, Mexico and the UK – and compared the performance of privatised firms with what their performance might have been had they not been privatised. The study concluded that in 11 of the 12 cases, privatisation resulted in large gains.

Ultimately, however, as the World Bank observes, the basic fact about privatisation is that there is a trade-off between the possibilities that, relative to its privatised incarnation, the objectives of the state-owned industry were socially more desirable but that these objectives were pursued less efficiently. In particular, the operation of the privatised industry could result in a diminution of consumers' welfare through efficiency losses caused by producing suboptimal quantities; on the other hand, the efficiency gains in production, in terms of producing in a least-cost way, that might result from privatisation, would lead to an improvement in such welfare. Whether privatisation does or does not lead to an improved performance on the part of the industry (or firm) is therefore an empirical question, the answer to which depends on the particular industry being considered and the social, political and economic context within which it is located. It is, most definitely, not a question that can be answered in purely ideological terms.

16 National Saving, Foreign Debt and Government Deficits

In Chapter 3, reference was made to the importance of national saving as a source of funds for the investment needed to improve the rate of productivity growth. If national saving was inadequate for this purpose, then a country would have no alternative but to either scale back the level of its investment or else to seek funds from abroad. This chapter details the relationship between government behaviour (as exemplified by its expenditure and revenue decisions which, in turn, determine the size of its budgetary surplus or deficit), national saving and foreign borrowing.

Trade between countries differs in two fundamental respects from trade between regions within a country. First, interregional trade is not subject to the restrictions that often exist on trade between countries. Thus, Scotch whisky travels freely from Edinburgh to London but supplies to Japan could be restricted by means of quotas imposed by the Japanese on British products. Secondly, trade between regions is conducted in a single currency whereas international trade involves several currencies and this leads to a host of problems connected with the determination of exchange rate values and the effects that such values have on the performance of the different sovereign economies.

As Paul Krugman and Maurice Obstfeld[1] observe, a few key issues dominate the subject of international economics. The first is that of gains from trade (and the related issue of the pattern of trade) which arises from the fact that countries trade with each other to their mutual benefit. The major insight here derives from David Ricardo and is enshrined in the *principle of comparative advantage*. This principle states that a country would gain by exporting those commodities which it was able to produce at comparatively lower per-unit costs (that is, those in which it had a comparative advantage) and by importing those commodities which it was able to produce at comparatively higher per-unit costs (that is, those in which it had a comparative disadvantage). Note that the comparison of costs is between commodities in a given country, not between countries for a given commodity. Thus, for example, the UK may be able to produce both cars and whisky more cheaply than Japan (that is, have an absolute advantage in both commodities over Japan) but may nevertheless choose to export whisky to and import cars from Japan because it enjoys a comparative advantage in the production of whisky over cars. If the UK tried to be self-sufficient in cars then it would be diverting resources to car production that could be more usefully employed in making whisky – much better to specialise in whisky manufacture and buy cars from the Japanese. Although trade implies specialisation, it does not imply complete specialisation; even though it imported cars from Japan, the UK might still have a domestic car industry.

This leads to the second important issue in international economics which is the imposition of restrictions on trade with a view to protecting domestic industry from foreign competition. This issue, of whether free trade is better than restricted trade, is reflected in the progressive liberalisation of trade that occurred, in the post-war period, through the General Agreement on Tariffs and Trade (GATT). The third issue that is of importance in international economics is that of imbalances in trade. These imbalances arise when the value of a country's exports is not equal to the value of its imports. Such imbalances invite two possible responses. The first is for a country to alter the value of its exchange rate and thereby affect trade flows by altering the prices of its exports and imports. The second possible response to an imbalance in trade is for a country, whose expenditure on imports exceeds its revenue from exports, to cover its deficit by borrowing from abroad. It is the relation between trade imbalances and foreign borrowing which is the subject of this chapter.

In order to analyse the relationship between trade imbalances and foreign borrowing, it is necessary to start with a framework for analysing a country's transactions with the rest of the world (RoW). This framework is provided by its balance of payments (BoP). In a country's BoP accounts all transactions that involve its selling something (good, service, or asset) to the RoW is entered as a credit transaction; conversely all transactions that result in its buying something from the RoW is a debit transaction. Thus, the export of Rover cars to Germany is entered as a credit transaction in the UK's BoP. In order to buy the cars, Germans need sterling and this they obtain by selling marks. As a consequence the UK's foreign exchange reserves rise. Debit items, on the other hand, lead to a diminution of such reserves – UK residents holidaying in Germany (that is, buying the services of the German tourist industry) need marks and these they obtain by giving up their pounds.

Exactly the same process applies to the sale and purchase of assets. A German buying property in the UK, or shares in a UK company or UK Government securities, causes UK foreign exchange reserves to rise, since these transactions are effected by Germans exchanging marks for the pounds needed to acquire the assets. The converse holds when UK residents buy foreign assets. There is, however, one very important difference between the sale and purchase of assets and that of goods and services. Unlike the sale of goods and services, the sale of an asset has to be 'serviced' by making the appropriate payment to the owner of the asset. Thus, the German owner of UK Government securities would receive regular interest payments made by the UK Government. These payments would be made in sterling but this would be exchanged, by the German beneficiary, for marks, through an appropriate transaction with the Bank of England. Since this would cause foreign exchange reserves to fall, the payment of interest would be recorded as a debit item, though the original asset sale was entered as a credit item.

The sequence of events, described in the preceding paragraph, reveals an important fact about international economics. When countries sell their assets to foreigners they are borrowing from abroad. This borrowing provides them with funds in the form of foreign exchange which can then be used in the manner they think best. However, this debt has to be serviced and the counterpart to the initial injection of funds from abroad is an outflow – in the form of rent, interest and dividends – of a stream of servicing payments. Should the foreign debt become so large that servicing it becomes a problem, then the country is in trouble. This was the situation that arose with Latin American countries in the 1980s (see below). Of course the real question is why do countries borrow from abroad and get themselves (sometimes) into serious trouble? To answer this question one must explore further the structure of its BoP.

The BoP is divided into two basic accounts: the current and the capital account. The current account is concerned with all transactions relating to trade in goods and services and with all flows of investment income either from or to abroad. The capital account is concerned with all transactions relating to the purchase and sale of assets. The difference between the total value of credits and debits on the current account defines the current balance: it is in deficit (surplus) if debits exceed (are less than) credits. These points are illustrated in Table 16.1.

For the UK (and other countries which also have a large oil production) the current account is also divided into an oil and non-oil account. Thus, it has a current balance on oil (determined entirely by oil transactions and, since it is a net exporter of oil, usually in surplus) and a current balance on non-oil (determined by all other current account transactions), the overall current balance being simply the sum of the oil and non-oil balances. The reason for this separation is that the non-oil account provides a better measure of the productive strength of the economy since the oil transactions result simply from the exploitation of a natural resource.

TABLE 16.1   *Components of the balance of payments*
(billion of pounds)

	Credits	Debits	Deficit–Surplus (−)	(+)
Oil	15.0	8.0	(A)	+7.0
Goods	63.0	72.0		−9.0
Services	24.0	18.0		+6.0
Balance of trade			(B)	−3.0
Investment income	53.0	60.0	(C)	−7.0
Current balance (A + B + C)				−3.0

The non-oil current account is further separated into transactions related to trade in goods and services and to those related to investment income. The surplus or deficit on the former is known as the balance of trade. Trade in goods (or merchandise) is known as the visible component of the balance of trade; trade in services (for example tourism, banking and insurance) is known as the invisible component of the balance of trade. The balance of trade is a very important indicator of a country's economic health. When the balance of trade is in deficit it indicates that a country's exports of goods and services are insufficient to pay for its imports of the same. To put it differently, a country with a balance of trade deficit is living beyond its means, since it is unable to pay for its purchases from foreigners by means of its sales to them. Of course, all countries cannot simultaneously be in deficit. Countries whose imports exceed their exports in value are counterbalanced by countries which have a trade surplus, that is, whose exports exceed their imports in value. Over the past decade, both the UK and the USA have suffered from large trade deficits – it is no coincidence that, over the same period, both Germany and Japan have had large trade surpluses.

Now when a country runs a current account deficit, most usually because the value of its imports exceed that of its exports, but sometimes also because net investment income flows are negative, it must find the necessary funds to enable it to, as it were, live beyond its means. There are essentially two ways in which it can acquire these funds. Either it can disinvest by selling some of the foreign assets it owns (for example, the UK Government can divest itself of some of its holdings of German securities) or it can borrow from abroad by selling some of its own assets to foreigners (for example, the UK Government can sell its securities to Germans). However, regardless of the method adopted – disinvestment, borrowing or a combination of the two – to raise finance, the current account deficit must be matched by a net inflow of funds on the capital account. As emphasised above, this net inflow

is required to finance the current account deficit. Thus, a sequence of current account deficits can transform a country from being a creditor to becoming a debtor. At the end of 1982, the value of the USA's net foreign assets[2] was $260 billion; then, during 1983–90, it had a string of large current account deficits so that, by the end of 1990, its foreign asset position was –$360 billion, representing a decline of $620 billion in its balance sheet position in less than a decade. The net inflow of capital, described in this paragraph, arose because the current account deficit had to be accommodated. In other words, a country's current account balance equals the change in its net foreign wealth.

A country's performance, in terms of its imports and exports can be viewed as part of a broader national picture which embraces the behaviour of its domestic sectors. The preceding discussion of current account balance and foreign borrowing can, therefore, be related to issues of national income and expenditure. The starting point for this relationship is to note that the demand for goods and services (whether produced at home or abroad) by, for example, UK residents may conceptually be separated into *consumption demand* (demand made mainly by households), *investment demand* (demand made mainly by firms) and *government demand* (demand made by central and local government and other public sector bodies). Denoting expenditures on these categories, in a given year, by respectively, £C, £I and £G billion, expenditure by UK residents, on goods and services, would, for that year, total £$(C + I + G)$ billion. As noted earlier, this includes expenditure on imported goods and services. Therefore, if the value of imports of goods and services into the UK was £M billion and this was subtracted from the total expenditure by UK residents, it would yield the total expenditure by UK residents *on domestically produced goods and services* $(C + I + G - M)$. Adding, to this latter quantity, foreign expenditure on UK-produced goods and services (which is the total value of UK exports of goods and services say, £X billion) would yield the total expenditure (that is, by UK residents and by foreigners) on UK-produced goods and services as £$(C + I + G + X - M)$ billion. If the value of UK output of goods and services (termed its gross domestic product or GDP) say, £Y billion is equated to its demand, *the GDP (or national income) identity* would obtain as

$$Y = C + I + G + X - M$$

This identity shows that the current account balance, $X - M$, is equal to $S - I$, that is to the difference between national saving, $S (= Y - (C + G))$ and national investment, I. The quantity, S, is regarded as national saving because it is the difference between national income, Y and national consumption (that

is, consumption effected through household and government expenditure on goods and services), $C + G$. In other words, S represents the amount of national income that, in a given year, has not been *consumed* either by the private or the public sector and is therefore available for *investment*, where the amount of investment expenditure undertaken is £I billion. This then yields the important identity

$$I = S + (M - X)$$

The importance of this identity lies in the fact that it points to the alternative sources of funding investment expenditure that exist in an open economy. Thus, if a UK electricity company wanted to build a new generating station it could look to domestic sources for funds. However, for such funding to be forthcoming, national saving, S, would have to rise to accommodate the higher level of investment. If it was not possible to generate additional domestic saving, then building the generating station would require that the investment funds were procured through foreign borrowing. The UK company could import the materials it needed from, for example, Germany and borrow German funds to pay for them. As a result of these imports, the UK current balance would deteriorate, that is $X - M$ would become (even more) negative, and this growing deficit would be financed by German savers who would supply the UK with the necessary investment funds.

However, a country cannot continue to meet its investment needs by borrowing indefinitely from abroad. As mentioned earlier, if foreign debt became very large, then the servicing of the debt, through payments of interest, could itself become a problem resulting in the debtor country being perceived as a bad risk. In 1982, Mexico notified its foreign creditors that it could no longer meet scheduled payments on its foreign debt of $80 billion and requested a rescheduling of such payments. In the same year, Brazil (with a debt of $88 billion) and Argentina (with a debt of $40 billion) found that foreign lenders were unwilling to lend them further sums. By the end of 1986, more than 40 countries, mainly in Africa and Latin America, had severe financing difficulties. If such problems are to be avoided, then dependence on foreign borrowing must be reduced. As the second identity, defined above shows, this can only be achieved, *without jeopardising the current level of investment*, if national saving rises so as to fill the gap.

Running parallel to the national rate of saving is the national rate of investment. In the course of a year, households, businesses and government, through their respective investment projects, increase the stock of productive assets in their country. Countries for which the national saving rate is less than the rate of national investment (that is, the level of national investment expressed as a percentage of GDP) have to seek funds from abroad, that is they are debtor nations. On the other hand, countries whose rate of national saving exceeds their national rate of investment supply funds to other countries, that is they are creditor nations. Two good examples of debtor and creditor countries are, respectively, the USA and Japan. During 1975–85, the Japanese rate of national saving averaged 18 per cent and this comfortably exceeded the average rate of 17 per cent national investment. By contrast, over the same period, the average US rate of national saving of 3.5 per cent was minuscule in relation to Japan and it also fell short of the average US rate of investment of 4.3 per cent.

There are two important conclusions that can be drawn from this. First, Japan invests a great deal more in its economy than does the USA. Second, it funds this investment out of domestic saving and has something left over to lend to foreign borrowers. By contrast, countries such as the USA and the UK which have low rates of national saving are faced with a choice between two unpleasant alternatives: either they scale down their investment to match their low saving rate, in which case they are likely to fall even further behind their major competitors like Japan and Germany or they borrow heavily from abroad, in order to maintain a high rate of investment, in which case they risk having the potential problem of growing indebtedness, referred to above.

Thus, if the level of national investment is to be maintained and perhaps increased, without increasing foreign indebtedness, then the level of national saving has to rise. To achieve this requires greater thrift on the part of *both households and government.* This is because S, the volume of national saving is the sum of household saving (S_h) and government saving (S_g), that is $S = S_h + S_g$. Household saving, S_h, is the surplus of after-tax income over consumption, that is national income less tax over household consumption expenditure, C ($S_h = Y - T - C$, where T represents tax payments). Government saving, S_g, is the difference between the government's revenue and expenditure, that is $S_g = T - G$. Hence,

$$S = (Y - (C + G)) = [(Y - T) - C] + [T - G] = (S_h + S_g)$$

A government deficit ($T < G$ or, equivalently, $S_g < 0$) reduces national saving, S and the larger the deficit, the smaller, for a given level of household saving S_h, will be the level of national saving. During 1960–90, of the Organization for Economic Co-operation and Development (OECD) countries, Japan had the highest rate of national saving (31 per cent) and the UK and the USA, at 17 and 18 per cent, respectively, the lowest rates. In both the UK and the USA, large budgetary deficits were responsible for the low rates of national saving. Thus, during 1981–8, the USA had a rate of private saving (that is, household saving, S_h, as a percentage of after-tax income, $Y - T$) of 8.7 per cent and in conjunction with a government deficit that was 4.5 per cent of national income (that is, S_g as a percentage of Y) this yielded a national saving rate (that is, the volume of national saving, S, as a percentage of national income, Y) of only 4.2 per cent.

The link between a government's budgetary deficit and the deficit on the current account of its country's BoP arises for the following reason. Typically households in, for example, the UK supply their savings for UK industry to invest. If this saving exactly matched the investment needs of UK industry then there would be no need to seek additional sources of borrowing. A problem arises when household savings fall short of the investment needs of industry. Industry then has to borrow the balance from elsewhere and this could be either from the UK Government and/or abroad. However, a major problem arises when the government runs a budgetary deficit. Then the government too has to borrow to cover the excess of its expenditure over revenue. Instead of the government being a source of funds for industry, a situation then occurs in which both the UK Government and UK industry are competing for the savings of UK households. Thus, even if UK savings were adequate to meet the borrowing needs of industry (which, because of the low UK saving ratio, they are not), they are likely to be woefully inadequate in meeting the combined borrowing needs of both industry and government. Thus, both industry and government in the UK have no alternative but to tap foreign sources of finance for their needs.

A low rate of national saving is, therefore, the ultimate constraint on increasing investment and thereby improving the rate of growth in productivity.[3] It prevents any significant expansion of productive capacity without reliance on foreign borrowing. In turn, to attract foreign funds to finance their investment, countries have to offer high rates of interest. This inhibits domestic investment and also leads to exchange rate values that are not in consonance with the needs of industry. The only way out of this impasse is to increase the rate of national saving. This can be done in two ways: by increasing the volume of private saving and by reducing the size of the government deficit. In both the UK and the US there is mounting concern about the effects of large deficits on the long- and medium-term prospects for their economies. For example, the UK Government's borrowing requirement during 1993 was expected to be over £50 billion or almost £1 billion per week. Of course some of this was due to the effects of the recession – when unemployment is high, tax receipts are low and benefit payments are high. However, even with growth, the borrowing requirement was not expected to fall below £25 billion. To bridge the gap between expenditure and revenue requires some painful choices to be made. To raise even £10 billion from revenues would mean raising the basic income tax rate from 25 to 33 per cent or increasing VAT from 17.5 to 21.5 per cent or imposing VAT at the existing rate on (currently zero-rated) items such as food and public transport.[4]

The alternative to increasing revenue would be to reduce public spending. Here the Welfare State provides a tempting target since expenditure on health, education and social security constitutes 61 per cent of public spending in the UK. However, the methods proposed for addressing the general problem of high spending on welfare are different, depending on the component of welfare that is being considered. For example, the problem with controlling expenditure on health is one of people living longer and thereby costing the state more in the final years of their lives. In 1992, the NHS spent £1000 per person over 75 years as against £250 for every person under 65 years. One solution to the problem of escalating health costs is higher 'co-payments' from patients: in continental Europe, out of pocket charges contribute 15 per cent to health spending while in the UK less than 4 per cent of health spending is met through payments by patients.[5]

With social security payments, the main area of concern is the move away from universal benefits to targeted benefits. The UK Government estimates, on the basis of its *Households Below Average Income* statistics for 1991, that one-quarter of the £80 billion spent on social security goes to persons with above-average incomes, many of them in the 6.9 million families receiving Child Benefit and the 9.9 million pensioners. For the richest 20 per cent of pensioners their state pension is, on average, one-quarter of their income. The necessity for tackling the 'pensions problem' is made even more urgent because demographic changes mean that the worker to pensioner ratio is declining: in 1945 there were seven persons of working age to every pensioner; today the ratio is just 3.3 per pensioner and in 50 years this is expected to decline to 2 per pensioner.

In addition to cutting the size of the government deficit, policies to raise the rate of national saving should also emphasise private saving. A major cause of the decline in household saving in the UK, during the latter part of the 1980s, was the boom in house prices when people who owned their houses responded to the increase in their wealth by increasing their consumption. An important aspect of policies to encourage household saving must be measures to bring stability into the housing market. In terms of business saving, a major area of concern in the UK and the USA is the size of dividend payments and, consequently, the low level of retained profits. This, in turn, carries the adverse implication that companies in the UK and USA, relative to Japan and Germany, are excessively reliant on funds from financial institutions for implementing their investment plans. A corollary of such dependence is an undue emphasis on short-term returns, since the need to keep shareholders happy and creditors at bay means that long-term projects are eschewed.[6]

This chapter has emphasised the importance of a high rate of national saving in improving a country's long-term economic performance. In macroeconomic policy, however, the long-term is usually the enemy of the short-term. In the short-term, raising national saving will retard the efforts of an economy seeking to climb out of a recessionary trough. Cuts in government spending, increases in household saving and more profits retained by businesses will all dampen demand and delay prospects for recovery. The problem is, that for nearly half a century, economic policy making in the UK has emphasised the short-term. Perhaps the time has come to refocus our sights, away from the valley of short-term macroeconomic demand management to the uplands of higher productivity and long-term growth.

Notes

CHAPTER 1: COMPETITIVENESS

1. Whose rise as an economic power is (see Table 1.1) almost as spectacular as that of Germany.
2. See N.F.R. Crafts, *Can De-Industrialisation Seriously Damage Your Wealth?*, Hobart Paper 120 (London: Institute of Economic Affairs, 1993).
3. See R. Dornbusch, J. Porteba and L. Summers, *The Case for Manufacturing in America's Future* (Rochester: Eastman Kodak Company, 1988).
4. A.S. Englander, R. Evenson and M. Hanazaki, 'R&D Innovation and the Total Factor Productivity Slowdown', *OECD Economic Studies*, no. 11, (Autumn 1988).
5. House of Lords, *Select Committee on Science and Technology* (London: HMSO, 1991), p. 3.
6. See, *inter alia*, the symposium on competitiveness in *Science*, vol. 241 (15 July 1988) and The President's Commission on Industrial Competitiveness, *Global Competition: the New Reality* (Washington DC: US Government Printing Office, 1985).
7. For example, 'list' prices for many products may be reviewed only biannually.
8. R.E. Hall and C. Hitch, 'Price Theory and Business Behaviour', *Oxford Economic Papers,* vol. 2 (1939), pp. 12–45.
9. Though the argument could be easily extended to cover other types of cost.
10. We emphasise foreign currency (taken here as dollars) because competitiveness is most important in export markets.
11. See Lawrence R. Klein, 'Components of Competitiveness', *Science*, vol. 241, (15 July 1988), pp. 308–13.
12. That is, the labour costs of producing a unit of output.
13. Expressed as pounds per hour or per person.
14. Expressed as output per hour or as output per person depending on how wage rates (see note above) are defined.
15. Real wages are defined as the purchasing power of money wages, that is as money wages divided by the price level. It follows that the rate of growth in real wages is the difference between the rates of growth in money wages and prices.
16. See Paul Krugman, *Peddling Prosperity: Sense and Nonsense in the Age of Diminished Expectations* (New York: Norton and Co., 1994) and for a critique of his views, Benjamin Friedman, 'Must We Compete?', *The New York Review of Books,* vol. XLI, (20 October 1994), pp. 14–20.
17. That is the exchange rate goes down from say, $2.00 per pound to $1.50 per pound.
18. See Lawrence Klein, *op. cit.*
19. Fred Bayliss, *Does Britain still have a Pay Problem?* (London: Employment Policy Institute, 1993).
20. OECD *Economic Outlook* (June 1992).
21. Defined as the rate at which exports exchange for imports.

22. Use of monetary policy to ensure exchange rate stability could, therefore, lead to interest rate volatility.
23. Many of the realignments have involved long and difficult bargaining sessions, see Gros and Thygesen, *op. cit.*, Chapter 3.
24. Paul Krugman, *Peddling Prosperity: Economic Sense and Nonsense in an Age of Diminished Expectations* (New York: Norton and Company, 1994).
25. D. Gros and N. Thygesen, *op. cit.*
26. This period of extreme stability was largely a result of the Basle–Nyborg Agreement which was arrived at when it was generally perceived that the realignment of currencies in January 1987, was brought about by speculative forces rather than by macroeconomic divergences between the members of the ERM. The agreement involved the enlargement of credit arrangements generally, together with a call for greater coordination of monetary policy between member states.
27. That is, 1 Deutschemark exchanged for one Ostmark, instead of the pre-unification 20 Ostmarks.

CHAPTER 2: ACCOUNTING FOR GROWTH AND THE PRODUCTIVITY SLOWDOWN

1. Sometimes also called multifactor productivity.
2. Improvements in the quality of capital and labour (for example, through education) can be thought of as increases in supply.
3. Pioneered by R.M. Solow, 'Technical Change and the Aggregate Production Function', *Review of Economics and Statistics*, vol. 39 (1957), pp. 312–20. See also E.F. Denison, *Accounting for United States Economic Growth, 1929–70* (Washington DC: The Brooking Institution, 1974).
4. The weights for capital and labour are as defined by their factor shares.
5. This decomposition is only possible under certain assumptions of which the most important are that technology is characterised by *constant returns to scale* so that a doubling, say, in input quantities leads to a doubling of the output produced, all producers are *profit maximisers* and markets are *competitive* by which is meant that no buyer or seller has sufficient market power to be able to alter prices, through altering their demand–supply decisions.
6. This definition of TFP growth is conceptually identical to its definition as a weighted average of capital and labour productivity.
7. The reason that these differences in annual growth rates of output are important is due to the magic of compound interest rates: when GDP is growing at an annual rate of 4 per cent it doubles every 18 years, while at an annual growth rate of 2 per cent, it doubles every 35 years.
8. John Page, 'The East Asian Miracle: Four Lessons for Development Policy', in S. Fischer and J. Rotemberg (eds), *NBER Macroeconomics Annual 1994* (The MIT Press: Cambridge, Mass., 1994). See also Dani Rodrik, 'Getting Interventions Right: How Korea and Taiwan Grew Rich', *Economic Policy*, (vol. 19 April 1995), pp. 53–108.
9. See, for example, Martin Baily, 'What has Happened to Productivity Growth', *Science*, vol. 239 (October 1986), pp. 443–51; A.S. Englander and A. Mittelstadt,

'Total Factor Productivity: Macroeconomic Aspects of the Slowdown', *OECD Economic Studies* (1988), no. 10, pp. 8–56; A.S. Englander, R. Evenson and M. Hanazaki, 'R&D, Innovation and the Total Factor Productivity Slowdown', *OECD Economic Studies* (1988), no. 11; 'Symposium on the Slowdown in Productivity Growth', *Journal of Economic Perspectives*, vol. 2 (1988), pp. 3–97.

10. *Op. cit.*

11. For France, the UK and the USA, defence-related R&D spending is an important part of total R&D expenditure. If one recognises that such spending affects TFP growth less strongly than non-defence R&D spending, then these three countries were (and continue to be) particularly disadvantaged relative to Germany and Japan where almost all of R&D spending is for civilian purposes.

12. M.N. Baily and A.K. Chakrabarti, 'Innovation and Productivity in U.S. Industry', *Brookings Papers on Economic Activity*, vol. 2 (1985), pp. 609–39.

13. Zvi Griliches, 'Productivity Puzzles and R&D', *Journal of Economic Perspectives*, vol. 2 (1988), pp.9–21.

14. In 1972 the price of Middle East light crude (in constant 1982 prices) was $3.86 per barrel and this price had remained virtually unchanged for over a decade; by 1974 it had risen to $20.33 per barrel representing a rise of over 400 per cent. The Iranian revolution of 1978 led to a second wave of oil price increases over the next 2 years.

15. This argument is made by Griliches, *op. cit.*

16. M. Olson, 'The Productivity Slowdown, the Oil Shocks, and the Real Cycle', *Journal of Economic Perspectives*, vol. 2 (1988), pp. 43–69.

17. Rising inflation rates co-existing with high unemployment rates.

18. E.A. Hudson and D.W. Jorgenson, 'U.S. Energy Policy and Economic Growth, 1975–2000', *The Bell Journal of Economics and Management Science*, vol. 5 (1974), pp. 461–514; D.W. Jorgenson, 'Productivity and Postwar U.S. Economic Growth', *Journal of Economic Perspectives*, vol. 2 (1987), pp. 23–41.

19. Canada, France, Germany, Italy, Japan, the UK and the USA.

20. A.S. Englander and A. Mittelstadt, *op. cit.*

21. Remembering that TFP growth is what remains when output growth is adjusted for the growth in inputs, a higher growth in capital, for a given growth in output, implies lower TFP growth.

22. See Baily, *op. cit.* for a discussion of these effects. The numbers are from A.S. Englander and A. Mittelstadt, *op. cit.*

23. From Paul Krugman, *Peddling Prosperity: Economic Sense and Nonsense in the Age of Diminished Expectations* (New York: Norton and Company, 1994).

CHAPTER 3: ECONOMIC POLICY AND PRODUCTIVE PERFORMANCE

1. Value added is calculated by subtracting from the value of output the cost of all raw materials and intermediate goods services used in the production of output. It is the income actually earned by labour and capital.

2. The previous chapter looked at differences, across countries, in productivity *growth rates.*

3. For example, in a comparison between the UK and the USA the basket might contain apples and pears but the proportion in which apples and pears should be included might vary with tastes between the countries.
4. Reported in the *Financial Times* (22 October 1993).
5. Respectively, 24, 16 and 15 per cent higher.
6. Respectively, 24, 33 and 28 per cent lower.
7. See D.M. Hitchens and J.E. Birnie, 'The United Kingdom's Productivity Gap: its Size and Causes', *Omega*, vol.17 (1989), pp. 209–21.
8. *Financial Times* (23 December 1991).
9. George N. Hatsopoulos, Paul R. Krugman and Lawrence H. Summers, 'U.S. Competitiveness: Beyond the Trade Deficit', *Science* (15 July 1988) vol. 241.
10. Several economists have drawn attention to the link between high investment rates and high growth rates. See, for example J.F. Helliwell and Alan Chung, 'Aggregate Productivity and Growth in an International Setting', in Bert Hickman (ed.), *International Productivity and Competitiveness* (Oxford: Oxford University Press, 1992).
11. Taken from M.L. Dertouzos, R.K. Lester and R.M. Solow, *Made in America: Regaining the Productive Edge* (Cambridge, Mass.: MIT Press, 1989).
12. The real interest rate is the nominal interest rate less the rate of inflation. It expresses the idea that lending yields interest income but the purchasing power of this income depreciates with inflation. It measures therefore the real income that is received from lending (and paid out for borrowing). There is a considerable degree of international convergence in real interest rates since investors will shift their funds to countries offering the highest rates of return.
13. *Financial Times* (1 June 1990).
14. For a discussion of such interconnections see Lester Thurow, *Head to Head: the Coming Economic Battle Among Japan, Europe and America* (New York: William Morrow and Company, 1992).
15. Walter Eltis, 'How Macroeconomic Policy Can Best Assist UK Industry', *Economics and Business Education*, vol. 1 (1993), pp. 60–8.
16. *Op. cit.*
17. Kim B. Clark, W. Bruce Chew and Takahiro Fujimoto, 'Product Development in the World Auto Industry: Strategy, Organisation and Performance', *Brookings Papers on Economic Activity*, vol. 3 (1987), pp. 729–81.
18. *International Herald Tribune* (3 February 1992).
19. The favourable tax treatment afforded to owner–occupiers in the UK biases the direction of household saving towards housing and away from industry.

CHAPTER 4: HUMAN CAPITAL, EDUCATION AND TRAINING

1. Adam Smith, *An Enquiry into the Nature and Causes of the Wealth of Nations*, 1776 (republished) (London: Home University, 1910).
2. G. Becker, *Human Capital* (New York: Columbia University Press, 1964).
3. E.F. Denison, *The Sources of Economic Growth in the United States and the Alternatives Before Us* (New York: Committee for Economic Development, 1962).

4. Theodore Schultz, 'Investment in Human Capital', *American Economic Review*, vol. 51 (1961), pp. 1–17.
5. S.J. Prais, *Economic Performance and Education: The Nature of Britain's Deficiencies* (London: NIESR Discussion Paper no. 52, 1993).
6. David Raffe, *Participation of 16–18 Year Olds in Education and Training* (London: National Commission on Education, Briefing Paper, no. 3, 1992).
7. S.J. Prais, *op. cit.*
8. H. Steedman and K. Wagner, 'A Second Look at Productivity, Machinery and Skills in Britain and Germany', *National Institute Economic Review*, vol. 122 (1987), pp. 84–95.
9. S.J. Prais and K. Wagner, 'Productivity and Management: the training of foremen in Britain and Germany', *National Institute Economic Review*, vol. 123 (1988), pp. 34–47.
10. N. Oulton, *Workforce Skills and Export Competitiveness* (London: NIESR Discussion Paper (New Series) no. 47, 1993).
11. Introduced in 1983, the YTS is central to the UK system of training. It provides 16 and 17 year old school leavers with 2 years of work-related training including up to 20 weeks off the job training and is delivered primarily through employers with the quality of training being monitored by a Training Standards Advisory Service.
12. Which involves either staying on in school or enrolling at a college of further education and may involve either pursuing vocational and technical courses or academic-type courses.
13. Typically involving study at a university.
14. R. Bennett, H. Glennester and D. Nevison, 'Investing in Skill: to Stay On or Not to Stay On?', *Oxford Review of Economic Policy*, vol. 8 (1992), pp. 130–41.
15. Which involves 2 years of academic study after compulsory schooling.
16. This is not withstanding the fact that the YTS often provides neither adequate training nor 'real' work, *Financial Times* (18 January 1994). See also I. Jones, 'An Evaluation of the YTS', *Oxford Review of Economic Policy*, vol. 4 (1988), pp. 54–71.
17. See J. Cassells, *Britain's Real Skills Shortage* (London: Policy Studies Institute, 1990).
18. YTS trainees receive an allowance whereas (the parents of) those in further education receive a much smaller amount in Child Benefit.
19. See Bennett *et al.*, *op. cit.*
20. The argument about the lack of demand for trained workers is detailed in D. Finegold and D. Soskice, 'The Failure of Training in Britain: Analysis and Prescription', *Oxford Review of Economic Policy*, vol. 4 (1988), pp. 21–53.
21. *Op. cit.*
22. See D. Raffe, *op. cit.*
23. D. Soskice, 'UK's Wrong Turning on Training', *Financial Times* (6 January 1994); D. Soskice, 'Social Skills From Mass Higher Education: Rethinking the Company-based Initial Training Paradigm', *Oxford Review of Economic Policy*, vol. 9 (1993), pp. 101–13.
24. Austria, Germany, Japan, The Netherlands, the Scandinavian countries and Switzerland.

25. For evidence of such demand in the UK see D. Gallie and M. White, *Employer Commitment and the Skills Revolution: First Findings from the Employment in Britain Survey* (London: Policy Studies Institute, 1993).
26. M. Wiener, *English Culture and the Decline of the Industrial Spirit* (Cambridge: Cambridge University Press, 1981).
27. See G. Williams, 'British Higher Education in the World League', *Oxford Review of Economic Policy*, vol. 8 (1992), pp. 146–58, for details of funding systems in other countries.
28. D. Finegold and D. Soskice, *op. cit.*
29. *Financial Times* (18 January 1994).
30. D. Soskice, *op. cit.*
31. *The Economist* (12 March 1994).
32. See James Murphy, 'A Degree of Waste: the Economic Benefits of Educational Expansion', *Oxford Review of Education*, vol. 19 (1993), pp. 9–31.
33. These problems are discussed in Chapter 8.
34. *The Economist, op. cit.*

CHAPTER 5: THE MEASUREMENT OF UNEMPLOYMENT

1. This chapter was written at a time when the EU contained 12 countries, that is, before its enlargement to include Austria, Norway and Sweden.
2. Richard Layard, Stephen Nickell and Richard Jackman, *The Unemployment Crisis* (Oxford: Oxford University Press, 1994), p. 1.
3. See note 1.
4. Commission of the European Communities, *Growth, Competitiveness, Employment: the Challenges and Ways Forward into the 21st Century* (Luxembourg: Office for the Official Publications of the European Communities, 1993).
5. Edward Balls and Paul Gregg, *Work and Welfare: Tackling the Jobs Deficit*, The Commission on Social Justice, Discussion Paper no. 3 (London: Institute of Public Policy Research, 1993).
6. Job search might take a number of forms: visits to a job centre, enrolment on a recruitment agency's register, inspection of job advertisements and the advertisement of one's own availability and direct approaches to employers.
7. The overall unemployment rate for the economy would have to be inferred from the sample surveyed.
8. These estimates are published in the spring of each year, the published figures being based on the survey carried out 12 months earlier. From 1992 they will be published quarterly with a time lag, between survey and publication, not exceeding 6 months.
9. Published regularly by the Department of Employment's *Employment Gazette*.
10. The claimant count measure, as a by-product of the system for administering unemployment, is estimated to be six times less expensive than the quarterly LFS, Employment Policy Institute, *Economic Report*, vol. 8 (March 1994).
11. The claimant count measure offers detailed breakdowns by sex, age and locality.
12. In the UK these are published monthly with a lag of a month between publication and data collection.

13. See Employment Policy Institute, *op. cit.* For an assessment of these changes see Paul Gregg, *Out for the Count Again? A Social Scientist's Analysis of Unemployment Statistics in the UK;* Discussion Paper no. 25 (London: National Institute of Economic and Social Research, 1992).

14. Either because they have a job or because they do not meet the job search/availability conditions of the LFS definition.

15. Of these 60 per cent were women, reflecting the fact that women – because they are more likely to work part-time and to have interrupted spells of employment – are less likely, than men, to build up a contribution record that would make them eligible for Unemployment Benefit; at the same time married women are often not entitled to claim Income Support (and, therefore, again excluded from the claimant count) but instead are included in the husband's claim for means-tested benefits.

16. The LFS defines anyone working for more than 1 hour in the week prior to the interview as being employed. Since claimants of unemployment-related benefits are allowed to earn up to specified amounts and since these amounts might involve them working hours in excess of the LFS threshold, they could fail the LFS 'jobless' test but yet be legitimate claimants. Hence, the existence of 'employed' claimants, who comprised 40 per cent of the 660000 claimants excluded from the LFS count of the unemployed, is not necessarily evidence about the scale of the 'black economy'.

17. Described in detail in R. Layard and J. Philpott, *Stopping Unemployment* (London: Employment Institute, 1991), from which the abbreviated description presented in this chapter, is culled.

18. Of these, 410000 were claimants and 14000 were non-claimants, who had failed the LFS job search test but who nevertheless wanted employment.

19. John Wells, 'Unemployment in the UK: the Missing Million', *European Labour Forum* (1994), no. 13.

20. See Paul Gregg, *op. cit.* and The Employment Policy Institute, *Economic Report*, vol. 8 (March 1994).

CHAPTER 6: THE INFLATION–UMEMPLOYMENT TRADE-OFF

1. For example, producer price indices measure the cost of goods leaving factories for the domestic market; the GDP deflator, which measures the 'price' of domestically produced output, is an index of domestically produced inflation.

2. The switching of the tax burden from direct to indirect taxation, in recent years, in the UK has contributed to the general rise in prices. In order to allow for this the tax and prices index (TPI) measures the cost of purchasing a representative basket taking into account not just price changes but also changes to the direct tax system.

3. There are also a number of methodological problems connected with including mortgage interest payments in the RPI. For details of such problems see the *Bank of England Quarterly Bulletin* (February 1993).

4. Moreover, if the process of rising prices is unattended to then it may turn into hyperinflation – an explosive and seemingly uncontrollable inflation in which money very rapidly loses value. Philip Cagan, 'The Monetary Dynamics of

Hyperinflation', in Milton Friedman (ed.), *Studies in the Quantity Theory of Money*, (Chicago: University of Chicago Press 1956), regarded an inflation rate of 50 per cent per month (12875 per cent per year) as representing the dividing line between inflation and hyperinflation.

5. Countries like Germany and Japan, which historically have had low inflation rates, have also had low variability in these rates; on the other hand, the high inflation rates of Italy and the UK have also displayed considerable variability.

6. J.M. Keynes, *The General Theory of Employment, Interest and Money* (London: Macmillan, 1936).

7. G.L. Perry, 'Cost-Push Inflation', in J. Eatwell, M. Milgate and P. Newman (eds) *The New Palgrave: A Dictionary of Economics* (London: Macmillan, 1987).

8. C.L. Schultze, *Memos to the President: A Guide Through Macroeconomics for the Busy Policy Maker* (Washington, DC: The Brookings Institution, 1992).

9. A.W. Phillips, 'The Relation Between Unemployment and the Rate of Change in Money Wages in the United Kingdom, 1861–1957', *Economica*, vol. 25 (1958), pp. 283–99.

10. For Britain, over the period studied by A.W. Phillips (see note 9), an unemployment rate of 2.5 per cent was associated with wage growth of approximately 2 per cent per annum; allowing for productivity growth this was roughly consistent with stable prices. See *The Economist* (19 February 1994).

11. For example, Fred Bayliss, *Does Britain Still have a Pay Problem?* (London: Employment Policy Institute, 1993) argues that most employers in the UK regard it as self-evident that pay increases must, at a minimum, compensate workers for cost of living increases and, if possible, workers should receive something over and above this minimum.

12. As the UK Government of 1979 did with its medium-term financial strategy.

13. Assuming zero productivity growth.

14. Wage divided by price.

15. In the analysis below it is assumed that the size of the labour force is fixed so that a given change in employment implies an equal and opposite change in unemployment.

16. If this period exceeded the time until the next election then a government might regard such an expansion as politically attractive.

17. See W.D. Nordhaus, 'The Political Business Cycle', *Review of Economic Studies*, vol. 42 (1975), pp. 169–90.

18. *The Economist*, 19 February 1994, p. 95.

CHAPTER 7; UNEMPLOYMENT AND LABOUR MARKET (IN)FLEXIBILITY

1. In 1992, only 15 per cent of workers in the USA, but 30–40 per cent of workers in many countries of Europe, belonged to a trade union, *The Economist* (26 February, 1994).

2. See Fred Bayliss, *Does Britain Still Have a Pay Problem?* (London: Employment Policy Institute, 1993).

3. Lars Calmfors and John Driffill, 'Bargaining Structure, Corporatism and Macroeconomic Performance', *Economic Policy*, vol. 6 (1988), pp. 14–61.

4. Robert M. Solow, *The Labour Market as a Social Institution* (Oxford: Basil Blackwell, 1990).

5. Assar Lindbeck and Dennis Snower, *The Insider–Outsider Theory of Employment and Unemployment* (Cambridge, Mass.: MIT Press, 1989).

6. D. Blanchflower and R. Freeman, *Did the Thatcher Reforms Change British Labour Market Performance*, Discussion Paper no. 168 (London: LSE, Centre for Economic Performance, August 1993).

7. Through the Employment Acts of 1980, 1982, 1984 and 1988 which *inter alia* abolished the closed shop, allowed employers not to recognise unions at work places, limited picketing, required pre-strike ballots and strengthened employer power to get injunctions against unions.

8. *Financial Times* (25 June 1991).

9. *The Economist* (26 February, 1994).

10. For example, Edward Balls and David Goodhart, 'The High Price of Social Cohesion', in *Can Europe Compete?* (London: Financial Times) report that, in Spain, which has a highly protected labour market, nearly 40 per cent of the work-force, in 1994, were on temporary contracts because of the difficulty of firing people on standard contracts; by contrast, nearly two-thirds of workers in the USA were subject to instant dismissal.

11. After the recession of 1979–81, almost 2 years elapsed before the employment rose in response to the recovery in output.

12. The Redundancy Payments Act 1965 introduced statutory payments for workers made unemployed, the Industrial Relations Act 1971 established legal rights against unfair dismissal and the Employment Protection Act 1975 extended periods of notice before termination. In the 1980s these laws became less strict and, in particular, the laws against unfair dismissal no longer applied to workers employed for less than 2 years.

13. *Financial Times* (15 March 1994).

14. These issues are discussed in detail in the next chapter.

15. Many of these arguments as to why the UK labour market might have become more 'flexible' in the 1990s are set out in The Employment Policy Institute, *Economic Report*, vol. 7 (July 1993).

16. For example, the relative, regional unemployment rate is given by the ratio of the unemployment rate in a particular region to the average unemployment rate across all the regions. Intuitively speaking, the *variance* measures the spread of these rates around their mean value. The higher the variance, the greater the spread and, hence, greater the degree of mismatch.

17. Figures cited from Richard Layard, Stephen Nickell and Richard Jackman, *Unemployment: Macroeconomic Performance and the Labour Market* (Oxford: Oxford University Press, 1991).

18. *Op. cit.*

19. S. Nickell, 'Unemployment and the Benefit System', *Economic Report*, vol. 7 (October 1993).

20. R. Layard, S. Nickell and R. Jackman, *op. cit.*

21. S. Nickell, *op. cit.*

22. R. Layard, S. Nickell and R. Jackman, *op. cit.*

23. R. Layard and J. Philpott, *Stopping Unemployment* (London: The Unemployment Institute, 1991).
24. R. Layard, S. Nickell and R. Jackman, *op. cit.*
25. P. Warr, *Unemployment and Mental Health* (Oxford, Clarendon Press, 1987).
26. P. Heady and M. Smyth, *Living Standards During Unemployment* (London: HMSO, 1989).
27. The UK system has been described in Chapter 5.
28. S. Nickell, *op. cit.*
29. See R. Jackman, C. Pissarides and S. Savouri, 'Labour Market Policies and Unemployment in the OECD', *Economic Policy*, vol. 11 (1990), pp. 449–90, for a detailed account of such policies.
30. S. Nickell, *op. cit.*

CHAPTER 8: JOBLESS MEN AND WORKING WOMEN

1. Excluding students. In the remainder of this discussion, unless stated to the contrary, the male working-age population is defined so as to exclude students. Consequently, inactive males are jobless, non-student males, between the ages of 16 and 64 years, not actively searching for jobs.
2. John Schmitt and Jonathan Wadsworth, *Why are Two Million Men Inactive? The Decline in Male Labour Force Participation in Britain,* Working Paper no. 336 (London: LSE Centre For Economic Performance, March 1994).
3. *Op. cit.*
4. Edward Balls and Paul Gregg, *Work and Welfare: Tackling the Jobs Deficit*, The Commission on Social Justice, Discussion Paper no. 3 (London: Institute of Public Policy Research, 1993).
5. Focusing on prime-age males (rather than on working-age men) abstracts from international differences in participation rates in higher education (which affects young men) and in retirement rates (which affects older men).
6. Except in the USA where it fell slightly in the 1980s after rising in the 1970s.
7. Defined by Schmitt and Wadsworth, *op. cit.* (whose findings are cited later in the paragraph) as qualifications up to and including Certificate of Secondary Education.
8. The corresponding figures for male graduates were, respectively, 3.4 and 4.2 percentage points and 9 per cent.
9. On average, over the 1980s, 12 per cent of prime-age males in the USA were non-employed compared to 15 per cent in the UK, OECD, *Economic Outlook* (1992).
10. See E. Balls and P. Gregg, *op. cit.*
11. Adrian Wood, *North–South Trade, Employment and Inequality* (Oxford: Clarendon Press, 1994).
12. In 1955, manufactured goods constituted only 6 per cent of the South's non-fuel exports; by 1989, this share had risen to 71 per cent (A. Wood, *op. cit.*).
13. Indeed, some commentators use the language of warfare to describe the state of economic relations between nations. Edward Luttwak, *The Endangered American Dream: How to Stop the United States from Becoming a Third World Country and How to Win the Geo-economic Struggle for Industrial Supremacy*

(New York: Simon and Schuster, 1993), for example, speaks of expenditure on R&D conquering the industrial territory of the future 'just as in war [in which] artillery conquers by firepower, territory that the infantry can then occupy'.

14. The advantage of such a strategy is evident from the fact that hourly labour costs in 1993 were less than $1 in China and Thailand, $2.40 in Mexico, $4.90 in South Korea, $16–17 in the USA and Japan and $24.90 in Germany, *The Economist* (2 April 1994).

15. The importance of Third World competition as an explanation for a decline in the demand for unskilled labour in the North has, however, been downplayed by other economists who prefer, instead, to stress the role of technological change in bringing about this fall. See for example, Edward Balls and David Goodhart, 'The High Price of Social Cohesion', in *Can Europe Compete?* (London: Financial Times, 1994). They stress the importance of technological change but, unlike Adrian Wood, *op. cit.* presumably what they have in mind is autonomous, rather than trade-induced, change.

16. OECD, *Employment Outlook* (1993).

17. For example, employers in the UK can avoid paying National Insurance contributions if part-time workers are paid less than the qualifying threshold. During a recent study into pay into wages councils industries, of 91 vacancies in the retail trade all were part-time and all but four jobs paid above the national insurance threshold, Jonathan Fry, 'Low Pay Network', letter to The *Financial Times* (29 March 1994).

18. Most notably, the Burton retail group in the UK replaced 2000 full-time jobs with 3000 part-time positions. In such cases part-time appointments are no more than *de facto* job sharing.

19. For example, the average weekly income in respect of the 91 part-time vacancies cited in noted 18, was £39.05.

20. E. McLaughlin, 'Employment, Unemployment and Social Security', in A. Glyn and D. Miliband (eds), *Paying for Inequality: the Economic Cost of Social Injustice* (London: Oram Press, 1994).

21. See Barry McCormick, *Unemployment Structure and the Unemployment Puzzle* (London: Employment Institute, 1991), for evidence on this point.

22. £5 per week for married women and £15 per week for single mothers.

23. Although the wife, if her earnings were low, would be entitled to claim family credit (the income supplement paid to low earners) the family would lose assistance with mortgage interest payments and free school meals that come with income support but not with family credit. See Patricia Hewitt, *About Time: the Revolution in Work and Family Life* (London: IPPR/Rivers Oram Press, 1993).

24. Richard Thomas, 'Right Jobs for the Right People', letter to the *Financial Times* (15 March, 1994).

25. See Christopher Jencks, 'Is the American Underclass Growing?', in C. Jencks and P.E. Peterson (eds), *The Urban Underclass* (Washington, DC: The Brookings Institution, 1991).

26. Richard Freeman, *Crime and Disadvantaged Youth*, Working Paper no. 3875 (Boston: National Bureau of Economic Research, 1990), points out that the increase in imprisonment in the USA was concentrated among Black, male, high school drop-outs. In 1986, 26 per cent of this group were in prison.

27. These are described in detail in Paul Peterson, 'The Urban Underclass and the Poverty Paradox', in C. Jencks and P.E. Peterson, *op. cit.*

28. C.A. Murray, *Losing Ground: American Social Policy, 1950–1980* (New York: Basic Books, 1984) and also *The Emerging British Underclass* (London: Institute of Economic Affairs, 1990).

29. C.A. Murray, *op. cit.*

30. For a useful review see Christopher Jencks, *Rethinking Social Policy: Race, Poverty and the Underclass* (Cambridge, Mass: Harvard University Press, 1992).

31. *Op. cit.*

32. Elijah Anderson, 'Neighbourhood Effects on Teenage Pregnancy', in C. Jencks and P.E. Peterson, *op. cit.*

33. W.J. Wilson, *The Truly Disadvantaged* (Chicago: University of Chicago Press, 1987).

34. L. M. Mead, *The New Politics of Poverty* (New York: Basic Books, 1992).

35. See *The Economist,* 30 July 1994.

CHAPTER 9: INEQUALITY

1. See Paul Krugman, *Peddling Prosperity: Economic Sense and Nonsense in the Age of Diminished Expectations* (New York: Norton and Co., 1994), Chapter 5 for a critique of this argument.

2. See Dinesh D'Souza, *Illiberal Education* (New York: The Free Press, 1991). He estimated that, at the University of California, Berkeley, because of the university's affirmative action policies, Black and Hispanic applicants were 20 times more likely to be accepted for admission than Asian-American applicants with the same academic qualifications.

3. A.K. Sen, *Inequality Reexamined* (Oxford: Clarendon Press, 1992).

4. That is, the variable on which the analysis of equality focuses.

5. A further property associated with this principle is that of transfer sensitivity. Suppose £100 was transferred from a richer to a poorer person, both high up in the income scale; suppose the same amount was similarly transferred but this time between two persons lower down the income scale than the first pair. By the *principle of transfers*, the value of an inequality index should fall for either transfer; however, if the index records a larger fall for the second transfer than for the first, it is *transfer sensitive*; if it records the same fall in both cases it is *transfer neutral*.

6. So that the relative position of each person in the income scale remains unaltered, notwithstanding the fact that mean income has changed.

7. By contrast, *absolute inequality indices* are invariant to equal (absolute) additions to all incomes.

8. In the jargon, they embody different degrees of 'transfer sensitivity'.

9. Note that the total area under the diagonal would not change. The Gini coefficient would take the value zero if the curve coincided with the diagonal (perfect equality) and the value unity if the curve was a right angle (complete inequality with all of income accruing to a single household).

10. For the single person family there would be no difference between its adjusted and unadjusted income.

11. See T.M. Smeeding, *op. cit.*

12. This is not surprising given that heads of families between 35 and 45 years of age have higher incomes than their counterparts in other age brackets.
13. Alissa Goodman and Steven Webb, *For Richer, For Poorer: The Changing Distribution of Income in the United Kingdom, 1961–91* (London: The Institute For Fiscal Studies, 1994).
14. That is before any tax and national insurance payments or transfer receipts.
15. This argument is forcefully made by A.B. Atkinson, M.A. King and H. Sutherland, 'Analysis of Personal Taxation and Social Security', *National Institute Economic Review* (November 1983) no. 106, pp. 63–74, reprinted in A.B. Atkinson, *Poverty and Social Security* (London: Harvester Wheatsheaf, 1989).
16. See Atkinson, King and Sutherland, *op. cit.*
17. One such survey in the UK is the Family Expenditure Survey (FES) which is an annual survey of the income and expenditure of approximately 7000 households encompassing some 20000 persons. The data can be analysed at the level of the household (persons living together), the family (single adult or couple and dependent children – if any) or individual.
18. This has been the philosophy behind a new generation of tax-benefit models. See A.B. Atkinson and H. Sutherland (eds), *Tax-benefit Models* (STICERD, London School of Economics, 1988). Most of the tax-benefit models for the UK are based on the FES.
19. The poverty trap refers to the situation where the marginal tax rate on increased earnings is very high through a combination of the loss of means-tested benefits and the payment of income tax on the higher earnings. The unemployment trap refers to a situation where income in work is not much greater than income out of work.
20. See A.B. Atkinson, M.A. King and N.H. Stern, 'The Poverty Trap in Britain', in House of Commons Treasury and Civil Service Committee (ed.), *The Structure of Personal Income Taxation and Income Support* (London: HMSO, May 1983), reprinted in A.B. Atkinson, *op. cit.* and also A.B. Atkinson and J. Micklewright, *Unemployment and 'Replacement Rates'*, Unemployment Project Working Note 8 (London: London School of Economics).

CHAPTER 10: POVERTY

1. Though policy relevance is not a central feature of poverty analysis; on this point see A.K. Sen, *Inequality Reexamined* (Oxford: Clarendon Press, 1992).
2. Adam Smith, *An Enquiry into the Nature and Causes of the Wealth of Nations*, 1776 (republished) (London: Home University, 1910).
3. See Sen, *op. cit.* for a discussion of income inadequacy.
4. M.C. Nussbaum and A.K. Sen (eds), *The Quality of Life* (Oxford: Clarendon Press, 1993).
5. There is also the related problem of adjusting the income of the unit for its size and composition. For example, a weekly income of £400 for a family consisting of husband, wife and child would lead to a lower level of welfare than the same income accruing to a single person. Details of how such adjustments are effected are to be found in Chapter 9.
6. Unlike the USA, Britain has no 'official' poverty line.

7. The changes are encapsulated in the fact that the old statistics were known as *low income families* statistics and the new ones were termed *households below average income* statistics.

8. See P. Johnson and S. Webb, 'Counting People with Low Incomes: the Impact of Recent Changes in Official Statistics', *Fiscal Studies*, vol. 10 (1989), pp. 66–82.

9. There are a number of ancillary problems relating, for example, to whether income should be considered on a weekly, monthly or annual basis, whether income should be current or normal income, how should non-cash benefits be taken account of and so on.

10. A.K. Sen, 'Poverty: an Ordinal Approach to Measurement', *Econometrica*, vol. 44 (1976), pp. 219–31.

11. Consequently, if incomes of the poor were, on average, raised by x per cent then poverty would be eliminated.

12. In the Sen index this is the Gini coefficient discussed in the previous chapter. Other distribution-sensitive poverty indices use different inequality indices.

13. T.M. Smeeding, 'Cross-national Comparisons of Inequality and Poverty Position', in L. Osberg (ed.), *Economic Inequality and Poverty: International Perspectives* (Armonk: M.E. Sharpe Inc., 1991).

14. That is, 5 per cent of persons in these countries had incomes less than half of their country's median adjusted disposable income.

15. I.V. Sawhill, *Anti-Poverty Strategies for the 1980s* (Washington: Urban Institute Discussion Paper, December 1986).

16. See Chapter 8 for further discussion of this point in relation to the 'underclass'.

17. V.K. Borooah, P.P.L. McGregor and P.M. McKee, *Regional Income Inequality and Poverty in the United Kingdom* (Aldershot: Dartmouth, 1991).

18. From the *Independent* (10 November 1993).

19. This last aim is pursued in the UK through the Child Support Agency which was established by the Child Support Act of 1990. It is estimated (*Financial Times*, 6 November 1993) that 70 per cent of absent parents make no maintenance payments and, for those that do, the average amount is £25 per week.

20. The *Independent* (10 November 1993).

21. This (essentially US) scheme is specifically targeted towards Aid to Families with Dependent Children (AFDC) recipients (mostly women) and requires them to work on community projects for their benefits.

22. See Lawrence Mead, *Beyond Entitlement: the Social Obligations of Citizenship* (New York: The Free Press, 1986).

23. Richard Layard and John Philpott in their book, *Stopping Unemployment* (London: Employment Institute, 1991), cite the case of West Virginia where participants on workfare programmes were less likely to be employed a year later than a control group of non-participants.

24. See I.V. Sawhill, *op. cit.*, for a discussion.

25. R. Layard and J. Philpott, *op. cit.*

CHAPTER 11: THE WELFARE STATE

1. The terms 'welfare system' are 'welfare spending' are used in their British sense. In the USA 'welfare spending' refers only to means-tested benefits and the totality of such benefits constitute its 'welfare system'.

2. See Nicholas Barr, 'Economic Theory and the Welfare State', *Journal of Economic Literature*, vol. XXX (1992), pp. 741–803.
3. Direct transfers could also include in-kind transfers. The Food Stamp and Medicaid programmes in the USA which provide, respectively, food coupons and free or subsidised medical services to low-income families are examples.
4. In 1992–3, total spending on welfare in the UK was nearly £160 billion of which nearly half was cash transfers.
5. See H.L. Wilensky and C.N. Lebeaux, *Industrial Society and Social Welfare* (New York: Free Press, 1965), for the distinction between residual and universal welfare systems.
6. A.B. Atkinson and John Hills, 'Social Security in Developed Countries: Are There Lessons for Developing Countries', in E. Ahmad, J. Dreze, J. Hills and A.K. Sen (eds), *Social Security in Developing Countries* (Oxford: Clarendon Press, 1991).
7. Income plus assets.
8. For example, in the USA, Aid to Families with Dependent Children (AFDC) is only paid to poor, female family heads with children under 18 years old; in the UK, Income Support is paid to those not in employment.
9. See J.-P. Jallade, 'Redistribution in the Welfare State: an Assessment of the French Performance', in J.-P. Jallade (ed.), *The Crisis of Redistribution in European Welfare States* (Stoke-on-Trent: Trentham Books, 1988).
10. See A.B. Atkinson, *The Western Experience with Social Safety Nets,* Discussion Paper No. 80 (London: LSE Suntory-International Centre for Economics and Related Disciplines (Welfare State Programme), November 1992).
11. Related to these questions of economic efficiency is that of administrative efficiency: the welfare system should be designed so as not to be open to abuse, while remaining both easy to understand and to administer.
12. These issues are discussed at length in A.B. Atkinson, 'Social Insurance and Social Assistance', in A.B. Atkinson (ed.), *Poverty and Social Security* (Hemel Hempstead: Harvester Wheatsheaf, 1989) and in Barr *op. cit.* from whom the subsequent discussion is taken.
13. Witness, for example, the several changes made to the eligibility conditions for receiving unemployment benefit in the United Kingdom, cf. A.B. Atkinson and J. Micklewright, 'Turning the Screw', in A. Dilnot and I. Walker (eds), *The Economics of Social Security* (Oxford: Oxford University Press).
14. For example, in the UK, many recipients of non-means-tested insurance-related unemployment benefit have also to collect means-tested Income Support.
15. See 'No Turning Back' Group of Conservative MPs, *Who Benefits? Reinventing Social Security* (London: Conservative Political Centre, 1993).
16. However, such disincentive effects may not be particularly important: a survey of unemployed men and women in the UK showed that only one in six men had replacement ratios in excess of 80 per cent. A. Garman, G. Redmond and S. Lonsdale, *Incomes in and Out of Work: a Cohort Study of Newly Unemployed Men and Women* (London: HMSO, 1992).
17. For people in employment in the UK, these are Housing Benefit and Family Credit.
18. John Hills, *The Future of Welfare: a Guide to the Debate* (York: Joseph Rowntree Foundation, 1993), constructs an example where a person earning

£150 per week is only £9 per week better off than someone earning £50 per week – the marginal 'tax rate' on the additional £100 is 91 per cent.

19. There is in fact little net gain from an occupational pension scheme until it reaches £50 per week; an occupational pension of £6 per week, for example, leaves a person only 87 pence per week better off than someone who had no occupational pension at all. See J. Collins, 'Occupational Pensions for the Less Well-off: Who Benefits?', *Watsons Quarterly*, vol. 28 (1993), pp. 4–7.

20. See Charles Murray, *Losing Ground* (New York: Basic Books, 1984) for a discussion of such effects.

21. Robert Moffitt, 'Incentive Effects of the U.S. Welfare System: a Review', *Journal of Economic Literature*, vol. XXX (1992), pp. 1–61.

22. *Aid to Families with Dependent Children* paid to poor female heads with children under 18 years, with increased earnings leading to benefit withdrawal on a dollar for dollar basis.

23. Most notably by Charles Murray, *op. cit.*

24. See Christopher Jencks, *Rethinking Social Policy: Race, Poverty and the Underclass* (Cambridge, Mass.: Harvard University Press, 1992).

25. John Hills, *op. cit.*

26. See Figure 11.2.

27. Robert Moffitt, *op. cit.*

28. See Rachel Hall, *Enterprise Welfare in Japan: Its Development and Role*, Discussion Paper no. 31 (London: LSE Suntory-Toyota International Centre for Economics and Related Disciplines Welfare State Programme, 1988). For example, the post-war consensus led to the creation of a comprehensive Welfare State in the UK, whereas in Japan it led to an overwhelming emphasis on economic growth and recovery. Many welfare benefits in Japan are company, rather than state, provided the effect of which is that employees devote their energies and talents to furthering the interests of their company

29. David Willetts, *The Age of Entitlement* (London: Social Market Foundation, 1993).

30. Andrew Dilnot and Paul Johnson, 'What Pensions Should the State Provide?', *Fiscal Studies*, vol. 13 (1992), pp. 1–20.

31. A.B. Atkinson, *State Pensions for Today and Tomorrow*, Discussion Paper no. 104 (London: LSE Suntory-Toyota International Centre for Economics and Related Disciplines Welfare State Programme, 1994).

32. *Op. cit.*

33. See also Amartya Sen; 'The Population Delusion', *The New York Review of Books* (22 September 1994) for a discussion of the global problem of population growth. Vol. XLI, pp. 62–71.

CHAPTER 12: HEALTH CARE

1. By contrast, contingencies like retirement and unemployment are addressed almost entirely from the perspective of income maintenance, with little or no attempt being made to address the condition itself. There is no necessity, however, for this: the condition of age-related retirement can be addressed through alterations in the statutory retirement age (for example, the abolition of statutory retirement

ages in some states of Australia); the condition of unemployment can be addressed through active labour market policies designed to help the unemployed to find jobs.

2. Through the two public insurance schemes, Medicare and Medicaid, designed to provide health care for, respectively, the old and the poor.

3. Adverse selection arises because of an asymmetry of information between insurers and their customers. The former do not know enough about the latter to customise premiums to individual risk and are forced, therefore, to charge premiums based on average risk; on the other hand customers know (or think they know) enough about themselves for some of them to regard the average premium as being 'too high'.

4. For example, some heavy smokers may regard themselves as being low health-risk persons because they are unaware (or do not wish to be made aware) of the dangers of smoking.

5. Henry J. Aaron and Barry P. Bosworth, 'Economic Issues in the Reform of Health Care Financing', in *Brookings Papers on Economic Activity (Microeconomics),* (Washington, DC: Brookings Institution, 1994), p. 258.

6. The force of this point may be gauged from the fact that, in the USA, even uninsured persons have access to emergency medical facilities; this reassurance would diminish the risks faced by the uninsured.

7. See Nicholas Barr, 'Economic Theory and the Welfare State', *Journal of Economic Literature,* vol. XXX (1992), pp. 741–803.

8. Henry Aarons and Barry Bosworth, *op. cit.*

9. See David M. Cutler, 'A Guide to Health Care Reform', *Journal of Economic Perspectives,* vol. 8 (1994), pp. 13–29.

10. For example, it would be absurd to defend the proposition that a woman with a family history of breast cancer should pay a higher premium than one without such a history; such a proposition may be efficient, but most persons would reject it on the ground that such discrimination is highly inequitable.

11. For example, an extended stay in hospital after an operation might be pleasant and convenient, but not essential.

12. Moral hazard, is but one source of this anxiety. Another source, particularly in the USA, is that administrative costs form a significant proportion of health care expenditure; for example, administrative expenditure absorbs approximately 22 per cent of health care expenditure in the USA. See David J. Himmelstein and Steffie Woodhandler, 'Cost Without Benefit: Administrative Waste in the United States Health Care', *New England Journal of Medicine,* vol. 314 (1986), pp. 1253–7.

13. In health care, where 'consumer' decisions about the appropriate level and form of health care are greatly influenced by medical advice, it is difficult to separate demand and supply decisions.

14. *The Economist* (29 May, 1993).

15. A standard Medicare assumption is that physicians will raise volume to compensate for only half of any fee constraint imposed by Medicare, cited in Joe White, 'Paying the Right Price: what the United States can Learn from Health Care Abroad', *The Brookings Review,* vol. 12 (1994), pp. 6–11.

16. Fee schedules may embody exceptions. For example, prices for medical care outside national standards (for example, cosmetic surgery) may be exempt.

17. See Joe White, *op. cit.*

18. A potential problem with DRGs is that there may be wide variations in patient health within a DRG, thus offering providers an incentive to 'cream-skim' by choosing the cheapest patients from within a DRG. However, the evidence does not indicate that this is a serious problem, see A.J. Culyer, 'Health Care Insurance and Provision', in Nicholas Barr and David Whynes (eds), *Current Issues in Economic Welfare* (London: Macmillan, 1993).

19. Compared to fee for service health plans, savings under HMOs would appear to be 10–15 per cent. David Cutler, *op. cit.*

20. *Op. cit.*

21. Though companies with 5000 workers or more could form their own, individual alliances.

22. The first wave of NHS trusts in 1990 included 25 acute hospitals, six mental health and mental handicap services and three ambulance services.

CHAPTER 13: THE ECONOMIC ROLE OF GOVERNMENT

1. Economists regard an outcome as being 'efficient' if there are no other outcomes in which, relative to the original outcome, some persons are better off without anyone being worse off. If such 'better' outcomes exist, then the original outcome is termed inefficient.

2. The fact that competition leads to efficiency is known as the first fundamental theorem of welfare economics. See K.J. Arrow and F.H. Hahn, *General Competitive Analysis* (San Francisco: Holden Day, 1971), for an authoritative account of how competitive economies work.

3. This last statement is known as the second fundamental theorem of welfare economics.

4. Robert Solow, 'Blame the Foreigner', *The New York Review of Books*, vol. XL (1993), no. 21, pp. 7–13.

5. J.E. Stiglitz, *On the Economic Role of the State* (Oxford: Basil Blackwell Ltd, 1989).

6. Sometimes people should not (as opposed to cannot) be excluded from consumption of certain goods. Such goods (for example, education and health) are called *merit goods* and they too provide a case for public provision.

7. Or receiving any benefit depending upon the nature of the by-product.

8. A.C. Pigou, *The Economics of Welfare* (London: Macmillan, 1920).

9. Assuming the externality was a 'bad'. A subsidy would be appropriate if the externality was a 'good'.

10. Ronald Coase, 'The Problem of Social Cost', *Journal of Law and Economics*, vol. 3, pp. 1–44, 1960.

11. Now sanctified as the *Coase theorem*.

12. Though the initial allocation of rights would determine the financial gainers and losers.

13. See Joe Alper, 'Protecting the Environment with the Power of the Market', *Science*, vol. 260 (1993), pp. 1884–5.

14. See D. Rodrik, 'Political Economy and Development Policy', *European Economic Review*, vol. 36 (1992), pp. 329–36; D.M. Newbery (1992), 'The Role

of Public Enterprises in the National Economy', *Asian Development Review* vol. 10, pp. 1–34.

15. M. Aoki, *Information, Incentives and Bargaining in the Japanese Economy* (Cambridge: Cambridge University Press, 1988).

16. David Newbery, *op. cit.*

17. Lester Thurow, *Head to Head: The Coming Economic Battle Among Japan, Europe and America* (New York: William Morrow and Company, 1992).

18. *Op. cit.*

CHAPTER 14: THE GROWTH OF GOVERNMENT

1. Income maintenance issues are discussed in Chapter 11.

2. For example, in the UK, government expenditure (measured in constant 1985 prices) grew, during 1960–91, at an average, annual rate of 2.8 per cent; the corresponding growth rate for GDP (at constant prices) was 2.4 per cent. Although, over this period, the annual growth rates for both GDP and government expenditure varied, in every year the former growth rate was greater than the latter.

3. See W.J. Baumol, 'The Macroeconomics of Unbalanced Growth', *American Economic Review,* vol. 57 (1967), pp. 415–26.

4. See Dennis Mueller, *Public Choice II* (Cambridge: Cambridge University Press, 1989).

5. For example, the public sector, in the UK, employed 5.4 million persons at the beginning of the decade and approximately 5.2 million at its end.

6. See Andrew Adonis' series of articles on the UK public sector in the *Financial Times* (July–August, 1991).

7. Andrew Adonis, *op. cit.*

8. A. Wagner, *Finanzwissenschaft,* vols I and II (Leipzig: C.F. Winter, 1890).

9. Reported in the *Independent* (7 January 1991).

10. Interestingly 67 per cent of Conservative supporters favoured higher public expenditure.

11. G.J. Stigler, 'Directors' Law of Public Income Distribution', *Journal of Law and Economics,* vol. 13 (1970), pp. 1–10.

12. Julian Le Grand and David Winter, 'The Middle Classes and the Welfare State under Conservative and Labour Governments', *Journal of Public Policy,* vol. 6 (1987), pp. 399–430.

13. Both because they are more aware of the importance of such services and also because they live longer than working-class families.

14. H. Glennerster, 'The Determinants of Public Expenditure', in T. Booth (ed.), *Planning for Welfare: Social Policy and the Expenditure Process* (Oxford: Blackwell, 1979).

15. P. Self, 'Public Expenditure and Welfare', in M. Wright (ed.), *Public Spending Decisions* (London: Allen and Unwin, 1980).

16. The dependency ratio is the ratio of the total number of dependents (that is, both young and old) to the size of the working-age population.

17. Organization for Economic Co-operation and Development, *OECD Economic Studies* (Paris: Organization for Economic Co-operation and Development, 1991).
18. Nominal spending deflated by health care price indices.
19. Jenny Church (ed.), *Social Trends* (London: CSO, 1994).
20. *OECD Economic Studies, op. cit.*
21. HM Treasury, *The Next Ten Years: Public Expenditure and Taxation into the 1990s* (London: HMSO, 1984).
22. See A.K. Sen, *Poverty and Famines: An Essay on Entitlement and Deprivation* (Oxford: Clarendon Press, 1981).
23. A person's entitlements is the 'bundle' of commodities (for example, food, shelter, health care, personal security) to which he (or she) has legitimate access.
24. See J. Dreze and A.K. Sen, *Hunger and Public Action* (Oxford: Clarendon Press, 1989).
25. Amartya Sen, 'How is India Doing?', *New York Review of Books,* vol. 29 (16 December 1982), pp. 41–5.
26. See Dennis Mueller, *Public Choice II* (Cambridge: Cambridge University Press, 1989).
27. See the previous chapter for a discussion of market failure.
28. See D.C. North and J.J. Wallis, 'American Government Expenditures: a Historical Perspective', *American Economic Review (Papers and Proceedings),* vol. 82 (1982), pp. 336–40.
29. See W.A. Niskanen, *Bureaucracy and Representative Government* (Chicago: Aldine-Atherton, 1971).
30. Counter, that is, to the state of the business cycle.

CHAPTER 15: PRIVATISATION

1. See special issue on the Conservative Revolution, *Economic Policy,* vol. 5 (1987).
2. *The Economist* (21 August 1993).
3. In addition to transferring enterprises from public to private ownership, several government departments in the UK have been converted into agencies – remaining responsible to a government Minister but expected to finance their operations commercially – while others have been converted into public corporations. Examples of the former are the Royal Mint, HMSO and the Passport Agency; examples of the latter are the Post Office and London Transport.
4. John Vickers and George Yarrow, *Privatization: An Economic Analysis* (Cambridge, Mass.: MIT Press, 1989).
5. *The Economist* (21 August 1993).
6. Speaking sometime after that election one of Mrs Thatcher's advisers, Oliver Letwin, said of the privatisation policy 'We had no coherent policy. It was not the case that we knew that privatisation would bring in millions of new shareholders. It was not the case that we knew all these shareholders would benefit from premiums. It was not the case that we knew companies would do better in the private sector. Almost nothing that has happened since was known in advance. It came upon us gradually and by accident and by a leap of faith', in M. Walker, *Privatisation: Tactics and Techniques* (Edinburgh: The Fraser Institute, 1988), p. 50.

7. Or what the late Harold Macmillan, former Conservative Prime Minister, described as 'selling the family silver'.

8. In a characteristically blunt statement, the late Nicholas Ridley, former Secretary of State, referred to public organisations having the nation by the 'jugular vein' with 'the only feasible option [being] to pay up'.

9. The objective of promoting efficiency may conflict with that of raising finances through privatisation. For example, in order to secure a successful flotation a government may prefer to privatise a monopoly intact and tolerate the associated inefficiencies, rather than break it up into competitive companies.

10. See Michael Barrow and Adam Wagstaff, 'Efficiency Measurement in the Public Sector: an Appraisal', *Fiscal Studies,* vol. 10 (1989), pp. 72–97, for a detailed exposition.

11. For example, if it costs £100 to produce ten units of output and £120 to produce 11 units, then the *marginal cost* of the eleventh unit is £20.

12. This is known as the 'marginal-cost pricing rule'. If, however, marginal costs and prices do not reflect the social costs and benefits of production (that is, there are externalities) then this rule will not lead to the *socially optimum* level of output being produced. See Chapter 13 for a discussion of externalities.

13. The theory of contestable markets owes its origins to the work of William Baumol and his colleagues. See W.J. Baumol, J. Panzar and R.D. Willig, *Contestable Markets and the Theory of Industrial Structure* (New York: Harcourt Brace Jovanovich, 1982).

14. Contestability also requires ease of exit from a market. This requires the absence of sunk costs, for example investment in specialist equipment which has no resale value. Such sunk costs create a financial penalty for leaving a market and, hence, may deter entry.

15. However, it may be possible to introduce competition for the right to make use of the distribution network. Joint use of a distribution network by rival suppliers is known as *interconnection*. Even if interconnection is feasible and, thus, competition is introduced for the right to use the distribution network – and the most likely way of achieving this is via *franchising* – the problem remains of how the distribution network itself is to be provided.

16. Indeed, at times it was in the government's interest or at the government's direction, that there was productive inefficiency; for employment (and electoral!) reasons it was not unknown for government ministers to direct public organisations to produce at a suboptimal location or to continue with suboptimal production techniques.

17. As exemplified by a speech made by John Moore, then financial secretary to the Treasury, in July 1985, in which he said that 'privatisation policies have been developed to such an extent that regulated private ownership of natural monopolies is preferable to nationalisation'.

18. The alternative would have been to stick with public provision and to seek ways of encouraging productive efficiency.

19. This is in contrast to the USA where it is the rate of return on capital that is regulated.

20. See G.L. Priest, 'The Origins of Utility Regulation and the Theories of the Regulation Debate', *Journal of Law and Economics,* vol. 9 (1966), pp. 24–40.

21. For example, during 1987–92 construction costs in the UK, as a consequence of prevailing recessionary conditions, fell 20 per cent relative to the retail price

index. Given the scale of planned investment in the water industry, this had the effect of dramatically reducing costs in the industry. See OFWAT, *Report on Capital Investment and Financial Performance* (Birmingham: Office of Water Services, 1993).

22. Recommended by Stephen Littlechild at the time of the privatisation of British Telecommunications in 1984.

23. In order to encourage successful flotations there has been a tendency in the UK to encourage the regulator to set the initial value of X at an artificially low level with the intention of improving the profitability of the privatised firms. To the extent that this has occurred, it will have resulted in higher prices than need have been the case. Indeed, it is possible for X to be set at a negative value. This is the case for the privatised water companies in England and Wales where the general formula is given as RPI + K. The 'K' factor is to allow these firms in this industry to undertake much needed capital investment.

24. That is, apart from the technical difficulties associated with establishing the appropriate value of X.

25. Since any reduction in quality is likely to lead to lower production costs which, with a price fixed by the regulator, will result in higher profits.

26. See OFWAT, *The Cost of Quality* (Birmingham: Office of Water Services, 1992).

27. *Op. cit.*

28. Amersham, British Aerospace, Cable and Wireless, Enterprise Oil and Jaguar.

29. British Telecom, British Gas, Electricity and Water.

30. As Vickers and Yarrow, *op. cit.,* note, although privatisation may have many objectives other than the promotion of efficiency (extension of share ownership, raising revenue and taming public sector unions) these are of a secondary order of importance as compared to the efficiency criterion.

31. Dieter Helm and Najma Rajah, 'Water Regulation – the Periodic Review', *Fiscal Studies*, vol. 15 (1994), pp. 74–94.

32. Since privatisation, water prices in the UK have outpaced inflation by 10 percentage points.

33. See for example, O. Blanchard, R. Dornbusch, P. Krugman, R. Layard and L. Summers, *Reform in Eastern Europe* (Cambridge, Mass.: MIT Press, 1991).

34. Patrick Bolton and Gerard Roland, 'Privatization Policies in Central and Eastern Europe', *Economic Policy,* vol. 15 (1992), pp. 275–310.

35. See John Vickers discussing Bolton and Roland, *op. cit.*

36. A. Galal, L. Jones, P. Tandon and I. Vogelsang, *Welfare Consequences of Selling Private Enterprises* (Washington, DC: The World Bank, 1992).

CHAPTER 16: NATIONAL SAVING, FOREIGN DEBT AND GOVERNMENT DEFICITS

1. Paul Krugman and Maurice Obstfeld, *International Economics: Theory and Policy* (New York: HarperCollins, 1993).

2. Represented by the difference between US holdings of foreign assets and foreign holdings of US assets.

3. See Chapter 3 for a discussion of the link between investment and productivity growth.

4. *The Economist* (29 May 1993).
5. *The Economist* (29 May 1993).
6. This is discussed in more detail in Chapter 3.

Bibliography

Aaron, H.J. and Bosworth, B.P. 'Economic Issues in the Reform of Health Care Financing', *Brookings Papers on Economic Activity (Microeconomics)*, Washington D.C.: Brookings Institution, 1994.

Alper, J. 'Protecting the Environment with the Power of the Market', *Science*, vol. 260, pp. 1884–5, June 1993.

Anderson, E. 'Neighbourhood Effects on Teenage Pregnancy', in C. Jencks and P.E. Peterson, *The Urban Underclass,* Washington D.C.: The Brookings Institution, 1991.

Aoki, M. *Information, Incentives and Bargaining in the Japanese Economy*, Cambridge: Cambridge University Press, 1988.

Arrow, K.J. and Hahn, F.H. *General Competitive Analysis*, San Francisco: Holden Day, 1971.

Atkinson, A.B. 'Social Insurance and Social Assistance', in A.B. Atkinson (ed.) *Poverty and Social Security,* Hemel Hempstead: Harvester Wheatsheaf, 1989.

Atkinson, A.B. *The Western Experience with Social Safety Nets,* Discussion Paper No. 80, London: LSE Suntory-International Centre for Economics and Related Disciplines (Welfare State Programme) November 1992.

Atkinson, A.B. *State Pensions for Today and Tomorrow,* Discussion Paper No. 104, London: LSE Suntory-Toyota International Centre for Economics and Related Disciplines (Welfare State Programme), 1994.

Atkinson, A.B. and Hills, J. 'Social Security in Developed Countries: Are There Lessons for Developing Countries', in E. Ahmad, J. Dreze, J. Hills and A.K. Sen (eds) *Social Security in Developing Countries,* Oxford: Clarendon Press, 1991.

Atkinson, A.B., King, M.A. and Stern, N.H. 'The Poverty Trap in Britain', in House of Commons Treasury and Civil Service Committee, *The Structure of Personal Income Taxation and Income Support*, London: HMSO, May 1983. (Reprinted in A.B. Atkinson (ed.) *Poverty and Social Security,* London: Harvester Wheatsheaf, 1989.)

Atkinson, A.B., King, M.A. and Sutherland, H. 'Analysis of Personal Taxation and Social Security', *National Institute Economic Review*, November 1983. (Reprinted in A.B. Atkinson (ed.) *Poverty and Social Security*, London: Harvester Wheatsheaf, 1989.)

Atkinson, A.B. and Micklewright, J. *Unemployment and 'replacement rates'*, Unemployment Project Working Note 8, London School of Economics, 1982.

Atkinson, A.B. and Micklewright, J. 'Turning the Screw', in A. Dilnot and I. Walker (eds) *The Economics of Social Security,* Oxford: Oxford University Press, 1989.

Atkinson, A.B. and Sutherland, H. (eds), *Tax-Benefit Models*, STICERD, London School of Economics, 1988.

Baily, M.N. 'What has Happened to Productivity Growth', *Science*, pp. 443–51, October, 1986.

Baily, M.N. and Chakrabarti, A.K. 'Innovation and Productivity in U.S. Industry', Brookings Papers on Economic Activity, vol. 2, pp. 609–39, 1985.

Balls, E. and Goodhart, D. 'The High Price of Social Cohesion', in *Can Europe Compete?*, London: Financial Times, 1994.

Balls, E. and Gregg, P. *Work and Welfare: Tackling the Jobs Deficit*, The Commission on Social Justice, Discussion Paper No. 3, London: Institute of Public Policy Research, 1993.

Barr, N. 'Economic Theory and the Welfare State', *Journal of Economic Literature*, vol. XXX, pp. 741–803, 1992.

Barrow, M. and Wagstaff, A. 'Efficiency Measurement in the Public Sector: an appraisal', *Fiscal Studies*, vol. 10, pp. 72–97, 1989.

Baumol, W.J. 'The Macroeconomics of Unbalanced Growth', *American Economic Review*, vol. 57, pp. 415–26, 1967.

Baumol, W.J., Panzar, J. and Willig, R.D. *Contestable Markets and the Theory of Industrial Structure*, New York: Harcourt Brace Jovanovich, 1982.

Bayliss, F. *Does Britain still have a Pay Problem?*, London: Employment Policy Institute, 1993.

Becker, G. *Human Capital*, New York: Columbia University Press, 1964.

Bennett, R., Glennester, H. and Nevison, D. 'Investing in Skill: to stay on or not to stay on?', *Oxford Review of Economic Policy*, vol. 8, pp. 130–41, 1992.

Blanchard, O., Dornbusch, R., Krugman, P., Layard, R. and Summers, L. *Reform in Eastern Europe*, Cambridge, Mass.: MIT Press, 1991.

Blanchflower, D. and Freeman, R. *Did the Thatcher Reforms Change British Labour Market Performance*, Discussion Paper no. 168, London: LSE, Centre for Economic Performance, August 1993.

Bolton, P. and Roland, G. 'Privatization Policies in Central and Eastern Europe', *Economic Policy*, vol. 15, pp. 275–310, 1992.

Borooah, V.K., McGregor, P.P.L. and McKee, P.M. *Regional Income Inequality and Poverty in the United Kingdom*, Aldershot: Dartmouth, 1991.

Cagan, P. 'The Monetary Dynamics of Hyperinflation', in Milton Friedman (ed.) *Studies in the Quantity Theory of Money*, Chicago: University of Chicago Press, 1956.

Calmfors, L. and Driffill, J. 'Bargaining Structure, Corporatism and Macroeconomic Performance', *Economic Policy*, vol. 6, pp. 14–61, 1988.

Cassells, J. *Britain's Real Skills Shortage*, London: Policy Studies Institute, 1990.

Clark, K.B, Chew, W.B. and Fujimoto, T. 'Product Development in the World Auto Industry: Strategy, Organisation and Performance', *Brookings Papers on Economic Activity*, vol. 3, pp. 729–81, 1987.

Coase, R. 'The Problem of Social Cost', *Journal of Law and Economics*, vol. 3, pp. 1–44.

Collins, J. 'Occupational Pensions for the Less Well-Off: Who Benefits?', *Watsons Quarterly*, vol. 28, pp. 4–7, 1993.

Commission of the European Communities, *Growth, Competitiveness, Employment: the Challenges and Ways Forward into the 21st Century*, Luxembourg: Office for the Official Publications of the European Communities, 1993.

Crafts, N.F.R. *Can De-Industrialisation Seriously Damage Your Wealth?*, Hobart Paper 120, London: Institute of Economic Affairs, 1993.

Culyer, A.J. 'Health Care Insurance and Provision', in Nicholas Barr and David Whynes (eds) *Current Issues in Economic Welfare*, London: Macmillan, 1993.

Cutler, D.M. 'A Guide to Health Care Reform', *Journal of Economic Perspectives*, vol. 8, pp. 13–29, 1994.

D'Souza, D. *Illiberal Education*, New York: The Free Press, 1991.

Denison, E.F. *The Sources of Economic Growth in the United States and the Alternatives Before Us*, New York: Committee for Economic Development, 1962.

Denison, E.F *Accounting for United States Economic Growth, 1929–70*, Washington, D.C.: The Brooking Institution, 1974.

Dertouzos, M.L., Lester, R.K. and Solow, R.M. *Made in America: Regaining the Productive Edge*, Cambridge, Mass.: MIT Press, 1989.

Dilnot, A. and Johnson, P. 'What Pensions Should the State Provide?', *Fiscal Studies*, vol. 13, pp. 1–20, 1992.

Dornbusch, R., Porteba, J. and Summers, L. *The Case for Manufacturing in America's Future,* Rochester: Eastman Kodak Company, 1988.

Dreze, J. and Sen, A.K. *Hunger and Public Action,* Oxford: Clarendon Press, 1989.

Eltis, W. 'How Macroeconomic Policy Can Best Assist UK Industry', *Economics and Business Education*, vol. 1, pp. 60–8, 1993.

Englander, A.S., Evenson, R. and Hanazaki, M. 'R&D, Innovation and the Total Factor Productivity Slowdown', *OECD Economic Studies*, No. 11, Autumn 1988.

Englander, A.S. and Mittelstadt, A. 'Total Factor Productivity: Macroeconomic Aspects of the Slowdown', *OECD Economic Studies*, No. 10, pp. 8–56, Spring 1988.

Finegold, D. and Soskice, D. 'The Failure of Training in Britain: Analysis and Prescription', *Oxford Review of Economic Policy*, vol. 4, pp. 21–53, 1988.

Freeman, R. *Crime and Disadvantaged Youth,* Working Paper No. 3875, Boston: National Bureau of Economic Research, 1990.

Friedman, B. 'Must We Compete?', *The New York Review of Books,* vol. XLI, pp. 14–20, 20 October 1994.

Fry, J. The *Financial Times* (letter), 29 March 1994.

Galal, A., Jones, L., Tandon, P., Vogelsang, I. *Welfare Consequences of Selling Private Enterprises*, Washington, D.C.: The World Bank, 1992.

Gallie, D. and White, M. *Employer Commitment and the Skills Revolution: First Findings from the Employment in Britain Survey*, London: Policy Studies Institute, 1993.

Garman, A., Redmond, G. and Lonsdale, S. *Incomes in and Out of Work: a cohort study of newly unemployed men and women,* London: HMSO, 1992.

Glennerster, H. 'The Determinants of Public Expenditure', in T. Booth (ed.), *Planning for Welfare: Social Policy and the Expenditure Process,* Oxford: Blackwell, 1979.

Goodman, A. and Webb, S. *For Richer, For Poorer: The Changing Distribution of Income in the United Kingdom, 1961–91,* London: The Institute For Fiscal Studies, 1994.

Gregg, P. *Out for the Count Again? A Social Scientist's Analysis of Unemployment Statistics in the UK*, Discussion Paper No. 25, London: National Institute of Economic and Social Research, 1992.

Griliches, Z. 'Productivity Puzzles and R&D', *Journal of Economic Perspectives*, vol. 2, pp. 9–21, 1988.

Gros, D. and Thygesen, N. 'The EMS: Achievements, Current Issues and Directions for the Future', *CEPS Paper No. 35*, Brussels: Centre for European Policy Studies, 1988.

H.M. Treasury, *The Next Ten Years: Public Expenditure and Taxation into the 1990s,* London: HMSO, 1984.

Hall, R. *Enterprise Welfare in Japan: Its Development and Role,* Discussion Paper no. 31, London: LSE Suntory-Toyota International Centre for Economics and Related Disciplines (Welfare State Programme), 1988.

Hall, R.E. and Hitch, C. 'Price Theory and Business Behaviour', *Oxford Economic Papers*, vol. 2, pp. 12–45, 1939.

Hatsopoulos, G.N., Krugman, P.R. and Summers, L.H. 'U.S. Competitiveness: Beyond the Trade Deficit', *Science*, 15 July, 1988.

Heady, P. and Smyth, M. *Living Standards During Unemployment*, London: HMSO, 1989.

Helliwell, J.F. and Chung, A. 'Aggregate Productivity and Growth in an International Setting', in Hickman, B. (ed.), *International Productivity and Competitiveness*, Oxford: Oxford University Press, 1992.

Helm, D. and Rajah, N. 'Water Regulation – the Periodic Review', *Fiscal Studies*, vol. 15, pp. 74–94, 1994.

Hewitt, P. *About Time: the revolution in work and family life*, London: IPPR/Rivers Oram Press, 1993.

Hills, J. *The Future of Welfare: a guide to the debate,* York: Joseph Rowntree Foundation, 1993.

Himmelstein, D.J. and Woodhandler, S. 'Cost Without Benefit: Administrative Waste in the United States Health Care', *New England Journal of Medicine*, vol. 314, pp. 1253–7, 1986.

Hitchens, D.M. and Birnie, J.E. 'The United Kingdom's Productivity Gap: its Size and Causes', *Omega*, vol. 17, pp. 209–21, 1989.

Hudson, E.A. and Jorgenson, D.W. 'U.S. Energy Policy and Economic Growth, 1975–2000', *The Bell Journal of Economics and Management Science*, vol. 5, pp. 461–514, 1974.

Jackman, R., Pissarides, C. and Savouri, S. 'Labour Market Policies and Unemployment in the OECD', *Economic Policy*, vol. 11, 1990.

Jallade, J.-P. 'Redistribution in the Welfare State: an Assessment of the French Performance', in J.-P. Jallade (ed.) *The Crisis of Redistribution in European Welfare States,* Stoke-on-Trent: Trentham Books, 1988.

Jencks, C. 'Is the American Underclass Growing?', in C. Jencks and P.E. Peterson, *The Urban Underclass*, Washington D.C.: The Brookings Institution, 1991.

Jencks, C. *Rethinking Social Policy: Race, Poverty and the Underclass,* Cambridge, Mass.: Harvard University Press, 1992.

Johnson, P. and Webb, S. 'Counting People with Low Incomes: the Impact of Recent Changes in Official Statistics', *Fiscal Studies*, vol. 10, pp. 66–82, 1989.

Jones, I. 'An Evaluation of the YTS', *Oxford Review of Economic Policy*, vol. 4, pp. 54–71, 1988.

Jorgenson, D.W. 'Productivity and Postwar U.S. Economic Growth', *Journal of Economic Perspectives*, vol. 2, pp. 23–41, 1987.

Keynes, J.M. *The General Theory of Employment, Interest and Money*, London: Macmillan, 1936.

Klein, L.R. 'Components of Competitiveness', *Science*, vol. 241, pp. 308–13, 15 July 1988.

Krugman, P. *Peddling Prosperity: Economic Sense and Nonsense in the Age of Diminished Expectations,* New York: Norton and Co., 1994.

Krugman, P. and Obstfeld, M. *International Economics: Theory and Policy*, New York: HarperCollins, 1993.

Layard, R., Nickell, S. and Jackman, R. *Unemployment: Macroeconomic Performance and the Labour Market*, Oxford: Oxford University Press, 1991.

Layard, R. and Philpott, J. *Stopping Unemployment*, London: Employment Institute, 1991.

Layard, R., Nickell, S. and Jackman, R. *The Unemployment Crisis,* Oxford: Oxford University Press, 1994.

Le Grand, J. and Winter, D. 'The Middle Classes and the Welfare State under Conservative and Labour Governments', *Journal of Public Policy,* vol. 6, pp. 399–430, 1987.

Lindbeck, A. and Snower, D. *The Insider–Outsider Theory of Employment and Unemployment,* Cambridge, Mass.: MIT Press, 1989.

Luttwak, E. *The Endangered American Dream: How to Stop the United States from Becoming a Third World Country and How to Win the Geo-Economic Struggle for Industrial Supremacy,* New York: Simon and Schuster, 1993.

McCormick, B. *Unemployment Structure and the Unemployment Puzzle,* London: Employment Institute, 1991.

McLaughlin, E. 'Employment, Unemployment and Social Security', in A. Glyn and D. Miliband (eds), *Paying for Inequality: the Economic Cost of Social Injustice,* London: Oram Press, 1994.

Mead, L.M. *Beyond Entitlement: the Social Obligations of Citizenship,* New York: The Free Press, 1986.

Mead, L.M. *The New Politics of Poverty,* New York: Basic Books, 1992.

Moffitt, R. 'Incentive Effects of the U.S. Welfare System: a Review', *Journal of Economic Literature,* vol. XXX, pp. 1–61, 1992.

Mueller, D. *Public Choice II,* Cambridge: Cambridge University Press, 1989.

Murphy, J. 'A Degree of Waste: the Economic Benefits of Educational Expansion', *Oxford Review of Education,* vol. 19, pp. 9–31, 1993.

Murray, C.A. *Losing Ground: American Social Policy, 1950–1980,* New York: Basic Books, 1984.

Murray, C.A. *The Emerging British Underclass,* London: Institute of Economic Affairs, 1990.

Newbery, D.M. 'The Role of Public Enterprises in the National Economy', *Asian Economic Review,* vol. 10, pp. 1–34, 1992.

Nickell, S. 'Unemployment and the Benefit System', *Economic Report,* vol. 7, London: Employment Policy Institute, October 1993.

Niskanen, W.A. *Bureaucracy and Representative Government,* Chicago: Aldine-Atherton, 1971.

Nordhaus, W.D. 'The Political Business Cycle', *Review of Economic Studies,* vol. 42, pp. 169–90, 1975.

North, D.C. and Wallis, J.J. 'American Government Expenditures: a Historical Perspective', *American Economic Review (Papers and Proceedings)* vol. 82, pp. 336–40, 1982.

No Turning Back Group of Conservative MPs, *Who Benefits? Reinventing Social Security,* London: Conservative Political Centre, 1993.

Nussbaum, M.C. and Sen, A.K. (eds), *The Quality of Life,* Oxford: Clarendon Press, 1993.

OECD *Economic Studies,* Paris: Organisation for Economic Co-operation and Development, 1991.

OECD *Economic Outlook,* June 1992.

OFWAT, *The Cost of Quality,* Birmingham: Office of Water Services, 1992.

OFWAT, *Report on Capital Investment and Financial Performance,* Birmingham: Office of Water Services, 1993.

Olson, M. 'The Productivity Slowdown, the Oil Shocks, and the Real Cycle', *Journal of Economic Perspectives,* vol. 2, pp. 43–69, 1988.

Oulton, N. *Workforce Skills and Export Competitiveness*, London: NIESR Discussion Paper (New Series) no. 47, 1993.

Page, J. 'The East Asian Miracle: Four Lessons for Development Policy', in S. Fischer and J. Rotemberg (eds), *NBER Macroeconomics Annual 1994*, Cambridge, Mass.: The MIT Press, 1994.

Perry, G.L. 'Cost-Push Inflation', in J. Eatwell, M. Milgate and P. Newman (eds) *The New Palgrave: A Dictionary of Economics*, London: Macmillan, 1987.

Peterson, P. 'The Urban Underclass and the Poverty Paradox', in C. Jencks and P.E. Peterson, *The Urban Underclass*, Washington D.C.: The Brookings Institution, 1991.

Phillips, A.W. 'The Relation between Unemployment and the Rate of Change in Money Wages in the United Kingdom, 1861–1957', *Economica*, vol. 25, pp. 283–99, 1958.

Pigou, A.C. *The Economics of Welfare*, London: Macmillan, 1920.

Prais, S.J. *Economic Performance and Education: The Nature of Britain's Deficiencies*, London: NIESR Discussion Paper no. 52, 1993.

Prais, S.J. and Wagner, K. 'Productivity and Management: the training of foremen in Britain and Germany', *National Institute Economic Review*, vol. 123, pp. 34–47, 1988.

President's Commission on Industrial Competitiveness, *Global Competition: the New Reality*, Washington D.C.: US Government Printing Office, 1985.

Priest, G.L. 'The Origins of Utility Regulation and the Theories of the Regulation Debate', *Journal of Law and Economics*, vol. 9, pp. 24–40.

Raffe, D. *Participation of 16–18 Year Olds in Education and Training*, London: National Commission on Education, Briefing Paper, No. 3, 1992.

Rodrik, D. 'Political Economy and Development Policy', *European Economic Review*, vol. 36, pp. 329–36, 1992.

Rodrik, D. 'Getting interventions right: how Korea and Taiwan grew rich', *Economic Policy*, pp. 53–108, April 1995.

Sawhill, I.V. *Anti-Poverty Strategies for the 1980s*, Washington, D.C.: Urban Institute Discussion Paper, December 1986.

Schmitt, J. and Wadsworth, J. *Why are two million men inactive? The decline in male labour force participation in Britain*, Working Paper No. 336, London: LSE Centre For Economic Performance, March 1994.

Schultz, T. 'Investment in Human Capital', *American Economic Review*, vol. 51, pp. 1–17, 1961.

Schultze, C.L. *Memos to the President: A Guide through Macroeconomics for the Busy Policy Maker*, Washington, D.C.: The Brookings Institution, 1992.

Self, P. 'Public Expenditure and Welfare', in M. Wright (ed.) *Public Spending Decisions*, London: Allen and Unwin, 1980.

Sen, A.K. 'Poverty: an Ordinal Approach to Measurement', *Econometrica*, vol. 44, pp. 219–31, 1976.

Sen, A.K. *Poverty and Famines: An Essay on Entitlement and Deprivation*, Oxford: Clarendon Press, 1981.

Sen, A.K. 'How is India Doing?', *New York Review of Books*, vol. 29, pp. 41–5, 16 December 1982.

Sen, A.K. *Inequality Reexamined*, Oxford: Clarendon Press, 1992.

Sen, A.K. 'The Population Delusion', *The New York Review of Books*, 22 September 1994.

Smeeding, T.M. 'Cross-National Comparisons of Inequality and Poverty', in L. Osberg (ed.) *Economic Inequality and Poverty: International Perspectives*, Armonk: M.E. Sharpe Inc., 1991.

Smith, Adam, *An Enquiry into the Nature and Causes of the Wealth of Nations*, 1776, (republished) London: Home University, 1910.

Social Trends, London: CSO, 1994.

Solow, R.M. 'Technical Change and the Aggregate Production Function', *Review of Economics and Statistics*, vol. 39, pp. 312–20, 1957.

Solow, R.M. *The Labour Market as a Social Institution*, Oxford: Basil Blackwell, 1990.

Solow, R.M. 'Blame the Foreigner', *The New York Review of Books*, vol. XL, Number 21, pp. 7–13, 1993.

Soskice, D. 'Social Skills From Mass Higher Education: Rethinking the Company-based Initial Training Paradigm', *Oxford Review of Economic Policy*, vol. 9, pp. 101–13, 1993.

Soskice, D. 'UK's wrong turning on training', *Financial Times*, 6 January 1994.

Steedman, H. and Wagner, K. 'A Second Look at Productivity, Machinery and Skills in Britain and Germany', *National Institute Economic Review*, vol. 122, pp. 84–95, 1987.

Stigler, G.J. 'Directors' Law of Public Income Distribution', *Journal of Law and Economics,* vol. 13, pp. 1–10, 1970.

Stiglitz, J.E. *On the Economic Role of the State*, Oxford: Basil Blackwell Ltd, 1989.

The Employment Policy Institute, *Economic Report*, vol. 7, July 1993.

The Employment Policy Institute, *Economic Report*, vol. 8, March 1994.

Thomas, R. The *Financial Times*, (letter) 15 March, 1994.

Thurow, L. *Head to Head: the Coming Economic Battle Among Japan, Europe and America*, New York: William Morrow and Company, 1992.

Vickers, J. and Yarrow, G. *Privatization: An Economic Analysis,* Cambridge, Mass.: The MIT Press, 1989.

Wagner, A. *Finanzwissenschaft*, vols. I and II, Leipzig: C.F. Winter, 1890.

Walker, M. *Privatisation: Tactics and Techniques,* Edinburgh: The Fraser Institute, 1988.

Warr, P. *Unemployment and Mental Health*, Oxford, Clarendon Press, 1987.

Wells, J. 'Unemployment in the UK: the missing million', *European Labour Forum*, no. 13, 1994.

White, J. 'Paying the Right Price: what the United States can learn from health care abroad', *The Brookings Review,* vol. 12, pp. 6–11, Spring 1994.

Wiener, M. *English Culture and the Decline of the Industrial Spirit*, Cambridge: Cambridge University Press, 1981.

Wilensky, H.L. and Lebeaux, C.N. *Industrial Society and Social Welfare,* New York: The Free Press, 1965.

Willetts, D. *The Age of Entitlement,* London: Social Market Foundation, 1993.

Williams, G. 'British Higher Education in the World League', *Oxford Review of Economic Policy*, vol. 8, pp. 146–58, 1992.

Wilson, W.J. *The Truly Disadvantaged*, Chicago: University of Chicago Press, 1987.

Wood, A. *North–South Trade, Employment and Inequality*, Oxford: Clarendon Press, 1994.

Index

Index by Auriol Griffith-Jones